"Launius and Hassel scaffold feminist analysis in a way that makes its underlying components highly accessible to novice students. This textbook provides students with a critical framework, while giving the instructor the flexibility to select companion texts for each of the threshold concepts."

—**Ann Mattis**, *Assistant Professor of English and Gender, Women's, and Sexuality Studies, University of Wisconsin—Sheboygan*

"Launius and Hassel are the mediums of metacognitive awareness in the field of Women's and Gender Studies, distilling threshold concepts so that students can become active agents in critiquing and shaping our gendered world. This book should be foundational in any Women's and Gender Studies program."

—**Tara Wood**, *Assistant Professor of English and instructor in Gender Studies, Rockford University*

"*Threshold Concepts* is my go-to foundational text for both teaching Women's and Gender Studies classes and facilitating Safe Zone training. The extensive end of chapter questions and learning roadblocks sections help students process and apply the information. I appreciate that the authors succinctly frame and contextualize complex gender studies topics."

—**Christopher Henry Hinesley**, *Associate Director, Women's and Gender Studies, Rochester Institute of Technology*

Threshold Concepts in Women's and Gender Studies

Threshold Concepts in Women's and Gender Studies: Ways of Seeing, Thinking, and Knowing is a textbook designed primarily for introduction to Women's and Gender Studies courses with the intent of providing both skills- and concept-based foundation in the field. The text is driven by a single key question: "What are the ways of thinking, seeing, and knowing that characterize Women's and Gender Studies and are valued by its practitioners?" Rather than taking a topical approach, *Threshold Concepts* develops the key concepts and ways of thinking that students need in order to develop a deep understanding and to approach material like feminist scholars do, across disciplines. This book illustrates four of the most critical concepts in Women's and Gender Studies—the social construction of gender, privilege and oppression, intersectionality, and feminist praxis—and grounds these concepts in multiple illustrations.

The second edition includes a significant number of updates, revisions, and expansions: the case studies in all five chapters have been revised and expanded, as have the end of chapter elements, statistics have been updated, and numerous references to significant news stories and cultural developments of the past three years have been added. Finally, many more "callbacks" to previous chapters have been incorporated throughout the textbook in order to remind students to carry forward and build upon what they have learned about each threshold concept even as they move on to a new one.

Christie Launius directs and teaches in the Women's and Gender Studies program at the University of Wisconsin, Oshkosh. She has taught the introductory course for over 20 years at six different institutions. She is also active in the field of working-class studies; she is the book review editor for the *Journal of Working-Class Studies* and served as president of the association from 2014 to 2015.

Holly Hassel has taught in the Gender, Sexuality, and Women's Studies program and the English department at the University of Wisconsin Colleges since 2004. Her work on teaching and learning in women's studies has been published in multiple books and journals. She is editor of the journal *Teaching English in the Two-Year College*.

Titles of Related Interest

Threshold Concepts in Women's and Gender Studies

Ways of Seeing, Thinking, and Knowing

Second Edition

Christie Launius and Holly Hassel

Routledge
Taylor & Francis Group

NEW YORK AND LONDON

Second edition published 2018
by Routledge
711 Third Avenue, New York, NY 10017

and by Routledge
2 Park Square, Milton Park, Abingdon, Oxon, OX14 4RN

Routledge is an imprint of the Taylor & Francis Group, an informa business

First edition published by Routledge 2015

Library of Congress Cataloging in Publication Data
Names: Launius, Christie, author. | Hassel, Holly, author.
Title: Threshold concepts in women's and gender studies : ways of seeing,
    thinking, and knowing / Christie Launius, Holly Hassel.
Description: Second edition. | Abingdon, Oxon ; New York, NY : Routledge,
    2018. | Includes bibliographical references and index.
Identifiers: LCCN 2017043817 | ISBN 9781138304321 (hardback) |
    ISBN 9781138304352 (pbk.) | ISBN 9780203730218 (ebook)
Subjects: LCSH: Women's studies. | Feminism. | Sex role.
Classification: LCC HQ1180 .L38 2018 | DDC 305.42—dc23
LC record available at https://lccn.loc.gov/2017043817

ISBN: 978-1-138-30432-1 (hbk)
ISBN: 978-1-138-30435-2 (pbk)
ISBN: 978-0-203-73021-8 (ebk)

Typeset in Adobe Caslon and Copperplate
by Apex CoVantage, LLC

Visit the eResources: www.routledge.com/9781138304352

Printed and bound in the United States of America by Sheridan

CONTENTS

PREFACE

Threshold Concepts in Women's and Gender Studies: Ways of Seeing, Thinking, and Knowing is a textbook designed primarily for use in the introductory course in the field of Women's and Gender Studies (WGS) with the intent of providing both skills- and concept-based foundation in the field. The text is driven by a single key question: "What are the ways of thinking, seeing, and knowing that characterize our field and are valued by its practitioners?" Through extensive review of the published literature, conversations with Women's and Gender Studies faculty across the University of Wisconsin System, and our own systematic research and assessment of student learning needs, we identified four of the most critical threshold concepts in Women's and Gender Studies:

- the social construction of gender
- privilege and oppression
- intersectionality
- feminist praxis

This textbook aims to introduce students to how these four concepts provide a feminist lens across the disciplines and outside the classroom. The term "threshold concept" is defined by Meyer and Land as a core disciplinary concept that is both troublesome and transformative. As they go on to explain, "A threshold concept can be considered as akin to a portal, opening up a new and previously inaccessible way of thinking about something. It represents a transformed way of understanding, or interpreting, or viewing something without which the learner cannot progress." A threshold concept is integrative, and when students cross the threshold and grasp a concept, "the hidden interrelatedness" of other concepts within that discipline becomes apparent (Cousin 4).

What Makes This Book Unique

The majority of WGS textbooks tend to be organized around the institutions that foster and reinforce gender hierarchies while also acknowledging the intersections of gender with race, class, and sexuality. Typical examples of these institutions include women and work, the family, media and culture, religion and spirituality, health and medicine, etc. Some focus exclusively on the U.S., while others integrate, to greater or lesser degrees, a global focus. Most also conclude with a chapter on activism. This approach privileges coverage of content over the disciplinary ways of seeing, thinking, and knowing. These textbooks certainly introduce and employ these four threshold concepts, but often as a one-shot definition, with the assumption that students will come to understand the concepts' centrality through encountering them repeatedly in the context of topical units, without their centrality being made explicit. What *Threshold Concepts in Women's and Gender Studies: Ways of Seeing, Thinking, and Knowing* does is not "cover" material but rather "uncover" the key threshold concepts and ways of thinking that students need in order to develop a deep understanding and to approach the material like feminist scholars do, across the disciplines. The advantage of this approach is that rather than the "one-shot definition" that characterizes most texts, students continually learn and relearn how the threshold concept is illustrated across multiple contexts, thus reinforcing their understanding in more substantive ways. Further, foregrounding the "learning roadblocks" that many students encounter as part of the learning process helps circumvent and move more quickly past those misconceptions that keep students from progressing in their understanding of Women's and Gender Studies.

In *Threshold Concepts in Women's and Gender Studies*, we make the assumption that ways of seeing, thinking, and knowing in Women's and Gender Studies must be made transparent to students, and that learning will be done most effectively if students understand the course goals, the pedagogical approach, and the potential roadblocks to understanding. We contend that the work happening on the part of the instructor and the work happening by students should not be "parallel tracks" that each negotiates independently, but part of the teaching and learning conversation itself, happening in and about the content, as part of the work of the classroom.

Features

Threshold Concepts in Women's and Gender Studies is organized strategically and conceptually in a reverse pyramid structure. That is, each threshold concept is introduced at a broad level as the key idea of the chapter, while subsequent chapter components add layers of depth and specificity. Each chapter contains the following elements:

- *Opening Illustration*: The opening illustration engages readers in the topic—typically these are drawn from historical, cultural, biological, or current events topics.
- *A Feminist Stance*: We use the framing concept of a "feminist stance" (Crawley, et al.) to help students continue to understand the nature and strategies of a feminist approach with each chapter they read. Our intent is not to suggest that there is a singular, monolithic feminist stance, or what that stance *is*; instead, we draw attention to what a feminist stance *does*—employ a critical lens using the threshold concepts.
- *Definition of the Threshold Concept*: Each chapter focuses on one of four threshold concepts. The chapter opens with a definition of the threshold concept, drawing from established and relevant research across interdisciplinary fields of study.
- *Framing Definitions and Related Concepts*: More specificity is offered by related concepts, or other explanatory terminology by scholars in the field that help students see how the threshold concept is supported and illustrated by related terms.
- *Learning Roadblocks*: Once students have an initial grasp of the concept and its related terms, the chapter introduces common "learning roadblocks" or misconceptions that many students encounter which prevent a full grasp of the idea. These misconceptions are directly

addressed along with tools that can serve as a "check for understanding" so students are able to understand not only why these
learning roadblocks crop up but also where their own learning is in
relation to the roadblocks. The goal of this feature is to help students identify common misunderstandings that prevent them from
"crossing the threshold."

- *Anchoring Topics*: To further develop students' understanding of the
  threshold concept, each chapter includes a discussion of it in relation to three anchoring topics: work and family, language, images,
  and symbols, and bodies. These three anchoring topics were chosen because of their centrality to feminist scholarship and activism.
  Selected issues within the anchoring topics are discussed through
  the prism of the particular threshold concept in an effort to help
  students develop a scaffolded, nuanced, and complex understanding
  of the cluster of related issues within the anchoring topics.

- *Case Study*: The case study offers an in-depth and analytical perspective on one key issue that should crystallize students' understanding of the concept. Case studies have been selected based on
  relevance to the threshold concept, and to represent a broad range
  of interdisciplinary issues.

- *Evaluating Prior Knowledge Activities*: As Ambrose and colleagues
  have observed, students' prior knowledge (particularly commonsense understandings or everyday use of discipline-specific terms)
  has a strong impact on how students absorb new knowledge. Activities that ask students to evaluate prior knowledge, to monitor their
  progress, and to develop a metacognitive understanding of their
  knowledge building stem from this learning principle.

- *Application Exercises and Skills Assessments*: Gender and women's
  studies classrooms typically emphasize several key related values
  focused on participatory learning: validation of personal experience,
  activism, reflexivity, action orientation, and local–global connections
  (see Crawley et al., 2008; Stake and Hoffman, 2000; Markowitz,
  2005; Maher, 1987; Shrewsbury, 1993). This praxis orientation (see
  Blake and Ooten, 2008) is reflected in application exercises and skills
  assessments for each chapter in which students are invited to connect
  disciplinary and interdisciplinary knowledge with lived experience.

- *Discussion Questions*: Consistent with the signature feminist pedagogies of Women's and Gender Studies classrooms that focus on collaboration, interconnectedness, and creating a community of learners (see Hassel and Nelson, 2012; Chick and Hassel, 2009), this book adheres to the convention of providing discussion questions for each chapter.
- *Writing Prompts*: The text includes writing activities that encourage students to process, reflect on, and integrate the course material.
- *Works Cited* and *Suggested Readings*: In this edition, we have separated the Works Cited section from the Suggested Readings. Because the text is intended to serve as a critical introduction to key concepts and not as a reader, we provide suggested, relevant readings that instructors can use to support and develop students' learning. In this way, we imagine the book to be part of a customized course in which the instructor can structure the curriculum around key ideas, then provide a deeper learning experience for students by adding primary documents, classic essays, or online texts to the course that reflect the instructor's specific learning goals and area of expertise.

Goals of the Book

As coauthors, our goals for this book have been to provide a text that reflects what we have learned about student learning needs in Women's and Gender Studies throughout our collective years of teaching in the field as well as current thinking in the field and in higher education more broadly about what it means to learn within a discipline or interdisciplinary area. The organization of the text around threshold concepts is intended to reflect what Lendol Calder calls an "uncoverage" model, one in which students learn to think, see, and know like feminist scholars rather than absorb a body of knowledge to be "covered."

As a result, our intent is to help students learn those ways of knowing and then be able to apply them to new subjects, in the way that feminist scholars do. We have tried to reflect in the text some of our shared values as teachers and writers. We have aimed to reflect an up-to-date sensibility in including recent data and research studies as well as current phenomena. Our tone emphasizes that arguments about sex and gender (and any number of other issues within feminist scholarship and activism) are unresolved, ongoing, and controversial, and the text contextualizes a feminist perspective by explaining what that perspective stands in contrast to.

While we treat each of the four threshold concepts in a separate chapter, which in one sense implies their separability and separateness, they are of course interconnected, and we strive to make those connections explicit within each chapter. In some instances this means returning to the same topic across chapters and highlighting different elements of it. For example, though feminist praxis has its own separate chapter, we have identified the ways that discussions of "problems" within Women's and Gender Studies can be responded to with action or different ways of thinking. Similarly, though intersectionality has its own chapter, we have attempted to incorporate an intersectional perspective and intersectional analysis *throughout* the book, addressing the interrelatedness of systems of privilege and oppression as part of an intersectional examination both across and within topics and themes.

Logistics of Using the Text

While individual programs and pedagogical approaches may vary, the threshold concepts we have identified are central to the content- and skills-based learning outcomes of a large number of Women's and Gender Studies programs nationally (see Levin and Berger and Radeloff). As such, we believe that using a text like ours can be helpful in making those programmatic learning outcomes explicit, and can support the assessment plans of programs and departments.

Logistically, one way to use this book in an introductory WGS course would be to assign all five chapters in succession over the first half of the semester before moving on to a varying number of topics (drawn from our anchoring topics or others of particular interest to the instructor) that would be spread out over the remainder of the semester. In this scenario, all of the threshold concepts would be revisited in the context of each topic.

A different approach to using this book in an introductory WGS course would be to spread the assignment and reading of the five chapters across the course of the entire semester, using one or more topics in relation to each threshold concept. This approach would allow for in-depth time with each individual threshold concept before moving on to the next.

Instructors can find more materials to support their work in the classroom using this text with the eResources (www.routledge.com/ 9781138304352). Materials available online include the following:

- web resources
- additional suggested readings
- full text journal articles for use with the text

A Note on the Second Edition

We are grateful for all of the feedback we have received since the book's publication in January of 2015. We have presented on the threshold concepts approach to teaching the introductory course at state, regional, and national conferences for the past several years, and have had many stimulating conversations with colleagues that have informed our revisions. We also received a wealth of constructive feedback from reviewers that was very useful to us as we began the process of working on the second edition. Overall, this edition includes a significant number of updates, revisions, and expansions. There are new opening illustrations in Chapters 4 and 5, and the case studies in all five chapters are either new or have been revised and expanded. In this edition, we have separated the Works Cited section from the Suggested Readings, and have significantly revised and/or expanded the end of chapter elements for every chapter. We have also, wherever possible, updated relevant statistics, and make numerous references to significant news stories and cultural developments of the past three years, including the 2015 Supreme Court decision, *Obergefell v. Hodges*, that legalized same-sex marriage, the 2016 U.S. presidential election, the Movement for Black Lives, and trans* rights activism (and backlash against it), just to name a few. We have also re-organized some sections, added many new examples, edited extensively for clarity, and moved some of the learning roadblocks so that they are more integrated into the relevant section. Finally, we have also incorporated many more "callbacks" to previous chapters throughout the textbook. As we have taught with the textbook, we have found it helpful to remind students to carry forward and build upon what they have learned about each threshold concept even as they move onto a new one.

Works Cited

Ambrose, Susan, et al. *How Learning Works: Seven Research-Based Principles for Smart Teaching*. Jossey-Bass, 2010.

Berger, Michelle Tracey, and Cheryl Radeloff. *Transforming Scholarship: Why Women's and Gender Studies Students Are Changing Themselves and the World*. Routledge, 2011.

Blake, Holly, and Melissa Ooten. "Bridging the Divide: Connecting Feminist Histories and Activism in the Classroom." *Radical History Review*, vol. 102, 2008, pp. 63–72.

Calder, Lendol. "Uncoverage: Toward a Signature Pedagogy for the History Survey." *Journal of American History*, vol. 92, no. 4, 2006, pp. 1358–1371.

Chick, Nancy, and Holly Hassel. "Don't Hate Me Because I'm Virtual: Feminist Pedagogy in the Online Classroom." *Feminist Teacher*, vol. 19, no. 3, 2009, pp. 195–215.

Cousin, Glynis. "An Introduction to Threshold Concepts." *Planet*, vol. 17, 2006, www.ee.ucl.ac.uk/~mflanaga/Cousin%20Planet%2017.pdf. Accessed 5 July 2017.

Crawley, Sara, et al. "Introduction: Feminist Pedagogies in Action: Teaching Beyond Disciplines." *Feminist Teacher*, vol. 19, no. 1, 2008, pp. 1–12.

Hassel, Holly, and Nerissa Nelson. "A Signature Feminist Pedagogy: Connection and Transformation in Women's Studies." In *Exploring More Signature Pedagogies*. Eds. Nancy L. Chick, Regan Gurung, and Aeron Haynie. Stylus Publishing, 2012, pp. 143–155.

Levin, Amy. "Questions for a New Century: Women's Studies and Integrative Learning." *National Women's Studies Association*, 2007, www.nwsa.org/Files/Resources/WS_Integrative_Learning_Levine.pdf. Accessed 5 July 2017.

Maher, Frances. "Inquiry Teaching and Feminist Pedagogy." *Social Education*, vol. 51, no. 3, 1987, pp. 186–192.

Markowitz, Linda. "Unmasking Moral Dichotomies: Can Feminist Pedagogy Overcome Student Resistance?" *Gender and Education*, vol. 17, no. 1, 2005, pp. 39–55.

Meyer, Jan, and Ray Land. "Threshold Concepts and Troublesome Knowledge: Linkages to Ways of Thinking and Practising within the Disciplines." *Enhancing Teaching-Learning Environments in Undergraduate Courses*. ETL Project. Occasional Report 4, 2003. https://kennslumidstod.hi.is/wp-content/uploads/2016/04/meyerandland.pdf. Accessed 5 July 2017.

Shrewsbury, Carolyn. "What Is Feminist Pedagogy?" *Women's Studies Quarterly*, vol. 3, 1993, pp. 8–16.

Stake, Jayne, and Frances Hoffman. "Putting Feminist Pedagogy to the Test." *Psychology of Women Quarterly*, vol. 24, 2000, pp. 30–38.

ACKNOWLEDGMENTS

We owe a deep debt of gratitude to our faculty colleagues in the University of Wisconsin System Women's Studies Consortium. This project emerged from conversations among our fellow Women's and Gender Studies teachers throughout the state of Wisconsin over several years. Their expertise, critical insights, years of teaching experience, and generosity of time and spirit shaped this project from start to finish.

In particular, we thank Helen Klebesadel, director of the Women's Studies Consortium for her tireless support and advocacy for this book; former UW System Gender and Women's Studies Librarian Phyllis Holman Weisbard offered research support in the early stages of the project; and we thank both Phyllis and JoAnne Lehman, editor of *Feminist Collections*, for suggesting that we write a review of introductory WGS textbooks for *Feminist Collections: A Quarterly of Women's Studies Resources*, published out of the UW System Office of the Women's Studies Librarian. We especially thank JoAnne Lehman for believing in the work and making publication possible.

We are also thankful to the UW System Office of Professional and Instructional Development for a conference mini-grant in 2011 that supported bringing together Women's and Gender Studies instructors to discuss threshold concepts in the field.

Christie would like to acknowledge the support of the University of Wisconsin Oshkosh Faculty Development Program, which funded her small grant proposal. Holly is grateful to the University of Wisconsin–Marathon County, which awarded her a Summer Research Grant to complete work on this project, as well as to the UW Colleges Women's Studies Program that has supported her work on threshold concepts in Women's and Gender Studies in material and immaterial ways. Thanks especially to Susan Rensing who helped us work through some of the initial organizational challenges of the text and provided many helpful suggestions along the way. And a thanks to our reviewers:

Courtney Jarrett	Ball State University
Beth Sertell	Ohio University
Daniel Humphrey	Texas A&M University
Jennifer Smith	Pacific Lutheran University
Tanya Kennedy	University of Maine
JoAnna Wall	University of Oklahoma
Shawn Maurer	College of Holy Cross
Danielle DeMuth	Grand Valley State
Desirée Henderson	University of Texas, Arlington
Beatrix Brockman	Austin Peay State University
Marta S. McClintock-Comeaux	California University of Pennsylvania
Lynne Bruckner	Chatham University
Angela Fitzpatrick	Coastal Carolina University
Harry Brod	University of Northern Iowa
Danielle Roth-Johnson	University of Nevada
Julia Landweber	Montclair State University
Lauren Martin	Pennsylvania State University
Murty Komanduri	Fort Valley State University
Jocelyn Fenton Stitt	University of Michigan—Ann Arbor
Katherine Pruitt	Indiana University—Purdue University—Fort Wayne
Ann Marie Nicolosi	The College of New Jersey
Hope Russell	Niagara University
Jan Wilson	University of Tulsa

And a number of other anonymous reviewers.

Christie Launius and Holly Hassel

1

INTRODUCTION

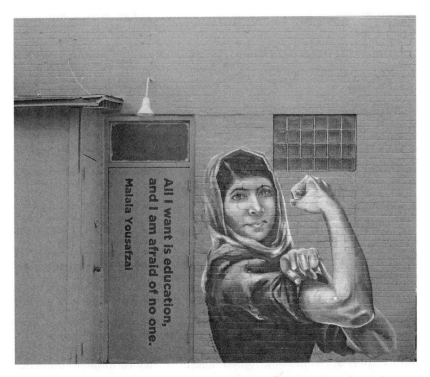

Figure 1.1 Artist Anat Ronen blends images and words of Malala Yousafzai with imagery of Rosie the Riveter

Source: www.anatronen.com

1

Why "Ways of Seeing, Thinking, and Knowing"?

Women's and Gender Studies (WGS) courses are a common feature on a large number of college and university campuses, with over 700 programs in the United States alone. Many students take an introductory WGS course as a part of their general education requirements, whereas others wind up in our classrooms as a result of word-of-mouth advertising from peers and roommates. A smaller number of students eagerly seek out WGS courses when they get to college after encountering Women's and Gender Studies in their high school curriculum.

In their book *Transforming Scholarship: Why Women's and Gender Studies Students Are Changing Themselves and the World*, Michele Tracy Berger and Cheryl Radeloff state that "students pursuing questions in women's and gender studies are part of an emerging vanguard of knowledge producers in the US and globally" (5). This is to say, WGS is an exciting, vibrant, and growing field. This textbook aims to introduce you to the ways of seeing, thinking, and knowing that characterize the field and are valued by its practitioners. These ways of seeing, thinking, and knowing can then be used throughout your academic study, not just in WGS courses. More fundamentally, these ways of seeing, thinking, and knowing can be (and perhaps should be) taken out of the classroom and into the world. In fact, the bridging of the divide between academia and the so-called real world is a big part of what Women's and Gender Studies is all about.

The image at the beginning of this chapter (see Figure 1.1) emphasizes this real-world engagement. The words and image of Malala Yousafzai, a young Pakistani woman, are highlighted because her struggle—to gain access to education for girls in a Pakistani area in which the Taliban has prohibited it—illustrates how feminist ways of seeing, thinking, and knowing are actualized. The image, invoking the historically significant "Rosie the Riveter" pose that has come to symbolize U.S. women's entrance into the workforce in the mid-20th century, shows the historical roots of feminist movement and how they continue to influence women's **activism** for gender justice worldwide.

Using This Book

As you approach this text, we want to direct your attention to the ways that we have organized it in order to provide an introduction to the ways of seeing, thinking, and knowing in Women's and Gender Studies. Each chapter is structured in purposeful ways in order to introduce you to the definitions of the **threshold concept** and to offer grounding examples that will deepen your understanding:

- The opening illustration in each chapter invites you to consider how the concept is relevant to day-to-day life, either current events, popular culture, historical moments, or other spaces.
- We have indicated in each chapter how the concept suggests a "feminist stance," or ways of looking at the world.
- Threshold concepts are defined, as are related or supporting concepts from research, theory, or scholarship that are critical to understanding the ideas in the chapter.
- Each chapter includes examples of "learning roadblocks," or the kinds of barriers to fully understanding the threshold concept that students typically encounter. We've drawn from our many years of teaching introductory Women's and Gender Studies courses as well as conversations with colleagues to identify these roadblocks as well as explain why they are common misconceptions, and how students can move past them.
- In order to illustrate in a fuller way how the threshold concept operates in interdisciplinary forms, each of the concepts is discussed through the lens of "anchoring topics," or key ideas that will root the concept within three overlapping and related areas of inquiry within Women's and Gender Studies: work and family; language, images, and symbols; and gendered bodies. As you engage with each of the chapters, you'll develop not only a new understanding of the threshold concept in that chapter, but an increasingly deepening sense of how each of the anchoring topics is "inflected" by the concepts.
- Each chapter contains a case study that, like the opening illustration, is intended to bring the threshold concept to life for readers and to help you see how it can be understood through specific cultural, historical, or other phenomena.
- Finally, at the end of the chapter, you'll find exercises and other ways to test your understanding of the chapter material, to engage in conversation with classmates, to write about the topic, and to apply what you've learned to other contexts.

We hope that this organizational structure will create multiple ways of "trying on" feminist ways of seeing, thinking, and knowing in academic and nonacademic spaces.

Feminism, Stereotypes, and Misconceptions

First and foremost, in order to understand terms like "feminist stance" and the idea that there are **feminist** ways of seeing, thinking, and knowing, some definitions of **feminism** are in order. As a term, feminism has a history; according to Estelle Freedman, it was "first coined in France in the 1880s as *feminisme*," (3) and made its way to the United States by the first decade of the 20th century. It was not used widely in the United States until the 1960s, however. In *No Turning Back: The History of Feminism and the Future of Women*, Freedman offers a four-part definition of feminism: "Feminism is a belief that women and men are inherently of equal worth. Because most societies privilege men as a group, social movements are necessary to achieve equality between women and men, with the understanding that gender always intersects with other social hierarchies" (7). In *Feminist Theory from Margin to Center*, bell hooks offers a succinct definition of feminism as "the struggle to end sexist oppression" (26). She goes on to argue that understanding and defining feminism in this way "directs our attention to systems of domination and the inter-relatedness of **sex**, race, and class oppression" (31). She concludes, "[t]he foundation of future feminist struggle must be solidly based on a recognition of the need to eradicate the underlying cultural basis and causes of **sexism** and other forms of group oppression" (31). Given these definitions, a feminist, then, is quite simply someone who advocates feminism. Each of the four threshold concepts that this book is structured around is implicit, if not explicit, in both Freedman's and hooks's definitions: the social construction of **gender**, the concepts of **privilege** and **oppression, intersectionality**, and **praxis**.

Advocating feminism or being a feminist can take many forms; in this book we emphasize the idea of taking a so-called feminist stance, which is to say, adopting a feminist perspective or way of looking at the world. As Crawley and colleagues assert,

> Although feminism is, in substance, always attentive to power
> differences that create inequalities, particularly those that create

differential opportunities for women and men (but also those that
create racial and ethnic, class-based, or sexuality-based inequalities), feminism is also an epistemological shift away from a history
of androcentric bias in the sciences, social sciences, and humani-
ties. As such, it is not just an "area study" (again, not just about
"women") but something much deeper: a way of orienting to academic work that is attuned to power relations, both within the
academy and within knowledge construction itself.

(2)

We will discuss this at more length in the section on the history of
Women's and Gender Studies as an academic field.

It also seems important to address here at the outset any lingering
misconceptions about feminism and feminists. Many stereotypes and
misconceptions about feminism, feminists, and the field of Women's
and Gender Studies circulate in our culture. These stereotypes and
misconceptions pop up in the right-wing blogosphere and so-called
lad mags like *Maxim,* but also in magazines like *Time* and *Newsweek,*
in Hollywood movies and television shows, and in everyday conversations. Most students taking this course have probably heard quite a few
of them. If you're curious about whether your friends, family, coworkers, and others believe those stereotypes and misconceptions, try this
exercise: make an announcement on the social media platform of your
choice that you're taking this class, and see what sorts of responses are
made and what sorts of conversations develop. Chances are, people will
supply some of the following (and maybe come up with different ones
as well):

- *Feminism is dead.* This misconception is invoked as a way to try to
  derail or shut down a discussion of gender inequality, a way to dismiss someone's critique by saying that we no longer need feminism
  because equality has already been achieved. The most charitable
  read on this stereotype is that people look at the real gains made
  by feminism and mistakenly assume that the need for feminism has
  passed. In this scenario, the person claiming that equality has already
  been achieved is likely experiencing the world from a position of

relative privilege. The misconception doesn't just get perpetuated on an individual level, however; it is a frequent headline in the news media. In response to *Time*'s cover story in 1998 declaring feminism dead, feminist writer Erica Jong noted that "there have been no less than 119 articles in the magazine sticking pins in feminism during the last 25 years." All of this raises the question, as Jessica Valenti puts it, "if feminism is dead, then why do people have to keep on trying to kill it?" (11).

- *Feminists are ugly, hairy, braless, don't wear makeup, etc. Emphasis on the ugly.* A feature called "Cure a Feminist," which appeared in the November 2003 issue of *Maxim*, does a good job of illustrating this stereotype.[1] It features four images of the same woman wearing different clothing and displaying different body language that purport to show the transformation from feminist to "actual girl." The "feminist" is wearing baggy jeans and a so-called wifebeater tank top with no bra. Her hair is messy, and her arm is raised to reveal a hairy armpit. She also has a cigarette dangling from her mouth, and she is standing with legs apart, with one hand hooked into the pocket of her jeans. By the end of her transformation, she is wearing nothing but a lacy bra and panties with high heels, standing with one hip jutted out and her hand tugging her underwear down. Her hair is styled and she is wearing makeup. The intent of this stereotype is fairly simplistic and transparent, but nonetheless hard to shake. As Jessica Valenti puts it, "[t]he easiest way to keep women—especially young women—away from feminism is to threaten them with the ugly stick. It's also the easiest way to dismiss someone and her opinions" (8–9).
- *Feminists hate men.* The *Maxim* piece hits this stereotype, too. The implication here is that feminism is a hate-filled vendetta against individual men. The thought bubble coming out of the so-called feminist's mouth says, "There'd be no more wars if all penises were cut off! Argh!" This misconception is a strategy to dismiss and mischaracterize feminism and feminists, by individualizing feminist concerns and seeing feminism as a battle of the sexes, rather than a structural analysis of systems of privilege and inequality. A more accurate characterization recognizes that feminism is interested in

critiquing and combating sexism and **patriarchy**, not hating or bashing individual men.

- *Only women can be feminists.* It is clear, in the *Maxim* feature and elsewhere, that the default assumption is that only women would *want* to be feminists, given that feminists hate men, and that only women stand to gain from feminism. This view is increasingly being challenged, not only because a growing number of men are committed to being strong feminist **allies** to the women in their lives, but also because men increasingly see the ways in which they are harmed by adhering to traditional masculine norms. These men are stepping outside of the so-called man box and are modeling feminist forms of **masculinity**.

- *Feminists are lesbians (or male feminists are gay).* This misconception often circulates as a dissuasion strategy that is sometimes referred to as "lesbian-baiting" or "gay-baiting," that is, as a way of capitalizing on social stigma within some communities to scare people away from openly identifying as feminist or even supporting key principles of gender equity. As philosopher Sue Cataldi has argued, "[t]he use of this word is a scare tactic. It is intended to frighten people away from affiliating with or associating with feminism" (80). In addition to harnessing the social power of **homophobia** to discredit **feminist action** and theory, this particular stereotype serves the purpose of reinforcing traditional gender scripts and sexualities. As Suzanne Pharr explains in "Homophobia as a Weapon of Sexism":

  > What does a woman have to do to get called a lesbian? Almost anything, sometimes nothing at all, but certainly anything that threatens the status quo, anything that steps out of role, anything that asserts the rights of women, anything that doesn't include submission or subordination.

  (73)

- *Feminism is solely for privileged (read: white, cisgender, straight, middle class) women interested in equality with similarly situated men.* This stereotype is a bit different than the others in that it is born out of a history of feminism in the U.S. that is marked by moments of outright exclusion of women of color, working-class women, and lesbians, as well as the downplaying or ignoring of issues important to them. The important point here is to acknowledge this past while also acknowledging that women of color, working-class women, lesbians, etc. have also always been engaged in feminist activism. In recent years, the contemporary feminist movement has made important strides toward becoming fully intersectional, even as it still has a long way to go, as evidenced by the January 2017 Women's March on Washington. While the march was initially referred to as the Million Women's March, intersectional feminists quickly pointed out that this replicated and appropriated the name of a march led by African American women in 1997. After this early organizing misstep, the march changed its name and came to be organized and led by a truly diverse group of women who crafted a deeply intersectional platform asserting that "Gender Justice is Racial Justice is Economic Justice." Even so, many women of color felt unwelcome at the march, and many white women bristled at being asked to check their (white) privilege.

The effect of these stereotypes and misconceptions: many people, particularly young women, are reluctant to identify as feminists. The title of Lisa Hogeland's oft-anthologized essay, originally published in *Ms.* Magazine in 1994, spells it out: "Fear of Feminism: Why Young Women Get the Willies." Hogeland explains, aptly and pointedly, that at least one reason is

> The central feminist tenet that **the personal is political** is profoundly threatening to young women who don't want to be called to account. It is far easier to rest in silence, as if silence were neutrality, and as if neutrality were safety.

That is, calling into question current gender arrangements requires people to actively and consciously challenge the ways that gender inequality persists instead of, as Hogeland states, "hide from feminist issues by not being feminists."

More recently, feminist blogger Julie Zeilinger has jumped into the fray, and the title of her book indicates that what she calls a "P.R.-problem" with feminism is still going on: *A Little F'd Up: Why Feminism Is Not a Dirty Word* (2012). Both Zeilinger and Jessica Valenti, among many others, bemoan what they call the "I'm not a feminist, but . . ." phenomenon, in which people express feminist ideas and opinions but disavow the label. Their response is to argue that most young people *are* feminists, but, as Zeilinger puts it, "They just don't know it" (79). Or as Valenti titles the first chapter of *Full Frontal Feminism: A Young Woman's Guide to Why Feminism Matters:* "You're a hardcore feminist. I swear" (5). In sum, while both Zeilinger and Valenti grant that the stereotypes and misconceptions about feminism and feminists continue to swirl through our news media and popular culture, and get internalized and perpetuated by many, they clearly believe that, with a dose of corrective information to counter the stereotypes, people can and do see them for what they are, which is an attempt to undermine feminism.

Proof that attitudes about gender equality have changed is abundant, as documented, for example, in the results of a survey by the Pew Research Center, which shows that almost three-quarters of young adults under the age of 30 seek equal partnership marriages (see Figure 1.2).

Stephanie Coontz cites this research as a positive sign of feminist progress, but she follows up by showing that in reality, many couples have a very hard time putting these aspirations into practice. In "Why Gender Equality Stalled," she argues that the

> main barriers to further progress toward gender equity no longer lie in people's personal attitudes and relationships. Instead, structural impediments prevent people from acting on their egalitarian values, forcing men and women into personal accommodations and rationalizations that do not reflect their preferences.

The structural impediments Coontz is referring to are the gender wage gap, the relative absence of family-friendly workplace policies, and the lack of high-quality affordable and accessible childcare. How does this

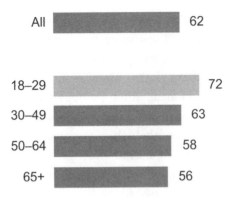

Figure 1.2 Young adults favor dual income marriage

Source: Pew Research Center survey, conducted Oct 1–21, 2010, N = 2, 691.

Q wording: What kind of marriage do you think is the more satisfying way of life? One where the husband provides for the family and the wife takes care of the house and children, or one where the husband and wife both have jobs and both take care of the house and children.

relate back to the stereotypes and misconceptions about feminism and feminists, you ask?

The fact that almost three-quarters of people under 30 aspire to an **egalitarian** marriage shows that the discrediting of feminism and feminist values through the dissemination of stereotypes has largely not succeeded, at least in terms of the attitudes documented by research. On the other hand, however, the demonization or dismissal of feminism *has* succeeded insofar as the couples who try and fail to enact their egalitarian values tend to think of their failure in personal, rather than political, terms. In other words, they think that the problem lies with them rather than with broader, structural factors outside of their immediate control. And most crucially, they are less likely to turn those feelings of personal failure into a recognition that this is a political issue that could be and is being addressed by feminists and feminist organizations. Debunking and offering rebuttals to those stereotypes about feminism and feminists is not just (or only) about countering myth with reality, then, but about helping to give people the necessary tools and perspectives they need to change the world in ways that allow them to, as Stephanie Coontz puts it, "put their gender values into practice." All of this illustrates why the feminist mantra of the second wave, "The personal is political," resonates across issues and experience.

Feminist ways of seeing, thinking, and knowing provide tools for the critical analysis of stereotypes about feminism and feminists. Calling yourself a feminist (or advocating feminism, as bell hooks puts it) may or may not be the outcome of trying on these ways of seeing, thinking, and knowing, and in any case, that's not the point. The point is to clear the space for everyone to consider feminism on its own terms, free from bias and distortion.

The History of Feminist Movement

The awareness of gendered inequality and women's (and male allies') efforts to eliminate inequality has a long history. However, in terms of organized activism on the part of women's groups in the United States to address long-standing oppressions such as a lack of civil rights, access to higher education and the professions, inequitable treatment by the legal system, and a lack of social and cultural status, the history is more recent.

It should be noted that the term most commonly used to describe feminist activism in the United States is **waves**, with chronological groupings of the first wave, beginning in the mid-19th century and progressing through the early 20th century; the second wave, starting in the mid-1960s; and the third wave, starting in the early 1990s. However, this is largely an organizational convenience and may not only overshadow the ongoing, active efforts on the part of many activists to challenge patriarchal values, norms, and practices, but also overemphasize the contributions of white and middle-class feminists. In what follows we will acknowledge the "waves" narrative while simultaneously complicating it.

The first wave of feminism is widely considered to have its origins in the activist efforts of a group of early feminists: Lucretia Mott and Elizabeth Cady Stanton attempted to attend the World Anti-Slavery Convention in London in 1840 and were barred from participating because of their sex. In 1848, Mott and Stanton joined Martha Wright, Mary Ann McClintock, and Jane Hunt in organizing a two-day meeting of women to be held at a church in Seneca Falls, New York. Several hundred people attended, and another 100 (68 women and 32 men) signed the document drafted by Stanton, "Declaration of Sentiments," modeled on the U.S. Declaration of Independence. It included the first formal demand for access to the "elective franchise," or voting rights, for women, and claimed:

> The history of mankind is a history of repeated injuries and usurpations on the part of man toward woman, having in direct object the establishment of an absolute tyranny over her. To prove this, let facts be submitted to a candid world.

The document not only made demands for property rights and the right to participate civically including voting, but also for recourse in the case of marital abuse and custodial authority over their children in the case of divorce. It also demanded greater participation in the activities of the church and access to educational and professional opportunities.

An issue that feminists and **suffrage** activists dedicated a great deal of attention to was the **Equal Rights Amendment (ERA)**, introduced in 1923 as an effort to cast in policy equal rights for women. However, it took 50 years before the amendment passed both houses of the legislature and ultimately, because it could not win the ratification requirements of 38 states, the amendment failed to be adopted. The text of the amendment reads as follows:

- *Section 1.* Equality of rights under the law shall not be denied or abridged by the United States or by any State on account of sex.
- *Section 2.* The Congress shall have the power to enforce, by appropriate legislation, the provisions of this article.
- *Section 3.* This amendment shall take effect two years after the date of ratification.[2]

Consider that, although many feminist organizations campaigned tirelessly for the passage of the ERA, a strong and vocal minority of women activists, notably Phyllis Schlafly, campaigned against it in the 1970s. They argued that it would eradicate a number of privileges that women enjoyed on the basis of their primary roles as wives and mothers, including entitlement to maintenance (alimony) and child support in the case of divorce and protection from being drafted in times of war. The ERA's opponents also attempted to incite fear and shore up opposition to the amendment by claiming that gender-segregated public restrooms would be illegal if the amendment passed. It is interesting to note that a similar kind of "bathroom panic" is in evidence in recent attempts to regulate which public restrooms transgender individuals can use.

The narrative of the first wave of feminism has been challenged by Paula Gunn Allen in her book *The Sacred Hoop*, where she notes that a full 250 years prior to the Seneca Falls convention, Iroquois women held great power and were respected within their communities. She argues that the women-led tribes of the American continent "provided the basis for all the dreams of liberation that characterize the modern world," although they are rarely credited with having done so. This supports some of the critiques that have been made in the past about early feminist movement, focusing primarily on the rights and activism of middle-class white women without a clear focus on equivalent civic activism for women of color and working-class women.

Since these early efforts at achieving suffrage—women were granted the right to vote in 1920 when the 19th Amendment was ratified—feminist activism since the late 1960s has focused on an array of issues widely considered to be the "second wave" of feminist activism. Early feminist activism in the U.S. focused on gaining rights for women *as citizens* of the United States; feminist activism starting in the 1970s maintained this focus while adding an additional focus on tackling the cultural and interpersonal dimensions of sexism. Issues during the 1960s and 1970s included: reproductive justice, including not just the ability to prevent conception and terminate unwanted pregnancy but also the freedom from involuntary sterilization; access to prenatal care and breastfeeding support; expanded educational and occupational opportunities; access to other political and civic rights; safety from violence; and elimination of cultural sexism including sexual **objectification**, lower social status, and the socialization of women to meet the needs of men. Strong, tangible gains were made in the 1960s and 1970s in particular, during the height of the second wave of feminism, including:

- National, legal access to contraceptive technologies, including the contraceptive pill, which was prohibited by law prior to 1965.
- National, legal access to abortion in the first trimester of pregnancy, with the landmark ruling in *Roe v. Wade* by the Supreme Court in 1973.
- The establishment of women's organizations such as the National Organization for Women (NOW), founded in 1966, largely focused on equal opportunity in the workplace.
- Advocacy for equal pay. In the 1970s, women made, on average, 52 cents to the average man's dollar; today, that hovers around 80.8 percent of the male dollar, still short of equality. When breaking these numbers down by race, they are even more troubling: as the Institute for Women's Policy Research documents, the percentages fall to 68.1 percent for black women and 59.3 percent for Hispanic women (Institute).
- Activism for legislation like the Equal Pay Act (1963), intended to ensure equal wages for all workers, prohibiting discrimination on the basis of sex; the Civil Rights Act (1964), for the protection from harassment on the basis of sex; the Pregnancy Discrimination Act (1978), which protected women from job loss or consequences on the basis of pregnancy.
- Prevention of gender-based violence, including establishment of **Take Back the Night** rallies (1976); creation of **Rape Shield Laws** in the 1970s and 1980s on the state level preventing a rape victim's past sexual history from being used as evidence in a rape trial; formation of the National Coalition Against Domestic Violence (1978); and the passage of the **Violence Against Women Act** (1994), which offered coordinated efforts to develop awareness and prevent violence.
- Passage of **Title IX**. This part of the Education Amendments of 1972 guarantees equal participation in any educational program or activity that receives federal financial resources. Although primarily associated with advancing women's equal participation in athletic activities, Title IX also affected women's achievement of

postsecondary degrees and pay equity within schools, and protection from any other discrimination taking place within an educational setting ("Fast Facts").

• Social advocacy for programs like affordable childcare; social safety nets to support poor women; and rape crisis centers and domestic violence shelters for women who have been victims of violence.

In addition to these tangible gains, second-wave feminism changed American culture in substantial ways. In *Feminism Unfinished*, historian Linda Gordon likens second-wave feminism to a "powerful and fast-flowing river" that

> radically changed the terrain. It moved rocks, carved out new courses, and deposited new soil, producing new gender structures. The new riverbed was felt everywhere: in health, in reproductive choices, media and culture, employment, parenting, education, sex, and man-woman, woman-woman, and parent-child relations.
>
> (75)

The changes brought about by feminist action were absorbed into the culture at large throughout the 1970s and 1980s, even as there was active resistance in the form of anti-feminist backlash, which will be discussed in more depth in Chapter 5.

A third wave of feminism arose in the early 1990s, sparked by the Supreme Court confirmation hearings of Justice Clarence Thomas. The hearings were marked by accusations that Thomas had sexually harassed Anita Hill when she worked for him at the Department of Education and the Equal Employment Opportunity Commission. The televised hearings riveted and outraged many, as Hill was subjected to harsh and dismissive questioning, and Thomas pushed back against the accusations, calling the hearings a "high-tech lynching." Thomas's remark referenced the nation's shameful history of white mobs lynching African American men for supposed sexual misbehavior, thus casting the hearings in a racial frame. Many others attempted to read the episode primarily using a gender frame, highlighting the ways that Hill's accusations of sexual harassment were belittled and dismissed by both Thomas and the white male senators conducting the hearings. Chapter 4's focus on intersectionality will delve further into the dangers of a single-axis analysis and explore the political and analytical developments of an intersectional approach that is able to analyze incidents such as this one in all its complexity.

Rebecca Walker, daughter of prominent second-wave feminist Alice Walker, penned what became the rallying cry for third-wave feminists. In her essay, "Becoming the Third Wave," Walker sounded the call for a revitalization of feminist activism that in particular was aimed at young women who were literally or metaphorically the daughters of second-wave feminists. Subsequently, feminist movement in the United States has focused on continued efforts for workplace rights for all women, **work–life balance** policies, elimination of rape culture and the reduction of violence against women; equality within **institutions** like religious institutions and the military; resistance to the objectification of women in the media and popular culture; racial justice; and **LGBTQ** rights. We will survey many contemporary feminist activist issues, tactics, and strategies in Chapter 5.

Contemporary feminism in the U.S. has also taken a more global turn, with the identification of issues that transcend national borders and the creation of transnational feminist organizations. Feminist activism and advocacy has particularly focused on girls and young women in recent years, especially girls' education, with a growing understanding that keeping girls in school is a key to improving their lives by a number of measures. And keeping girls in school requires tackling all of the factors that cause them to drop out, including not just child marriage, but also a lack of access to menstrual products, and lack of easy access to water (which in many parts of the world requires that girls spend large chunks of their days obtaining water and carrying it back to their homes). More broadly, global feminist activists focus on economic equality for women and the overall undervaluing of women's labor, equal political representation of women in leadership positions, as well as environmental issues. They also focus on preventing forms of patriarchal violence[3] like sex-selective abortion and son preference, **honor killings**, the treatment of women as a form of property, female **infanticide, female genital cutting/female circumcision, intimate partner violence** and marital rape, sex work and sex trafficking, and pornography. Feminists around the globe use a variety of strategies and tactics in their work on these issues. Sometimes they disagree about the best approach, as in the cases of sex work and pornography, in which some advocate legalization, reform, and regulation by the state, whereas others argue for abolition.

Returning to the second wave of feminism in the U.S., which arose in the late 1960s, part of that activist work centered on the dearth of scholarly and academic work by and about women, as well as the desire for an institutional and educational infrastructure that could support and implement feminist work. Out of these motivations, the field of women's studies emerged.

Women's and Gender Studies as an Academic Field

As a field of academic study, with courses, faculty, and majors and minors, Women's and Gender Studies stretches back over 40 years, with the first women's studies courses and programs created in the late 1960s and early 1970s.

The further away we get from the founding of the field, the harder it is to remember what higher education was like prior to its creation. In their Prologue to *Manifesta: Young Women, Feminism, and the Future*, Jennifer Baumgardner and Amy Richards open with a vignette about what life was like in the United States in 1970 (the year they were born). In the section on higher education, they remind us that in 1970 there were still a small number of colleges and universities that barred women from enrolling, and that women's colleges were still referred to as "girls' schools." They also note that many campuses maintained curfew times for female students who lived in the dorms.

The timing of the field's creation is no coincidence; as mentioned earlier, it came into being in the United States during the second wave of feminism, or the **women's liberation** movement. Indeed, for many years afterward, women's studies was often referred to as the academic arm of the women's movement. Professors and students who identified as feminists began questioning and critiquing many aspects of higher education, including *what* was being taught, *how* it was being taught, and *by whom*. They pointed out that women's experiences and perspectives were for the most part absent in the curriculum, and they also noted the relative absence of women in the ranks of professors and administrators. According to Marilyn J. Boxer, the absence of women's voices and perspectives in academia itself constituted a "hidden curriculum of women's second-class status." She continues, "[i]n this view, courses that ignored women's experiences and perspectives subtly reinforced old ideas about female intellectual deficiencies while also perpetuating women's social, economic, and political marginality" (43). For example, students and professors in English departments began to question why there were so few women authors included in literary anthologies and therefore on course syllabi. Professors' efforts to rectify that situation led to the exploration of broader issues such as canon formation and the role of publishers and critics. During this initial period of field development, the main question was, "Where are the women?"

In creating new courses and undertaking new research projects that focused on women and placed their experiences at the center of inquiry, early practitioners realized that they both wanted and needed to go beyond the boundaries of any single academic discipline. Feminist scholars interested in researching motherhood, for example, not only wanted to explore how motherhood had been represented in literature, but also wanted to look at psychological theories of motherhood, or sociological studies that were focused on interviewing women about their experiences of motherhood. The new courses and scholarship, then, frequently had a multidisciplinary or interdisciplinary approach. This emphasis has endured within the field; for example, the scholarship cited in this textbook comes from the fields of history, psychology, sociology, literary studies, public health, and media studies, to name a few. Today, Women's and Gender Studies programs have become the academic home of the courses and scholarship that go beyond the boundaries of a single discipline. In addition, disciplinary courses and scholarship with a feminist focus continue to thrive; the difference in these courses is that they are more focused on the conventions and conversations that practitioners of a single field are interested in.

Over the last four decades, women's studies has grown not just in terms of its numbers and reach across campuses, but also in terms of how it defines and understands its focus and objects of inquiry. For example, while the field first started as "women's studies," the forms of academic inquiry about gender, and new theories, paradigms, and empirical evidence, have resulted in a field of study more accurately titled "women's and gender studies," or "gender, sexuality, and women's studies," or sometimes more pointedly, "feminist studies." Titles of programs or departments or courses often reflect the interests and emphases of particular institutions or faculty in postsecondary education.

If the initial question of the field was "Where are the women?", by the 1980s that question had shifted to "Which women?" Feminist historian Estelle Freedman explains the shift this way: "I believe that we must question both the assumption that the term *man* includes woman as well as the assumption that the term *woman* represents the diversity of female experience" (8). It was during this period that one of the threshold concepts of this book, intersectionality, began to be developed by women of color who correctly noted the limitations of scholarship that did not incorporate considerations of difference. This concept is the focus of Chapter 4.

The name changes that included the terms gender and sexuality reflect the fact that today, research and teaching are often focused not exclusively on women, but also on men and masculinity, and look even further, to the questioning of gender as a binary construct. Thus, for example, we are seeing the emergence of courses on **trans*** issues and identities. At the same time, many programs have incorporated content and degree programs in LGBTQ Studies and the study of sexuality more generally. Finally, the field has also become increasingly global and comparative in focus. The National Women's Studies Association notes that the field draws on the "conceptual claims and theoretical practices of transnationalism, which focus on cultures, structures, and relationships that are formed as a result of the flows of people and resources across geopolitical borders."

Today, the glass is simultaneously half-full and half-empty. On the one hand, huge strides have been made in terms of the numbers of colleges and universities offering courses, minors, and majors in WGS; in terms of the broader integration of gender issues across the curriculum; and in terms of the numbers of women who are professors and administrators. Many students find that they are introduced to issues of gender and sexuality in any number of college courses, only some of which are explicitly designated as Women's and Gender Studies courses. On the other hand, however, women are still overrepresented among the ranks of temporary, part-time, and adjunct faculty, and are woefully under-represented in the science, technology, engineering, and mathematics (STEM) fields. According to the White House Office of Science and Technology Policy, for example, women today currently earn 41 percent of PhDs in STEM fields, but make up only 28 percent of tenure-track faculty in those fields.

Some disciplines more than others have been slow to integrate content on women, gender, and feminism into their curricula; philosophy is a good example. Not coincidentally, philosophy also has some of the lowest numbers of female faculty members. A *Chronicle of Higher Education* story explains that women earned

> 31 percent of bachelor's degrees in philosophy in 2006–7, compared with 41 percent in history, 45 percent in mathematics, 60 percent in biology, and 69 percent in English, to name several other fields. Moreover, women earned just 27 percent of philosophy doctorates in 2006, and they currently make up only 21 percent of professional philosophers.
>
> (Penaluna)

Some theories about these low numbers include explanations ranging from the content itself—the canon of philosophy is almost exclusively made up of male philosophers, or as Penaluna argues, "the canon is sexist and there is little being done about it." Other theories include the low regard for feminist philosophy, overt sexism or misogyny within the field of academic philosophy, and historical associations between men/masculinity and analysis and logic, the hallmarks of academic philosophy.

The progress that has been made in academic and nonacademic settings is in some ways a double-edged sword. As Howe explains:

> In short, students—and some younger faculty as well—may have two different kinds of experiences today: A majority may still be

where we were thirty years ago, unknowingly in a male-centered curriculum; a minority may think that women have always been a part of the curriculum.

(29)

This text aims to introduce you to the many important achievements of feminist work—as well as draw attention to how a feminist stance or lens can make visible the additional work to be done to gain full social equality for all.

Case Study: Assessing Pop Culture

Feminist critics apply the lens of gender (and race and sexuality) to a variety of settings; both inside and outside academia, those devoted to gender justice have devoted much time and attention to how popular culture can both reinforce and challenge dominant ideas about gender. Ellen Willis, Manohla Dargis, GLAAD, and Allison Bechdel have all created "tests" for critically evaluating pop culture artifacts.

In 1971 pioneering feminist rock critic Ellen Willis suggested a test for measuring sexism in the lyrics of songs—take a song written by a man about a woman, reverse the sexes, and analyze the assumptions that are revealed. In a 2011 post on *Jezebel*, Erin Carmon dusted off the test and applied it to Justin Bieber's "One Less Lonely Girl," pointing out that reversing the sexes in this song reveals a condescendingly sexist attitude.

In a 1985 comic strip, "Dykes to Watch Out For," Allison Bechdel introduced a method for assessing gender bias in narratives: fiction, film, TV shows—any text that offers a storyline. In order to pass the test, so to speak, the narrative must feature: 1) at least two women characters; 2) who speak to each other; 3) about something other than a man. Visit the Bechdel test website to see how your favorite (or least favorite) films pass or fail this test of gender and sexism in media.[4] Anita Sarkeesian discusses "The Oscars and the Bechdel Test" on her website, Feminist Frequency.[5] Keep this approach in mind as you read about gender and the Oscars in Chapter 2.

In a related vein, the Vito Russo test (named after the author of the groundbreaking 1981 book *The Celluloid Closet*, which explored

representations of gay characters in Hollywood film from the 1920s
forward) was created by GLAAD in 2013 to assess both whether and
how people with LGBT identities are depicted in films. The bar for
passing is a bit higher in the Russo test than the Bechdel test, which
mainly focuses on the presence or absence of women in a narrative, and
not what they say or how they are depicted. According to GLAAD,[6] in
order to pass the Russo test, a film must 1) contain a character who is
recognizably lesbian, gay, bisexual, and/or transgender; 2) that character
must not be defined solely by their sexual orientation or gender identity;
and 3) they must be embedded in the narrative in a meaningful way, as
opposed to being the object of humor, for example. GLAAD's purpose
in creating the Russo test is explicitly activist; the organization provides
a report each year on how many Hollywood films pass the test, with the
aim, as their website puts it, of providing a "standard GLAAD expects a
greater number of mainstream Hollywood films to reach in the future."

And finally, in 2016, film critic Manohla Dargis floated the idea of
a "Duvernay test," named after film director Ava Duvernay. Dargis was
responding to the fact that Duvernay's critically acclaimed film *Selma*,
about the 1965 civil rights march from Selma to Montgomery, AL, only
received two Oscar nominations, which was widely perceived as a snub,
and more specifically, as symptomatic of persistent racial inequality in
Hollywood. Dargis stated that in order to pass the test, a film would have
to have a narrative in which "African-Americans and other minorities
have fully realized lives rather than serve as scenery in white stories."
The overall *lack* of films featuring the stories of people of color, and
more specifically, the lack of recognition of the films that do, prompted
writer and editor April Reign to create the hashtag #oscarssowhite in
2015. As with GLAAD, the aim of Reign and Dargis is activist; in particular, Reign's hashtag, which went viral and received widespread media
attention, was intended not just to critique the Oscars, but to jolt the
film industry into change.

All of these tests show how critics use gender, race, and/or sexuality as
lenses to analyze pop culture artifacts, as well as how the results of those
tests can be used to advocate for change in the industries that produce
them. These tests also demonstrate how the work of feminist intellec-
tuals is not contained within academia but extends out to the general

public in an effort to increase levels of media literacy. We encourage you to give one or more of these measures a try next time you're listening to music, streaming a movie, or watching your favorite television show.

End of Chapter Elements

Evaluating Prior Knowledge

1. Where have you encountered feminism, feminist activism, or anti-racist gender justice efforts in other contexts—your family, friends, school, media and popular culture, etc.? What are your major assumptions about the goals of feminist movement?
2. Which of the stereotypes and misconceptions about feminism and feminists discussed in this chapter have you encountered before? Where and in what context?

Application Exercises

1. To further investigate the Bechdel test and the Russo test, select two or three of your favorite films. Watch them again with a specific and careful eye toward dialogue, action, and interaction between characters. Do they "pass" one or both tests? What would the films look like if they did? How would they look different, and what would need to be added or changed in order to increase the representation and depth of the women/LGBT characters in it?
2. View the 2004 film *Iron-Jawed Angels*, an account of the suffrage movement. Write out responses in which you explore the following questions: Why did 19th-century activists focus so heavily on women's right to vote? In what ways is it a significant form of civic participation? What other issues might have been neglected because of a focus on suffrage, and why?

Skills Assessment

1. Consider your own educational experiences. To what degree has the study of gender and the inclusion of women been (a) made visible? (b) part of the curriculum? (c) taken for granted? That is, in history courses, were you taught about women's roles and contributions, or

did your studies focus primarily on military and political history? In literature courses, did you read work by women writers? Are there other examples of gender equity or inequity that stand out to you from your own academic experiences? In your answers, consider your experiences in elementary school, middle school, high school, and college.

Discussion Questions

1. Feminist bell hooks argues in *Feminism Is for Everybody* that feminists in developed countries have oversimplified feminist thinking, charging that

> linking circumcision with life-threatening eating disorders (which are the direct consequence of a culture imposing thinness as a beauty ideal) or any life-threatening cosmetic surgery would emphasize that the sexism, the misogyny, underlying these practices globally mirror the sexism here in this country.

(47)

That is, bell hooks asks us to consider the relationship between various forms of social control over women's bodies and whether one is more horrific than another (and if not, whose interests are served by ranking them so). Do these parallels ring true to you? Why or why not?

2. Review the core principles of the ERA described in this chapter. What arguments can you see being made in favor of the ERA? What arguments do you imagine being made against it? Which do you see as more persuasive, and why?

3. Read the Unity Principles of the Women's March on Washington (www.womensmarch.com/principles/). What did you learn about the concerns and priorities of the contemporary feminist movement from this document? Were any of the issues surprising to you? If so, why?

Writing Prompts

1. *Reflection:* When people talk about feminism as "political," they often mean very different things. Critics of feminism and Women's

and Gender Studies argue that it's focused on electoral politics and partisan issues (like abortion or pay equity) and therefore is not academic. Proponents use "political" to mean that it is rooted in concepts of power. Which meaning resonates the most with you? What examples can you think of to illustrate it?

2.   Select one of the following feminist issues mentioned in this chapter and do some Internet research. What is the current status of that issue? What policy or legislative efforts are currently at work in that issue? How do you see the issue in your own day-to-day life?

- Access to **contraception**
- Access to safe, legal abortion
- Access to breastfeeding support and space
- Social support services including Temporary Assistance for Needy Families or Supplemental Nutrition Assistance Program funding
- Affordable childcare
- LGBTQ rights
- Trans* issues
- Media and popular culture images of women (and men)
- Working conditions, including recourse in the case of unequal pay, pregnancy discrimination, and sexual harassment
- Gender violence
- Women in **electoral politics**

Notes

1   www.about-face.org/maxim-magazine-considers-feminism-a-disease-to-be-cured/

2   www.gpo.gov/fdsys/pkg/GPO-CONAN-1992/pdf/GPO-CONAN-1992-8.pdf. "Proposed Amendments Not Ratified by States" *(PDF)*. United States Government Printing Office. Retrieved 3 August 2017.

3   bell hooks defines "patriarchal violence" in her book *Feminism Is for Everybody* this way: "Patriarchal violence in the home is based on the belief that it is acceptable for a more powerful individual to control others through various forms of coercive force. This expanded definition of domestic violence includes male violence against women, same-sex violence, and adult violence against children. The term 'patriarchal violence' is useful because unlike the more acceptable phrase 'domestic violence' it continually reminds the listener that violence in the home is connected to sexism and sexist thinking, to male domination. For too long the term domestic violence has been used as a 'soft' term which suggests it emerges in an intimate context that is

private and somehow less threatening, less brutal, than the violence that takes place outside the home. This is not so, since more women are beaten and murdered in the home than on the outside. Also most people tend to see domestic violence between adults as separate and distinct from violence against children when it is not. Often children suffer abuse as they attempt to protect a mother who is being attacked by a male companion or husband, or they are emotionally damaged by witnessing violence and abuse."

4   http://bechdeltest.com/
5   www.youtube.com/watch?v=bLF6sAAMb4s
6   www.glaad.org/sri/2016/vitorusso

Works Cited

Allen, Paula Gunn. *The Sacred Hoop*. Beacon Press, 1986.

Baumgardner, Jennifer, and Amy Richards. *Manifesta: Young Women, Feminism, and the Future*. Farrar, Strauss, and Giroux, 2000.

Berger, Michele Tracy, and Cheryl Radeloff. *Transforming Scholarship: Why Women's and Gender Studies Students Are Changing Themselves and the World*. Routledge, 2011.

Boxer, Marilyn J. "Women's Studies as Women's History." *Women's Studies Quarterly*, vol. 30, 2002, pp. 42–51.

Carmon, Erin. "The Willis Test Is the New Bechdel Test." *Jezebel*, 2 May 2011. http://jezebel.com/5797747/the-willis-test-is-the-new-bechdel-test. Accessed 23 January 2017.

Cataldi, Sue. "Reflections on Male-Bashing." *NWSA Journal*, vol. 7, no. 2, 1995, pp. 76–85.

Cobble, Dorothy Sue, Linda Gordon, and Astrid Henry. *Feminism Unfinished: A Short, Surprising History of American Women's Movements*. W.W. Norton, 2014.

Coontz, Stephanie. "Why Gender Equality Stalled." *New York Times*, 16 February 2013.

Crawley, Sara, et al. "Introduction: Feminist Pedagogies in Action: Teaching Beyond Disciplines." *Feminist Teacher*, vol. 19, no. 1, 2008, pp. 1–12.

Dargis, Manohla. "Sundance Fights Tide with Films Like 'The Birth of a Nation.'" *New York Times*, 29 January 2016. www.nytimes.com/2016/01/30/movies/sundance-fights-tide-with-films-like-the-birth-of-a-nation.html. Accessed 5 July 2017.

"Declaration of Sentiments and Resolutions." The Elizabeth Cady Stanton and Susan B. Anthony Papers Project. Rutgers. http://ecssba.rutgers.edu/docs/seneca.html. Accessed 5 July 2017.

"Fast Facts: Title IX." National Center for Education Statistics. U.S. Department of Education. 2014. https://nces.ed.gov/fastfacts/display.asp?id=93. Accessed 5 July 2017.

Freedman, Estelle. *No Turning Back: The History of Feminism and the Future of Women*. Ballantine Books, 2002.

Hogeland, Lisa. "Fear of Feminism: Why Young Women Get the Willies." *Ms. Magazine*, 1 December 1994.

hooks, bell. *Feminist Theory from Margin to Center*. South End, 1984.

——. *Feminism Is for Everybody: Passionate Politics*. South End Press, 2000.

Howe, Florence. "Still Changing Academe after All These Years." *Women's Studies Quarterly*, vol. 30, 2002, pp. 27–31.

Institute for Women's Policy Research. "Fact Sheet: The Gender Wage Gap, 2013: Differences by Race and Ethnicity No Growth in Real Wages for Women." March 2014. https://iwpr.org/publications/the-gender-wage-gap-2013-differences-by-race-and-ethnicity-no-growth-in-real-wages-for-women/. Accessed 5 July 2017.

Iron-Jawed Angels. Dir. Katja van Garnier. Perf. Hilary Swank, Margo Martindale, Anjelica Huston, Frances O'Connor, Vera Farmiga, and Lois Smith. HBO, 2004.

Jong, Erica. "Ally McBeal and Time Magazine Can't Keep the Good Women Down." *New York Observer*, 13 July 1998.

National Women's Studies Association. www.nwsa.org/. Accessed 5 July 2017.

Penaluna, Regan. "Wanted: Female Philosophers, in the Classroom and in the Canon." *The Chronicle of Higher Education*, 11 October 2009. www.chronicle.com/article/Wanted-Female-Philosophers/48729/. Accessed 5 July 2017.

Pharr, Suzanne. "Homophobia as a Weapon of Sexism." *Women's Voices, Feminist Visions: Classic and Contemporary Readings*. McGraw-Hill, 2007, pp. 71–74.

Sarkeesian, Anita. "The Oscars and the Bechdel Test." *Feminist Frequency*, 15 February 2012. https://feministfrequency.com/video/the-2012-oscars-and-the-bechdel-test/. Accessed 5 July 2017.

Valenti, Jessica. *Full Frontal Feminism: A Young Woman's Guide to Why Feminism Matters*. Seal Press, 2007.

Walker, Rebecca. "Becoming the Third Wave." *Ms. Magazine*, vol. 2, no. 4, 1992, pp. 39–41.

White House. "Women and Girls in Science, Technology, Engineering, and Math (STEM)." Department of Energy, 30 November 2011. https://energy.gov/sites/prod/files/White%20House%20OSTP%20Women%20in%20STEM%20Fact%20Sheet%202011.pdf. Accessed 5 July 2017.

Women's March on Washington. "Guiding Vision and Definition of Principles." https://static1.squarespace.com/static/584086c7be6594762f5ec56e/t/587b8e5b15d5db2c4ba884d1/1484492383110/WMW+Guiding+Vision+%26+Definition+of+Principles.pdf. Accessed 5 July 2017.

Zeilinger, Julie. *A Little F'd Up: Why Feminism Is Not a Dirty Word*. Seal Press, 2012.

Suggested Readings

Basu, Amrita. *Women's Movements in the Global Era: The Power of Local Feminisms*. 2nd ed. Westview Press, 2016.

Cobble, Dorothy Sue, Linda Gordon, and Astrid Henry. *Feminism Unfinished: A Short, Surprising History of American Women's Movements*. W.W. Norton, 2014.

Dicker, Rory. *A Brief History of U.S. Feminisms*. 2nd ed. Seal Press, 2016.

"Domestic Violence Prevention: A History of Milestones and Achievements." National Online Resources Center on Violence Against Women. VAWNet.org. 2011.

Ferree, Myra Marx, and Aili Mari Tripp, eds. *Global Feminism: Transnational Women's Activism, Organizing, and Human Rights*. New York University Press, 2006.

Freedman, Estelle, ed. *The Essential Feminist Reader*. Modern Library, 2007.

Gay, Roxane. *Bad Feminist: Essays*. Harper Perennial, 2014.

Kennedy, Elizabeth Lapovsky, and Agatha Beins, eds. *Women's Studies for the Future*. Rutgers University Press, 2005.

Orr, Catherine, Ann Braithwaite, and Diane Lichtenstein, eds. *Rethinking Women's and Gender Studies*. Routledge, 2011.

Seager, Joni. *The Penguin Atlas of Women in the World*. 4th ed. Penguin, 2009.

"The Women's Rights Movement, 1848–1920." *History, Art, and Archives. The United States House of Representatives.* https://memory.loc.gov/ammem/naw/nawstime.html. Accessed 5 July 2017.

Wiegman, Robyn, ed. *Women's Studies on Its Own: A Next Wave Reader on Institutional Change*. Duke University Press, 2002.

Yousafzai, Malala. With Christina Lamb. *I Am Malala: The Girl Who Stood Up for Education and Was Shot by the Taliban*. Back Bay Books, 2015.

2

THE SOCIAL CONSTRUCTION
OF GENDER

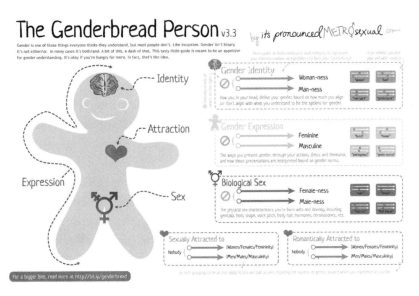

Figure 2.1 The Genderbread Person

Source: First published in *The Social Justice Advocate's Handbook: A Guide to Gender* by Sam Killermann, http://samuelkillermann.com

Opening Illustration

In 1972, at the heart of the second wave of feminist movement, Lois Gould published the fictional tale "X: A Fabulous Child's Story" in *Ms.* Magazine. The story's narrator describes an imaginary parenting scenario in which a baby is born, named "x," and under the guidance of scientists is deliberately raised in a gender-neutral way. The child is not subject to feminizing or masculinizing influences through toy selection and clothing coded as feminine or masculine, and is co-parented equally by different-sex parents. The story calls attention to the many gendered messages we experience on a daily basis:

> bouncing it up in the air and saying how strong and active it was, they'd be treating it more like a boy than an X. But if all they did was cuddle it and kiss it and tell it how sweet and dainty it was, they'd be treating it more like a girl than an X. On page 1654 of the Official Instruction Manual, the scientists prescribed: "plenty of bouncing and plenty of cuddling, both, X ought to be strong and sweet and active. Forget about dainty altogether.
>
> (Gould)

Gould's ultimate moral was that parenting that drew from a range of human virtues would produce well-adjusted, functional children who were free to express themselves and pursue their interests regardless of whether those expressions and pursuits were coded as masculine or feminine.

A contemporary version of this fictional tale made news headlines in recent years, with news journalists documenting the stories of two contemporary couples whose decision not to reveal their baby's sex (up until the child reached school age) earned them a great deal of public scorn and attention (Bielanko). As one of the parents, Beck Laxton, said in an interview with the *Cambridge News*, "I wanted to avoid all that stereotyping. Stereotypes seem fundamentally stupid. Why would you want to slot people into boxes?" ("Couple"). Laxton, a UK-based online editor, and her partner, Kieran Cooper, decided to keep Sasha's sex a secret when he was still in the womb. The birth announcement stated the gender-neutral name of their child but skipped the big reveal. Up until recently, the couple only told a few close friends and family members that Sasha was a boy and managed to keep the rest of the world "in the dark." Another couple announced the arrival of their baby with an email that read "We've decided not to share Storm's sex for now—a tribute to freedom and choice in place of limitation, a stand up to what the world could become in Storm's lifetime (a more progressive place? . . .)."

Gould's story and the contemporary versions of the Fabulous X simultaneously illustrate how gender is encoded and maintained through a variety of strong social cues (i.e., naming practices, parenting responsibilities, toys, clothing, games, interpersonal interactions, and media exposure) and the way that people struggle to carve out space and identities that resist normative constructions of gender. This chapter explores how a social constructionist approach to gender is a key feature of a feminist theoretical lens.

A *feminist stance* understands gender as a system of privilege and oppression; it also assumes that gender is socially constructed, and is deeply interested in mapping out how, where, and to what effect.

Why a Threshold Concept?

A core premise of feminist scholarship is that gender and sex are distinct from each other, and that our gender identities are socially constructed and not immutable. Key to this concept is that ideas and constructions of gender change across time, between and within cultures, and even within one's lifespan. The specific ways that gender is socially constructed at any given time also serve the purpose of establishing and perpetuating *sexism,* defined as prejudice and discrimination based on sex. Furthermore, racial, ethnic, and cultural identities frame expectations for appropriate gendered behavior, as does social class and sexuality. Simply put, feminist scholars focus on how gender is socially constructed, and to what ends, and they are simultaneously interested in how social constructions of gender are shaped by issues of race, class, age, ability, and sexual identity. This threshold concept, then, is deeply intertwined with both the concept of privilege and oppression, which is the focus of Chapter 3, and the concept of intersectionality, which is the focus of Chapter 4.

Framing Definitions and Related Concepts
Social Constructionism
One of the early foundational theories underpinning a social constructionist approach is C. Wright Mills's articulation of the concept

of the **sociological imagination**. In his 1959 book of the same name, Mills argues that

> the individual can understand his own experience and gauge his own fate only by locating himself within his period, that he can know his own chances in life only by becoming aware of those of all individuals in his circumstances.

(5)

Mills's claims became the foundation of social science and sociology as a discipline. As Mills contended, "[t]he sociological imagination enables us to grasp history and biography and the relations between the two within society" (6). As one of the foundations of feminist theory, **social constructionism** can be distinguished from other theories about sex and gender that are used to explain gender role socialization and how gendered systems are created and maintained. There are several hallmark concepts that distinguish a social constructionist approach to gender.

Sex and Gender

The "Genderbread Person" image that opens this chapter—and the accompanying controversies around it—is a case in point of the unsettled social understanding of the relationship between biological sex and the various ways that gender is created, expressed, and defined. What the image attempts to do is complicate our understanding of a binary gender system—boys and girls, men and women—and present a more varied spectrum of elements that make up sex, gender, and sexuality.

Although most scholars acknowledge that gender and sex exist on a continuum, a simple definition pulls apart these two commonly conflated terms into "sex," which focuses on the biological, genetic, and physiological features of people, and "gender," which characterizes the behavioral (and changeable/evolving) characteristics that we define as feminine and masculine. Physical features of sex include reproductive organs and secondary sex characteristics that develop at puberty, such as average difference and variation in muscle-to-fat ratios between men and women, and growth in body and facial hair. Gender, in contrast, is shaped by behavioral cues and social codes that are coded as "masculine" or "feminine." In the social constructionist understanding of gender, then, gender is performative, that is, something you "do" rather than something that is built into or programmed into you.

The work of feminist sociologist Judith Lorber serves as a touchstone in this area. Her work helpfully provides a number of terms that flesh out the idea of gender as a social construction. She makes clear that gendering is a *process* that has many dimensions and that occurs over time: first, there is the *assignment* of sex and gender, which quickly becomes a **gender status**, according to Lorber, through naming, clothing, and the choice of children's toys and room decor. From there, children continue to be socialized into their gender, developing a **gender identity**, which is a person's gendered sense of self. The expression of that gendered sense of self is referred to as one's **gender comportment**, which Susan Stryker defines as "bodily actions such as how we use our voices, cross our legs, hold our heads, wear our clothes, dance around the room, throw a ball, walk in high heels" (12). This category is referred to as **gender expression** in the Genderbread figure that opens the chapter. Lorber also uses the term **gender display**, defined as the presentation of self as a kind of gendered person through dress, cosmetics, adornments, and both permanent and reversible body markers.

A social constructionist approach to gender rejects the belief that there are only two sexes and two genders, arguing instead that our current binary **sex/gender system** is itself a social construction. Powerful evidence for this argument comes from the **intersex** community (those who are themselves intersexed, parents of intersex children, and researchers who focus on intersexuality). The Intersex Society of North America defines intersex as "a general term used for a variety of conditions in which a person is born with a reproductive or sexual anatomy that doesn't seem to fit the typical definitions of female or male" ("What Is Intersex?"). While it has been difficult to get a handle on how frequently intersex babies are born, Anne Fausto-Sterling estimates that intersex births account for 1.7 percent of all births. She helpfully puts this into perspective:

> a city of 300,000 would have 5,100 people with varying degrees of intersexual development. Compare this with albinism, another

relatively uncommon human trait but one that most readers can probably recall having seen. Albino births occur much less frequently than intersexual births—in only about 1 in 20,000 babies.

(51–53)

Another frequently cited point of reference is redheadedness: being intersex is about as common as being born with red hair. For those who believe that sex and gender are binary—that there are only two possibilities, male and female—intersex babies are "really" male or female, and medical management, including genital surgery, can bring their physical appearance in line with their "true" sex. By contrast, Anne Fausto-Sterling and many others argue that the birth of intersex babies indicates that sex and gender are not binary, that is, that there are more than two categories, male and female, and she envisions a future (an admittedly utopic one) in which a wide range of gender identities and expressions would be permitted, even encouraged. Toward this end, Fausto-Sterling and the Intersex Society of North America call for an end to infant genital surgery on intersex babies, both because they feel strongly that decisions about making any permanent changes to the appearance and sexual function of intersex people should be made by the people themselves, or at least in consultation with them, *and* because the genital surgeries reinforce the idea that there are really only two sexes. Cheryl Chase, founder of the Intersex Society of North America and herself born intersex, argues that "children should be made to feel loved and accepted in their unusual bodies" (Weil).

Recent legal victories would seem to suggest some small steps toward Fausto-Sterling's vision: India, Pakistan and New Zealand now recognize a third gender, and in 2013, Germany enacted a law that allows parents to refrain from marking "M" or "F" on their intersex baby's birth certificate. The law was intended to allow parents to defer the decision and allow the child to decide later on whether to identify as male or female; however, the law also stipulates that a child could continue to identify as intersex. In a move that echoes the Gould story that opens this chapter, Germans can choose to use an "X" in the gender field of their passport. And in 2016 in the United States, Kelly Keenan, at the age of 55, successfully had her birth certificate amended to read "intersex" rather than M or F, after finding out what had been kept a secret from her throughout her life. Keenan's is thought to be the first birth certificate to read "intersex" (Levin). (Note: Keenan was raised female, and continues to use feminine pronouns.)

While most people experience congruence between their **gender assignment**, gender identity, and gender expression, this is not automatically the case, and a growing number of people are exploring other identities and ways of being, and demanding legal recognition for their right to do so. The term **transgender** has many complex meanings and nuances, but a starting point is that it is used to describe an individual for whom there is a lack of congruence between their gender assignment and gender identity. In *Transgender History,* Susan Stryker uses the term "to refer to people who move away from the gender they were assigned at birth, people who cross over (*trans-*) the boundaries constructed by their culture to define and contain that gender" (1). While it used to be more common for that movement to remain within the boundaries of the binary gender system, that is, by seeking sex reassignment surgery and transitioning from identifying as a man to identifying as a woman (or vice versa), many trans* people today are increasingly identifying themselves and staking out territory outside the binary altogether. As Stryker points out, some people "seek to resist their birth-assigned gender without abandoning it," whereas others "seek to create some kind of new gender location" (19). Trans* people may or may not modify their bodies using surgery and/or hormones and may or may not seek legal recognition for their gender identity if it does not match the sex and gender they were assigned at birth.

Conversely, the terms **cisgender** and **cissexual** are used to describe people who experience congruence between their gender assignment and gender identity. Stryker points out that the creation of this term helps to name and mark that experience rather than assuming it as the norm. She writes, "[t]he idea behind the terms is to resist the way that 'woman' or 'man' can mean 'nontransgendered woman' or 'nontransgendered man' by default, unless the person's transgender status is explicitly named" (22).

Social media have also responded to the expanding understanding of gender identity that has emanated from a variety of sources, including the intersex and the trans* communities. For example, Facebook in 2014 changed the gender field of its profile options to allow for a wider range of user selections, moving from the binary "male/female" options to roughly 50 options including "cisgender," "trans male," "androgynous," and "genderqueer," among others (Henn). Although the opportunity to choose one's online gender identity, along with the legal recognition of a third gender in several countries, indicates that change is afoot and many people are actively working to create more cultural space for life beyond the binary, this is not to downplay or diminish the realities of **transphobia**, which Julia Serano defines as "an irrational fear of, aversion to, or discrimination against people whose gendered identities, appearances, or behaviors deviate from societal norms." Even as many, especially younger people, are actively embracing gender fluidity, there are powerful forces that are working actively to police the boundaries of sex and gender. A recent incident in the state of Colorado highlights the uneven nature of change; the Girl Scouts (GSUSA) found themselves under attack over the inclusion of Bobby Montoya, a grade-school-aged trans girl. In fact, Bobby's desire to join the Girl Scouts was initially thwarted by a troop leader who cited Bobby's "boy parts" as a barrier to joining, but that decision was quickly reversed based on national GSUSA policy. The FAQ section of the GSUSA website states that "if the child is recognized by the family and school/community as a girl and lives culturally as a girl, then Girl Scouts is an organization that can serve her in a setting that is both emotionally and physically safe." When Bobby's story hit the news, however, a group calling itself Honest Girl Scouts encouraged a cookie-buying boycott, citing GSUSA's "bias for transgenders [*sic*]" (Hetter). Many cities and states are also passing so-called "bathroom bills" which seek to prohibit trans men and women from using the bathroom that accords with their gender identity. Many of these bills constitute backlash to recent political gains for transgender rights, and proponents of them often disingenuously cite their desire to protect women and girls from being preyed upon by men in the restroom.

Gender Socialization

Having made an initial pass through an explanation of the distinction between sex and gender, as well as what gender *is* or consists of, we can now ask and answer the question of where and how we learn about gender in our culture. Where do we learn what it means to be a boy or girl in our culture, in terms of appearance and behavior, and what are the cues and messages that we receive, both implicitly and explicitly? That is, we can begin to think about where, but also how, we are socialized into our gender. Some of the primary sites and arenas of **gender socialization** include the family, education, religion, popular culture and the media, sports, and the legal and criminal justice systems. What follows are a few examples of how these societal institutions serve as a site of gender socialization (note: institutions as sites and mechanisms for structuring systems of privilege and oppression will be discussed in Chapter 3 as well).

Education

School settings are a key site of gender socialization. The messages children receive about appropriate behavior, attitudes, and appearance for their gender are both explicit and implicit, and come from school policies, teachers, fellow students, as well as the curriculum. Dress codes in middle schools and high schools are a good example of the role of school policy in shaping ideas around gender. An increasing number of schools have instituted dress codes that reinforce a double standard and convey the message to girls and young women that their bodies, by definition, are a distraction to boys and young men, and that it is their responsibility to cover themselves. Some of these dress codes can also have the effect of regulating the dress and appearance of trans* students. Many of these dress codes are ostensibly gender-neutral, but the language in them often reveals that women's bodies are the prime focus of the policy. In Appleton, WI, for example, the policy states that "[s]tudents may not wear scanty and/or revealing clothing," but then goes on to provide examples that are almost exclusively feminine: "short skirts (need to be mid-thigh) or revealing shorts, tube tops, halters, backless tops, spaghetti straps less than one inch, exposed midriffs or undergarments." Around the country, many students are resisting these dress codes and calling out the sexist assumptions that are implicit in them, as when a student in Appleton posted flyers urging administrators to "teach male students and teachers not to over-sexualize female body parts" (Zettel).

The role of peers in educational settings can be seen powerfully in discussions of boys' underachievement. A recent article by sociologist Michael Kimmel, "Solving the 'Boy Crisis' in Schools," drawing from qualitative evidence collected from surveys and interviews with middle school students, links expectations about gender norms for boys to attitudes about school, and more specifically, toward particular school subjects. Kimmel argues that "[h]ow little they care about school, about studying, about succeeding—these are markers of manhood in peer groups of middle and high school boys across the country." He further argues that "what boys think it means to be a man is often at odds with succeeding in school. Stated most simply, many boys regard academic disengagement as a sign of their masculinity." Kimmel concludes with a call to change the messages that boys receive in school settings, saying that "[w]e must make academic engagement a sign of manhood— which we can only do by interrupting those other voices that tell our young boys to tune out." On a related note, the values of compliance and obedience are a key feature in many school settings, a fact that has gendered (and racialized) implications. As Sadker and Zittleman explain, boys are more likely to be overdiagnosed with behavioral and emotional problems such as Attention Deficit Disorder, whereas girls' higher overall average grades and lower test scores may reflect what they note is an educational setting that values "following the rules, being quiet, and conforming to school norms" (78). In this way, particular behaviors are rewarded even if they are not ultimately those that will lead to "success" beyond school and in other settings that prize assertiveness and risk-taking behaviors.

School curricula also contain gendered messages that affect children's perceptions of intelligence, as illustrated by a recent study published in the journal *Science*. The study documented the shift that takes place as early as age 5 regarding children's perceptions of "brilliance" or intelligence. At 5, both boys and girls associated brilliance with their own gender; by 6 or 7, however, both boys and girls were significantly less likely to pick women as brilliant. That assessment was distinct from girls' beliefs about who does well in school, where girls were more likely to identify girls, suggesting that at least for girls, their beliefs about academic success were disconnected from their perceptions of who is "really, really smart," as the study framed the question to child participants. As the study concluded, by age 6, then, girls in the study were avoiding activities that were framed by the researchers as being for kids who were "really, really smart," and the authors assert that "[t]hese findings suggest that gendered notions of brilliance are acquired early and have an immediate effect on children's interests" (Bian, Leslie, and Cimpian).

Family Structures and the Workplace

Social and policy structures that assume female caretaking and the primacy of men's careers send strong reinforcing messages and logistical cues about the responsibility for childcare as women's work. For example, paid family and medical leave for the birth or adoption of a child (or to care for sick or elderly family members) does not exist on a standard national level in the United States (although it is common in other industrialized countries), and the status of the U.S. leave program as unpaid reinforces the notion that pregnant people can rely on the income of a (usually) male partner to support them during childbirth and throughout infancy. When these are heavily gendered responsibilities, messages about who belongs in the public sphere and who belongs in the private sphere are clear. Children also learn what is considered "women's work" and what is considered "men's work" by observing both the amount and kind of domestic and unpaid work performed by their parents and caregivers. Although the amount of housework performed by women has gone down over the last 30 years, and the amount of housework performed by men has gone up, a significant gap remains between the average weekly hours spent by men and women engaged in these tasks, with women still spending roughly twice as much time as men. As the Bureau of Labor Statistics notes, women do 10.8 hours more unpaid household labor than men, and among 25- to 34-year olds, women perform 31.7 hours of household work compared with men's 15.8 ("Hours"). And while recent studies show that men's share of meal preparation and childcare has increased, the biggest gap is around cleaning.

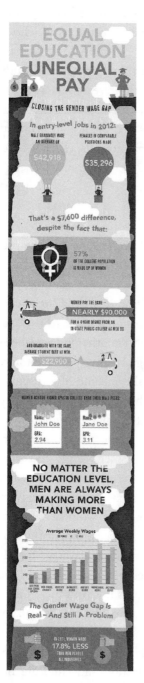
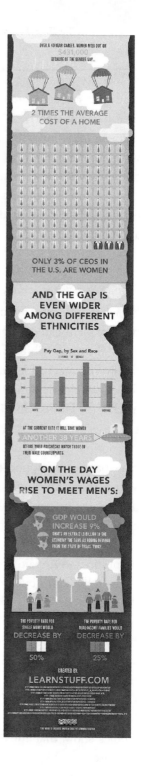

Figure 2.2 Equal Education, Unequal Pay

Source: LearnStuff.com

These messages are not just conveyed through observation of adults, however; children are also socialized into their gender through the chores they are (or aren't) asked to perform around the house, and the money they may receive in the form of an allowance. The Allstate Foundation's 2014 Teens and Personal Finance Survey revealed that more boys than girls reported receiving an allowance from their parents (67 percent v. 59 percent). A 2007 study by the University of Michigan Institute for Social Research found that "girls spend more time doing housework than they do playing, while boys spend about 30 percent less time doing household chores than girls and more than twice as much time playing." And finally, several studies have shown that in families where both boys and girls get allowances, boys' allowances are higher (Dusenbery). Taken together, these findings suggest that chores and allowances are key sites of boys' and girls' gender socialization.

Religions

Most major religions are based on a heavy foundation of **masculine god language**, and masculine iconography as omniscient and omnipotent; major religions are centered on male prophets and gods and around strict rules for men's and women's conduct, particularly regarding sexuality, reproduction, and marriage. Masculine god language that refers to deities as "Him" and "Our Heavenly Father" reinforce an image of an all-powerful male ruler. Religious texts as well often communicate oppressive notions about gender relationships, such as Biblical passages regularly referenced in Christianity including:

> Women should keep silence in churches. For they are not permitted to speak, but should be subordinate, as even the law says.
>
> (1 Cor. 14:34)

> I would have you know that the head of every man is Christ; and the head of the woman is the man; and the head of Christ is God.
>
> (1 Cor. 11:3)

> Wives, submit yourselves unto your own husbands, as it is fit in the Lord.
>
> (Col. 3:18)

Let the woman learn in silence with all subjection. But I suffer not a woman to teach, nor to usurp authority over the man, but to be in silence.

(1 Tim. 2:11–15)

Further, in a number of faiths, women are excluded from religious practices. For example, Hindu women perform rituals of self-denial, such as fasting, in order to create positive energy and power for their husbands. The self-sacrifice of a woman for her husband is understood to be a religious offering. Men do not perform such rituals for their wives (Burn). Women are often also excluded from leadership positions. Female ministers, bishops, priests, rabbis, mullahs, gurus, or sadhus remain relatively rare or nonexistent in many religious traditions. Children who attend worship services learn by observing the roles played by both children and adult men and women in those places of worship, and they also absorb explicit and implicit messages about their "proper" roles.

It should also be noted, however, that many women, both feminist religious scholars and everyday activists, continue to work to challenge power imbalances, including segregated and exclusionary practices, and thereby send a different set of messages to their religion's practitioners, including children. For example, Kristine Stolakis's documentary, *Where We Stand*, traces the work of stay-at-home-mom Abby Hansen's advocacy for women's ordination in the Mormon church, also known as the Church of Jesus Christ of Latter-Day Saints (Parker). Ordination of women as Catholic priests is also among the many issues tackled by the Women's Ordination Conference, an organization described on its website as "A Voice for Women's Equality in the Catholic Church." And finally, Muslim women have opened a number of women's mosques in various parts of the world; the first in the U.S. opened in Los Angeles in 2015. These mosques feature women imams (prayer leaders) and are seen as a part of women's empowerment efforts within Islam.

Popular Culture

From birth, children are exposed to gendered messages in the form of pink or blue blankets and baby name signs, in the gendered division of toy store aisles, and in TV shows geared toward girls or boys, as well as the dominance of male characters in children's media. Regarding children's media, research from the Geena Davis Institute on Gender in Media found that girl characters are outnumbered by boy characters by a ratio of 3 to 1 (Smith). Another example comes from looking at recipients of Best Picture Oscar awards. For example, films that have been praised and rewarded in the film industry are almost universally male-centered. A brief review of the films receiving the Best Picture award over the last two decades demonstrates that male-centered narratives are most typically perceived as worthy of adulation.

For example, the majority of the films center on a heroic male protagonist who overcomes a significant obstacle (such as *The Departed*'s focus on the main character's navigation of his life as a double agent; *A Beautiful Mind*, documenting the main character as a genius suffering from a mental illness; or Oscar Schindler's acts of heroism during the Holocaust in *Schindler's List*). Films such as *The Silence of the Lambs*, while including a central female character, largely are driven by her interaction with or attempts to understand a more significant male character (in that film, Hannibal Lecter). Other filmic conventions rewarded include vengeance stories, such as a male character seeking out revenge for a wrong done to a woman (*Unforgiven*); or the emotional life of a male character presumed to be of depth and thus interest to a viewer, such as *The English Patient* or *American Beauty*. Films centered on war or battle are also overrepresented (such as *Braveheart*, *Platoon*, *Gladiator*, *Lord of the Rings*, *The Hurt Locker*, and *Schindler's List*) relative to their overall proportion of film plots. This emphasis on male-centered narratives and male-identified events and activities (war, battle, math, detective work, the Old West) communicate strong messages about what is culturally valuable and what (and who) is interesting. On a similar note, a recent analysis of the roles played by the winners of the Best Actress Oscar showed that almost a third of the winners played roles that were defined primarily through relationship to a man or men; that is, as wives, mothers, sisters, daughters, or girlfriends. Tellingly, there was no parallel "relational" category for the Best Actor winners. While the number of relational roles among the Best Actress nominations has slowed in recent years, Brie Larson won the Best Actress Oscar in 2016 for her role in *Room*, about a mother and son who survived long-term kidnapping. In addition, in the last decade more films featuring central girl or women characters have been among Best Picture nominees, including *Million Dollar Baby* (2004), *Little Miss Sunshine* (2006), *Juno* (2007), *Precious* (2009), *Black Swan* (2010), *The Help* (2011), *Zero Dark Thirty* (2012), and *Beasts of the Southern Wild* (2013). Recent progress is uneven: in 2013, four of nine nominated films featured a woman as protagonist, but in 2015, *none* of the eight films nominated featured a woman as protagonist. And in terms of box-office success, as of May 2014, two of the top three movie releases of 2013 featured female protagonists: *The Hunger Games: Catching Fire* and *Frozen*, evidence which counters the notion that male viewers are not interested in paying to see films that feature female protagonists and female-centered storylines. In early 2017, the film *Hidden Figures*, about three African American women mathematicians whose work was instrumental to the U.S. effort during the Cold War space race, was doing extremely well at the box office and had netted a Best Picture Oscar nomination. Recall the Case

Table 2.1 List of Best Picture Award Winners

2016 – *Moonlight*	
2015 – *Spotlight*	1999 – *American Beauty*
2014 – *Birdman or (The Unexpected Virtue of Ignorance)*	1998 – *Shakespeare in Love*
2013 – *Twelve Years a Slave*	1997 – *Titanic*
2012 – *Argo*	1996 – *The English Patient*
2011 – *The Artist*	1995 – *Braveheart*
2010 – *The King's Speech*	1994 – *Forrest Gump*
2009 – *The Hurt Locker*	1993 – *Schindler's List*
2008 – *Slumdog Millionaire*	1992 – *Unforgiven*
2007 – *No Country for Old Men*	1991 – *The Silence of the Lambs*
2006 – *The Departed*	1990 – *Dances With Wolves*
2005 – *Crash*	1989 – *Driving Miss Daisy*
2004 – *Million Dollar Baby*	1988 – *Rain Man*
2003 – *The Lord of the Rings: The Return of the King*	1987 – *The Last Emperor*
2002 – *Chicago*	1986 – *Platoon*
2001 – *A Beautiful Mind*	
2000 – *Gladiator*	

Study in Chapter 1 on using media tests as a way of critically examining gender, sexuality, and race in film.

Athletics

Sports is a primary site of gender socialization, especially for adolescents. Cheerleading in its earliest incarnations was a male activity, developed in 1898 as "pep clubs" (International). Charged with generating crowd enthusiasm, cheer clubs were male-only until 1923, but by the 1940s women became the majority of cheerleaders in the United States. Today, 96 percent of cheerleaders are female (Bettis and Adams). Cheerleading is suggestive of male-centeredness; as a "corollary" or "add-on" to, initially, exclusively male athletic events, primarily football and basketball, cheerleading has evolved to function as a method of (1) drawing attention to the athletic activities and achievements of a group of culture-dominant men, and (2) demanding particular highly compliant, traditionally feminine, and surface-focused standards from its female participants. By the 1970s, the emergence of professional cheerleading squads popularized the erotic image of the female cheerleader and her support of the athletic prowess of her team. As Bettis and Adams observe, "erotic tensions . . . creep into the language, practices, and policies of cheerleading squads at all levels, from preadolescent All-Star squads to collegiate competitive squads" (123). With current cheerleading choreography including what Bettis and Adams call "sexually suggestive" and "sexually provocative" moves, cheerleading becomes outward-looking in its emphasis on drawing attention to male athletics and in the efforts of female participants to garner social status through male attention to the often erotic performance of cheerleading routines. Competitive cheer has evolved as an offshoot of traditional cheerleading; its growing popularity can be seen in movies like *Bring it On* (2000) and the television show *Glee*, which features an award-winning squad called the Cheerios. Many people consider competitive cheer to be a sport, and organizing bodies within the field have petitioned the NCAA to officially recognize it as such on the collegiate level. Some cynically see the push to have competitive cheer recognized as a collegiate sport as a way for universities to comply technically with Title IX regulations while not supporting more traditional sports for women athletes. Proponents of recognizing cheerleading as a sport argue that competitive cheer is highly athletic, and that those participating in it run the risk of incurring severe sports-related injuries. But while competitive cheer draws its own audience (as opposed to being on the sidelines of another sporting event), it arguably maintains the requirement of traditionally feminine appearance and sexually suggestive choreography.

Figure 2.3 Relational Roles and Best Actress Oscars

Source: Infographic by Jan Diehm for the *Huffington Post*, www.huffingtonpost.com/2014/01/16/best-actress-winners_n_4596033.html

Electoral Politics

As of January 2017, according to United Nations data, there were ten women serving as Head of State and nine serving as Head of Government. Fifteen percent of the world's lawmakers were female in 2003; by 2016, that number had risen to 23 percent (UN Women). In the United States, women are extremely underrepresented in elected office relative to their numbers in the general population. As of 2017, according to the Center for American Women and Politics, women represent 19.4 percent of Congress and 24.8 percent of state legislators; only 10 percent of governors are women. And while the U.S. came close to electing its first woman as president (Hillary Clinton won the popular vote in the 2016 presidential election), Clinton was ultimately defeated. The causes of Clinton's defeat are numerous and complex, but sexism was clearly among them.

When compared to women's representation in elected office in other countries, it appears that the United States is *losing* rather than gaining ground. For example, in 1997, the United States ranked 52nd in the world for women's representation in government; as of 2016, that ranking had fallen to 97th. The short answer for why we are losing ground, according to Sarah Kliff and Soo Oh, is that, unlike in other countries around the world (Sweden, Rwanda, Bolivia, Canada, Mexico, and France, just to name a few) neither the U.S. government nor the country's major political parties have made increasing women's participation a priority through instituting quotas.

The patterns and expectations are set at an early age, with many high schools and universities electing fewer young women to student government positions. For example, in 2013 at Phillips Academy, an elite prep

U.S. STATE LEGISLATORS ARE

75% MEN AND 25% WOMEN, INCLUDING 5% WOMEN OF COLOR.[1]

Figure 2.4 Gender and Race Breakdown of U.S. Legislators

Source: Hill, Catherine. "Barriers and Bias: The Status of Women in Leadership." *American Association of University Women.* 2016. www.aauw.org/research/barriers-and-bias/, accessed 5 July 2017

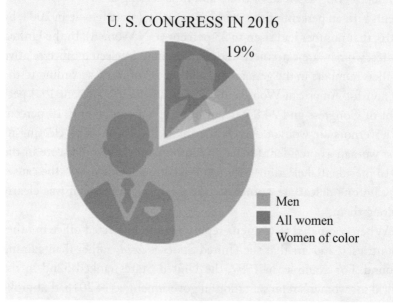

The gap is even worse in the U.S. Congress ...

U. S. CONGRESS IN 2016

19%

- Men
- All women
- Women of color

Figure 2.5 U.S. Congressional Demographics

Source: Hill, Catherine. "Barriers and Bias: The Status of Women in Leadership." *American Association of University Women*. 2016. www.aauw.org/research/barriers-and-bias/, accessed 5 July 2017

school in Andover, Massachusetts, students spoke out about the lack of female student leadership since the school opened its ranks to female students in 1973. According to a *New York Times* article written about the campus controversy, only four young women have been elected to the position of school president in the past 40 years. In an effort to increase female representation in student government, the school's administration adopted a co-president model in the hope that mixed-gender groups would run for office. Although the intended effect was not produced in 2013 (when two young men were elected), each pair of finalists in the 2014 election consisted of one young man and one young woman, ensuring the election of a woman to the co-presidency (Seelye). At the postsecondary level, the American Student Government Association estimates that 40 percent of student presidents are women, also noting, however, that that number does not distinguish between two-year and four-year campuses; the assumption is that the number of women presidents on four-year campuses is lower (Johnson). A May 2013 report by the Center for Information and Research on Civic Learning and Engagement adds nuance to the discussion of women's underrepresentation in political office by pointing out that although women are "severely underrepresented at virtually all levels of elected office," girls and young women outpace their male peers "on many indicators of civic engagement, including volunteering, membership in community associations, and voting" (Kawashima-Ginsberg and Thomas 2). The report attempts to explain what leads to and creates the gender gap in leadership, and several of those factors clearly stem from the differing gender socialization of boys and girls. More specifically, they point to a gap in both confidence and expectations. They cite survey data from the Higher Education Research Institute that shows that women in their first year of college "are far less likely to claim personal characteristics such as leadership and public speaking skills, competitiveness, social skills, and popularity, all of which are commonly named characteristics of a political leader" (4), and they note that the gap has not narrowed in the past 50 years. Finally, they cite a study from American University that found that 30 percent of young college women had been encouraged to run for office, compared to 40 percent of young college men. More specifically, women "were less likely to be encouraged by parents, grandparents, teachers, religious leaders, coaches, and even friends" (6). In sum, both the implicit and explicit gendered messages boys and girls receive about political leadership shape the paths they pursue in adolescence and adulthood.

The Legal System

Broadly speaking, the legal system, including courts of law, the police, and the prison system, are sites that convey powerful messages about gender. According to the Sentencing Project, over half of incarcerated women are mothers of children under the age of 18. And the number of incarcerated women has grown enormously over the past

30 years, more than 700 percent, from 26,378 in 1980 to 215,332 in 2014. While there continue to be far more men than women in prison, "the rate of growth for female imprisonment has outpaced men by more than 50 percent between 1980 and 2014." Children, then, are increasingly learning about the criminal justice system from an early age as a result of having an incarcerated parent, an increasing number of whom are mothers. According to the Pew Research Center, there were 2.7 million children in the U.S. with an incarcerated parent as of 2010 (Reilly). However, in spite of the fact that the numbers of incarcerated women have grown tremendously in recent decades, women (particularly white women) are treated more leniently than men (both white men and men of color) within the criminal justice system, by a number of measures. According to a study entitled "From Initial Appearance to Sentencing: Do Female Defendants Experience Disparate Treatment?," which analyzed almost 4,000 felony cases from 2009, they are less likely to be detained while awaiting trial, their bond amounts are lower than men's, and they are less likely to be sentenced to prison. Racialized gender stereotypes, then, clearly operate within the criminal justice system in ways that directly impact both men's and women's experiences.

Children and teens are also increasingly encountering the criminal justice system through what has been termed the school-to-prison pipeline, which describes the ways that some K–12 students are being pushed out of schools and into the criminal justice system as a result of increased police presence in schools and the criminalization of minor infractions of school rules. This so-called pipeline disproportionately affects students of color and disabled students, and also has a gendered dimension, according to a 2015 report from the African American Policy Forum entitled "Black Girls Matter: Pushed Out, Overpoliced, and Underprotected." According to Kimberlé Crenshaw, one of the authors of the report, the disparity in punishment between black girls and white girls is greater than the disparity between black and white boys. In an interview with NPR News's Karen Grigsby Bates, Crenshaw hypothesizes that this disparity is a result of the fact that black girls are targeted for school discipline not only because of their race, but also because their behavior does not conform to normative expectations of white femininity. In short, black girls are often misperceived as defying authority because their gender expression is not seen as properly feminine.

A social constructionist approach argues that our gender identity, that is, our personal understanding of our own gender, is shaped by the intersection of experience and institutions. We receive implicit and explicit messages through our interactions with each of these institutions that fundamentally shape our understandings of ourselves and our beliefs about the world.

A final point here is that as we learn about gender through these societal institutions, masculinity and **femininity** are defined in relation to one another. More specifically, masculinity is defined in opposition to femininity. As Raewyn Connell puts it, "'[m]asculinity' does not exist except in contrast with 'femininity'" (252). In *Full Frontal Feminism*, Jessica Valenti puts a finer point on it: "masculinity is defined as whatever *isn't* womanly" (185). The oppositional and relational nature of socially constructed masculinity and femininity is evident in Table 2.2.

Gender Norms, Gender Policing

Reinforced across institutions and ideologies, gender norms are communicated in many settings that individuals experience throughout their lives. In the discipline of psychology, gender norms might be called

Table 2.2 Stereotypical Gender Qualities

"Masculine" Qualities	*"Feminine" Qualities*
aggressive/assertive	passive
logical/analytical	indirectly aggressive ("catty")
physically strong, athletic	sensitive
responsible	other-oriented
protective	physically weak/er
self-oriented	compromising
emotionally unexpressive	emotionally expressive
in control	collaborative
authoritative	submissive
invulnerable	nurturing
sexually aggressive	chaste or pure

"gender roles," while sociologist Lisa Wade uses the term "gender rules." Whatever the term, those messages communicate our society's norms or expectations for gender, in ways that we may only dimly be aware of. It is often only when we inadvertently break a gender rule that we become consciously aware that it exists.

Gender norms of both masculinity and femininity are maintained through many mechanisms, including what is referred to as "policing." In this context, "gender policing" means monitoring behavior or gender display, and granting or withholding social approval based on those behaviors. Gender norms are internalized to greater or lesser degrees by everyone, and we all participate (again, to greater or lesser degrees) in policing our own and others' gender expression. An example of this type of policing is the phenomenon of **"slut shaming,"** in which a woman's sexual choices and behaviors (or presumed choices and behaviors) are critiqued by others; gender studies scholar Leora Tanenbaum's book-length study, *Slut!*, traces how women who violate traditional sexual expectations for their gender are subject to direct and indirect social consequences ranging from virtual or real-life name-calling, harassment, and assault. When oppressed groups police other members of that group, this is referred to as **horizontal hostility**, a phenomenon that will be discussed more fully in Chapter 3.

Gender Ranking

The concept of gender ranking helps us understand the purpose and function of gender rules or norms. Masculinity and femininity are not valued equally in our culture; instead, greater value is typically attached to masculine qualities than feminine qualities. In *The Gender Knot: Unraveling Our Patriarchal Legacy*, Johnson argues that *androcentrism*, or centering on and valuing of those qualities associated with masculinity, is a part of our cultural norms. This male-centeredness becomes visible through a close look at how status and power are distributed in our society. With positions of power that are male-dominated, and higher value attached to masculine personality traits like

> control, strength, competitiveness, toughness, coolness under
> pressure, logic, forcefulness, decisiveness, rationality, autonomy,

self-sufficiency, and control over any emotion that interferes with other core values (such as invulnerability) . . . these male identified qualities are associated with the work valued most in patriarchal societies—business, politics, war, athletics, law, and medicine.

(7)

This **gender ranking** is often framed as both biological in origin and immutable, with masculine qualities defined in opposition to—and more culturally valued than—feminine qualities.

Within a society that engages in gender ranking, it is important to police people's gender expression in order to ensure the "proper" distribution of rewards and punishments. Within a sex/gender system that privileges masculinity, a certain latitude is given to girls and women to emulate masculinity. In other words, we have space in our culture for girls to be "tomboys," because there is a certain logic in many people's minds to why a girl would want to adopt masculine styles of dress, behavior, and play. But because femininity is devalued, boys who are termed "sissies" frequently endure merciless teasing. In adulthood, masculine styles of dress, within certain parameters, are open to women; think, for example, of the popularity of "boyfriend" jeans, chinos, sweaters, and button-down shirts. The same cannot be said of men's clothing; there is no parallel "girlfriend" styling of men's clothing. This point will be explored visually in the "Bodies" portion of the Anchoring Topics section.

But aside from clothing, the emulation of masculinity by adult women can be fraught. There is a double standard of behavior for men and women in the workplace and in politics, for example, where the same behavior is judged very differently depending on whether the person engaging in the behavior is a man or woman. Sheryl Sandberg's Lean In organization is attempting to raise awareness of one manifestation of this double standard with its "Ban Bossy" campaign. As the campaign's website puts it, "When a little boy asserts himself, he's called a 'leader.' When a little girl does the same, she risks being branded 'bossy.'"

Closely related to this concept of a **gendered double standard** of behavior is the idea of the **double bind**, whereby women in the public sphere

are faced with two less-than-desirable options of adhering to or rejecting feminine gender norms, risking negative repercussions either way.
Amanda Fortini captured this double bind in an article she wrote about
the 2008 U.S. presidential race, in which Hillary Clinton sought the
Democratic presidential nomination and Sarah Palin was the Republican vice presidential candidate. Clinton's style was deemed more
masculine, whereas Palin's was more traditionally feminine, but both
received negative media attention. Fortini's title: "The 'Bitch' and the
'Ditz' (How the Year of the Woman Reinforced the Two Most Pernicious Sexist Stereotypes and Actually Set Women Back)". This gendered
double standard also has everything to do with race and class; traditional femininity is often implicitly coded as both white and middle-
class. African American women in positions of power in the workplace
and in politics, for example, have to negotiate a gendered double standard that is also interwoven with racial stereotypes, such as the Angry
Black Woman trope.

Associations between traditionally gendered behavior—and unequal
penalties for men and women who do not adhere to expectations—is
illustrated in a series of public columns by Sheryl Sandberg and Adam
Grant, who examine how biases and assumptions about the superiority
of masculine qualities—but the simultaneous social consequences for
women who behave in traditionally 'masculine' ways—operates in the
workplace. For example, Grant and Sandberg report on a study that

> asked managers to read a transcript from a job interview of a
> candidate described as either female or male. At the end of the
> interview, the candidate asked for higher compensation and a
> nonstandard bonus. . . . they were 28 percent less interested in
> hiring the female candidate. They also judged her as 27 percent
> less likable. The same information did not alter their judgments of
> male candidates.
>
> (Grant and Sandberg, 2014)

Only being told that stereotypes exist had a negative impact on
participants' abilities to moderate their stereotypes, but if they were
told not only that stereotypes were present but also that most people

work to be aware of and act in ways that counter them, people in the study were much less likely to have discriminatory reactions. As Grant and Sandberg report, "[w]ith this adjustment, discrimination vanished in their studies. After reading this message, managers were 28 percent more interested in working with the female candidate who negotiated assertively and judged her as 25 percent more likable." What this demonstrates is the complicated relationship between gendered behaviors and qualities and the lived experience of gender—and the complex challenges of navigating institutions that have been built upon and around traditional ideas about gender rules and gender roles.

Reimagining Masculinity

Gender ranking serves the purpose of maintaining and perpetuating *sexism*, that is to say, a system of male dominance. However, there is a growing realization that boys and men often experience deep and lasting harm as a result of adhering to, striving to adhere to, or failing to adhere to the very masculine gender norms that form the foundation of sexism. Paul Kivel's articulation of the contents of the **act-like-a-man box**, as well as its purpose and function, has been key in this area. He calls it a box to emphasize the rigidity, narrowness, and confining aspects of the social construction of masculinity. He writes,

> [I]t feels like a box, a 24-hour-a-day, seven-day-a-week box that society tells boys they must fit themselves into. One reason we know it's a box is because every time a boy tries to step out he's pushed back in with names like wimp, sissy, mama's boy, girl, fag, nerd, punk, mark, bitch, and others even more graphic. Behind those names is the threat of violence.

(148)

Kivel points out that this policing of boys can come from other boys, but also from girls, who "don't seem to like us when we step out of the box" (148). This policing can also come from adults, who "seem convinced that if they 'coddle' us, we will be weak and vulnerable" (148). A graphic illustration of the policing of the "act-like-a-man-box" can be found in the story of a young boy in Raleigh, North Carolina, who attempted suicide in February 2014 after a long period of being bullied because he was a fan of the television show *My Little Pony*.

A growing body of psychological and medical research has linked boys' and men's adherence to traditional masculine gender norms with a number of connected negative outcomes: loss of intimate friendship, high rates of depression, and lower life expectancy. Regarding friendship, according to sociologist Lisa Wade, the qualities needed to extend and receive friendship are coded feminine in our culture, thus causing a gender role conflict for men. She writes,

> To be close friends, men need to be willing to confess their insecurities, be kind to others, have empathy and sometimes sacrifice their own self-interest. "Real men," though, are not supposed to do these things. They are supposed to be self-interested, competitive, non-emotional, strong (with no insecurities at all), and able to deal with their emotional problems without help. Being a good friend, then, as well as needing a good friend, is the equivalent of being girly.

She cites research by psychologist Niobe Way that found that younger boys report having close, intimate friendships with other boys, but that there is a shift around the age of 15 or 16, when boys "start reporting that they don't have friends and don't need them." Later in adulthood, however, many adult men report wanting intimate friendships but are not sure how to forge them. This example not only illustrates the limitations of adhering to traditional norms of masculinity, but it also reveals the need to consider how the social construction of masculinity changes across an individual's life span. Put differently, these examples show the importance of thinking about gender in relation to age.

Beyond identifying the limitations and harm of traditional masculinity, a growing number of men are making strides in their personal, professional, and activist lives toward reimagining masculinity. Guante, a hip hop artist, poet, and social justice educator, has a spoken word piece, "Ten Responses to the Phrase 'Man Up,'" that resonates deeply with audiences. Another poet, Carlos Andres Gomez, published a book entitled *Man Up: Reimagining Modern Manhood* in 2012. Both men offer analysis of masculinity as a forced performance, make public declarations that they reject traditional masculinity, and instead claim for themselves a reimagined manhood that, as Guante puts it, entails having meaningful, emotional relationships with other men, admitting weakness, and being "strong in a way that isn't about physical power or dominance." Indeed, a huge emphasis of the work of men like Guante and Gomez, and groups like A Call to Men, is reimagining masculinity toward the end of preventing violence, whether that's men's violence against women, against themselves, or against other men. Men's work to reimagine masculinity benefits girls and women, then, in the sense that it is focused on reducing violence against women, but it also benefits boys and men per se, in the sense that it can result in raising their quality of life, even as it may entail giving up some of the unearned privileges of masculinity.

The examples described in this section give a sense of how complex the gender landscape is in the 21st century. Many people, young and old, chafe against the restrictions of the gender binary that dictate that masculinity and femininity are relational and oppositional, and that masculinity is more highly valued. Simultaneously, however, other individuals, along with structural forces, work hard, in ways both visible and invisible, to shore up traditional norms and gendered expectations.

Learning Roadblock

"It's how you were raised." It can be tempting to analyze gender through a lens that imagines family structures are the sole and most important influence on a person's gender identity. Typically, these binary characterizations of gender are psychoanalytic in origin. Psychoanalytic theories typically explain gender differentiation through relationships to others. Such theories originated from two different sources: **Freudian** views and those of other psychologists about how humans develop their sense of gender identity from deep roots in their childhood experience of family origin (experiences that are gendered); and theories that build on

those psychological evolutions by positing essentialized views of masculine and feminine ways of developing psychologically, morally, and emotionally. Freudian theories undergird the psychological approach because of Freud's role in laying the groundwork for the study of the human psyche. Freud's theory of the Oedipus complex is sometimes used to explain the difference between male and female development of identity; in sum, Freud theorized that male children must individuate from their primary (female) caretaker and identify with the male parent in order to fully develop into an adolescent and adult. Freud's theory supposed a deep and unconscious basis in an unrealized sexual desire for the mother, one that is displaced by identification with the father. In contrast, female children do not need to individuate and become independent in their identity formation because their primary caretaker is the same-sex parent. Thus, boys and men, in this view, develop an identity characterized by separation, independence, and individuality whereas girls maintain an emphasis on identification, interdependence, and cooperation/mutuality.

Other theories, such as that of feminist Carol Gilligan (in response to Lawrence Kohlberg), challenge assumptions about moral development that emphasize independent decision-making based on a moral truth and disconnected from the needs of others as the pinnacle. By this logic, women (in general) were perpetually "immature" in their moral development because they were more likely to be driven by moral decision-making that accounted for the needs and feelings of others—the emotional or affective dimension—than by disconnected or objective applications of a moral principle. Psychoanalytic theories typically use essentialist assumptions about the moral or psychological orientation of men and women; as such, psychoanalytic explanations of occupational segregation focus on women's attraction to and suitability for relational care work and work guided by a sense of moral obligation to others. Conversely, more independence, or what Gilligan calls an "ethic of justice," is ascribed to men, which purportedly explains their attraction to fields that provide work that is objective, mechanical, or conducted independently.

However, as this chapter illustrates, families themselves are subject to and part of structural and cultural contexts that grant privileges to certain types of family structures and withhold them from others; parents themselves absorb and reproduce cultural values about gender. Family structures are part of larger institutional contexts that reproduce values around class, race, gender, sexuality, and other categories of identity—values that do not begin and end around the boundaries of families of origin. In short, it's not inaccurate to say that "how you were raised" shapes one's ideas about gender, but what *is* inaccurate is the assertion that the only necessary changes that need to be made to the structure of gender can be brought about through child-rearing practices.

Learning Roadblock

"*Women and men are naturally* _____." Historically and in our contemporary "commonplace" understandings of gender, *biology* holds a great deal of explanatory power, because physical differences between men and women are typically the first "cues" we experience about gender identity. Biological determinist explanations for gender role development are rooted in assumptions about men's greater average muscle mass and physical strength, in theories about genetics and hormonal differences between men and women, and in claims about reproductive strategies and the influence of women's reproductive life cycles, for example, on the development of their emotional and psychological priorities. A biological determinist looks at the occupational segregation of labor and locates the explanation for this division in genetic, biological, and evolutionary differences. The determinist might assert that because women are biologically responsible for reproduction, gestation, and lactation, as well as, because of these physiological realities, caring for children, that women are attracted to fields that make use of these "natural" dispositions. Lower-compensated and lower-status work such as early childhood education, childcare, social work, secretarial work, and nursing are naturally suited to women's biological and evolutionary impulse toward caring for others, they would argue. On the flip side, the physically demanding occupations such as logging and construction, for example, are occupied by men, whose larger bodies and greater muscle strength make them physically suited for this work. Further, historical associations between men and logic as well as spatial skills (borne out by some neurological research) are used to justify the concentration of male workers in fields like law, architecture, and engineering.

Although the idea that gender and sex are biologically and genetically determined can have great explanatory power, scientific research as well as careful reflection reveal that many of the gendered behaviors we take for granted are actually highly socially constructed by the overlapping institutions we experience on a daily basis: the family, media, medical communities, religion, educational institutions, and so forth. The scientific and historical evidence of the malleability of gender—the wide range of sexualities across cultures; the range of expectations for masculine and feminine behavior across culture, time, and even an individual's life span; and the significant cultural energy spent on ensuring that boys and girls conform to particular gendered ideologies (through such mechanisms as gay- and lesbian-baiting, stigmatizing gender nonconforming behavior, and maintaining policies and practices that reward traditional gendered behaviors)—suggests that gender is not quite as "natural" as we suppose. A story featured in the online arts and culture magazine *Slate* showcases the strong explanatory power of biological and genetic explanations for gender differences. Calling attention to the media coverage of two studies published in the prestigious scholarly journal *Nature*, the story observes that

> [t]he *Huffington Post* quoted one of the studies' authors as saying that these "special" genes "may play a large role in differences between males and females." Yet what the *Nature* articles *actually* show is the exact opposite. The 12 genes residing on the Y chromosome exist to ensure sexual *similarity*.
>
> (Richardson)

Although the original study findings emphasized sexual similarity, the story was "translated" to emphasize sexual difference—even though this was not actually borne out by the research.

Taken together, these interrelated framing concepts—social constructionism, the relationship between sex and gender, gender socialization, gender identity, gender expression, and gender ranking—are all part of understanding how a social constructionist approach is critical to feminist analysis.

Anchoring Topics through the Lens of Social Constructionism

Work and Family

One way of understanding the varying theories about gender construction is to look at the phenomenon of what is called **occupational segregation of labor** and how it illustrates gender ranking and gender role socialization. Specifically, the predominance of men in some occupations and women in others both communicates expectations about work and gender, and is valued and compensated differently based on the predominance of men or women in that workforce.

Overview of Gender Wage Gap/Occupational Segregation of Labor

As research from the Bureau of Labor Statistics and other sources consistently shows, occupations are strongly separated by gender; that is, particular segments of the labor market are occupied by women, and men are clustered in other labor segments. As the chart below illustrates in broad terms, particular types of work such as administrative and clerical work are fields that women are concentrated in; by contrast, production and craft work is largely done by male workers (91 percent).

A more fine-grained analysis suggests that very particular jobs such as secretaries and administrative assistants are mostly done by women (97 percent); work that involves small children is almost entirely performed by female workers (preschool teachers, 97.7 percent). By contrast, male-dominated occupations—those that typically pay significantly higher wages—are also as disproportionately dominated by men as those clerical positions are by women. Law enforcement officers are 84.5 percent male, 98 percent of automotive technical work is performed by men, and 97 percent of construction workers are men. Occupational segregation of labor is a useful and robust topic through which to develop a more complicated picture of how the **gender wage gap**—the common gap between men's and women's earnings, with women generally receiving lower pay—is promoted and reproduced. However, for the purposes of

Table 2.3 Gender Differences in Occupational Distributions among Workers

Occupation	Percentage of occupation that are men	Percentage of occupation that are women	Men		Women	
			Number (in thousands)	Percentage of all men employed in each occupation	Number (in thousands)	Percentage of all women employed in each occupation
Total	…	…	67,334	100.0	59,787	100.0
Managerial	54	46	11,005	16.3	9,387	15.7
Professional and technical	46	54	12,063	17.9	13,552	23.3
Sales	52	48	7,601	11.3	6,953	11.6
Clerical and administrative support	21	79	3,751	5.6	14,128	23.6
Service	39	61	6,465	9.6	10,066	16.8
Production and craft	91	9	3,516	20.1	1,283	2.1
Operatives	76	24	9,302	13.8	3,007	5.0
Laborers	78	22	3,631	5.4	1,011	1.7

Note: The Index of Dissimilarity across all occupations in 2001 was 31.1.

Source: www.bls.gov/opub/mlr/2007/06/art2full.pdf

this chapter the topic is discussed to illustrate various theories about how and why men and women occupy different labor market segments. As Gabriel and Schmitz explain, "31 percent of men or women (or a combination of percentages that add up to 31 percent) would have to change occupations for there to be complete gender equality in occupational distributions" (19). The social construction of gender is both reflected and reinforced by the gendered segregation of labor.

Two terms that capture the issues in labor segregation include **vertical segregation of labor** and **horizontal segregation of labor**. For example, women are more likely to work in administrative and clerical positions whereas men are more likely to work in manufacturing and skilled labor; this is the horizontal segregation of labor, and this clustering of women in lower-paying occupations partly explains the gender wage gap. Vertical segregation takes place simultaneously, and refers to the fact that even in fields where there is a more even mix of men and women working, women tend to be clustered in positions with lower pay and prestige. For example, as the U.S. Department of Labor notes, more women than men work in professional fields, but women are more likely to be found in health and education professional fields (68 percent of women in this category worked in these types of fields compared with 30 percent of men) and are paid less than those occupied by men, such as computer science and engineering. For example, "[i]n 2015, 9 percent of women in professional and related occupations were employed in the relatively high-paying computer and engineering fields, compared with 45 percent of men" (2). Other notable statistical information includes the higher proportion of female workers in part-time positions—as the Department of Labor data show, "[w]omen who worked part-time made up 26 percent of all female wage and salary workers in 2010. In contrast, 13 percent of men in wage and salary jobs worked part-time" (2). Even within the same field, for example, medical professions, women are more likely to occupy lower-paying specialties such as public health or pediatrics, with men in higher-paid specialties like neurosurgery or internal medicine.

In this way, thinking back to Table 2.2 in this chapter, the connections between traditional notions about gender—and socialization into these qualities—maps fairly clearly on to the occupational segregation of labor. Occupations that focus on managing the emotions, logistics, or bodies of others (education of young children, administrative support for professions, hands-on healthcare fields) are vastly female-dominated, while occupations that focus on interactions with objects or things and that call for objectivity, mechanical skills, and less human care work are male-dominated. The relationship between traditional ideas about masculinity and femininity, gender role socialization, and reproduction of gender norms, in this way, is complicated and recursive. As women and men cluster in particular occupations, this communicates a "norm" about the gendered nature of types of work; this, in turn, is represented through other institutions like education or media, which are thus part of creating a network of images and symbols that shape perceptions of gendered norms.

Notably, then, gender ranking is demonstrated by the occupational segregation of labor by the different compensation that single-gender dominated fields receive. For example, on average, according to the Bureau of Labor Statistics, returning to the highly single-gender dominant fields mentioned at the start of this section, average wage comparisons reveal how fiscal value follows gender ranking, considering the level of postsecondary education required for these trade and technical fields:

Table 2.4 Comparison of Single-Gender Dominant Occupations and Annual Wages

Occupation	Percent Gender	Average Annual Wage
Preschool teachers	97.7% women	$32,500
Secretaries and administrative assistants	79% women	$39,360
Law enforcement officers	84.5% men	$56,860
Construction trades workers	98% men	$46,290
Automotive technical work	98% men	$41,290

Source: https://www.bls.gov/cps/cpsaat39.htm

Certainly some of this differential valuing comes from cultural assumptions about the relative difficulty of types of work. Work that requires physical labor rather than emotional or social labor has been valued as more challenging. Feminist sociologists and feminist scholars from other fields continue to reframe this assumption in order to make the cognitive and emotional work required to do quality care work visible and press for compensation that appropriately values that work.

For women in elite and/or corporate positions, the construction of leadership itself may be gendered. For example, as Joan Williams and Rachel Dempsey discuss in *What Works for Women at Work: Four Patterns Working Women Need to Know,* even as women make up the majority of college students and have made inroads into many professions, positions of power remain starkly gendered masculine. Just 3.6 percent of Fortune 500 CEOs are women, for example (4), and just 15 percent of law firm partners are women. Workplace values centered on the unencumbered worker—historically, a male employee with few if any commitments outside the workplace—exert unequal pressures on men and women workers. Williams and Dempsey report that motherhood is the strongest trigger for bias: women with children are 79 percent less likely to be hired, only half as likely to be promoted, and earn a lot less money than women with identical resumes but without children, while this bias was untrue for men with children (5). A 2013 research study showed that women CEOs were more likely to be fired than their male counterparts—38 percent versus 27 percent, partly because they tend to be "riskier" hires brought in at times of corporate crisis (Duberman). Leadership qualities that require unencumbered workers and that are synonymous with traditionally masculine characteristics—self-assuredness, assertiveness, daring, and authoritative and commanding demeanors—all work against women and construct leadership work as masculine in nature. Further, expectations about women's roles within the workplace often reproduce the social expectations of other environments. As Grant and Sandberg discuss, women workers who demonstrated stereotypically feminine behaviors were neither helped nor hurt by their conformity to gender socialization; however, women who did not conform experienced social and economic consequences. Reporting on a study by psychologist Madelin Heilman, the *New York Times* column shows that when comparing the performance of two employees who were asked to stay late to help with preparations for an important meeting the next day,

> [f]or staying late and helping, a man was rated 14 percent more favorably than a woman. When both declined, a woman was rated 12 percent lower than a man. Over and over, after giving identical

help, a man was significantly more likely to be recommended for promotions, important projects, raises and bonuses. A woman had to help just to get the same rating as a man who didn't help.

(Grant and Sandberg, 2015)

Differential penalties between men and women for similar behaviors like those documented by Grant and Sandberg are illustrative of the key concepts in this section: gender ranking, the double bind, and a gendered double standard.

Methods of untangling socially constructed gender norms from biological ones are complicated but still present a strong picture of the gap between "natural" or "biological" explanations and the realities of gender construction. For example, although there is a stereotype that boys and men are better at mathematics and related fields than girls are, the gap in performance on standardized tests between boys and girls has narrowed. Further, gaps in standardized math test scores vary by country—there are no sex differences between boys and girls in Russia, India, and Japan, and in Iceland and Japan, girls *outscored* boys on math tests. Were mathematical or other abilities fixed, we would not see cross-cultural variation at this rate, nor could we explain the increase in the number of women engineers from 0.3 percent of bachelor of science degrees in 1970 to 18.9 percent in 2012.

Further, cross-cultural expectations for gender vary widely, suggesting that, were genetics or biology at work in shaping an immutable set of expectations around men and women, boys and girls, we would not see so much variation between cultures and nations about what is considered masculine and what is considered feminine, nor occupational segregation at the rate we see it in the United States.

Language, Images, and Symbols

As mentioned previously, a key aspect of assigning a gender to infants when they're born happens through the naming process (side note: many parents find out the sex of their baby, using ultrasound technology, in utero, which means that the process of gender assignment begins even *before* birth, particularly if parents-to-be take seriously the suggestion to talk to the fetus and begin addressing it by name while still in the womb). In the United States, the majority of given names are unambiguously gendered and considered appropriate only for girls or only for boys, although there are exceptions that add nuance to this discussion.

Studies have looked at how names that were historically considered masculine, like Ashley or Courtney, have been claimed and appropriated as girls' names. There are two related aspects of this sort of shift that connect to how gender operates in our culture. In terms of explaining *why* parents have chosen "boy" names for their daughters, it would seem that *gender ranking* comes into play here, meaning that within the logic of patriarchy, giving a girl a boy's name is an act of emulating privilege. That same "logic" also explains why there has been no parallel trend of parents choosing "girl" names for their sons; giving a boy a girl's name would be adopting the status of the less-valued gender (an interesting take on this issue can be found in Johnny Cash's classic country song, "A Boy Named Sue"). In terms of the *consequences* of parents choosing "boy" names for their daughters, we see that as more parents choose these names for their daughters, *fewer* parents choose those same names for their sons. In effect, then, there seems to be a tipping point; if too many parents choose a "masculine" name for their daughter, parents of male children avoid that name as it comes to be seen as feminine.

The popular website Nameberry, which tracks baby naming trends, has noted, however, that some new trends may be emerging. The site reports, in a 2012 post, seeing "parents 'reclaiming' for their sons unisex names that had veered girlward and names rising in tandem for both sexes." Another phenomenon that has yet to be quantified but has been reported anecdotally is that more parents are deliberately choosing gender-neutral names. Some parents, for example, are choosing not to find out the sex of their baby before its birth and decide on a name that could be used for either a boy or a girl.

Fast forwarding to adulthood, two recent studies that focus on gender bias in the workplace highlight the role that gendered names play in maintaining inequality. In one study referenced perhaps most notably by Sheryl Sandberg in her *Lean In*-based TED Talk, a business school professor gave his students a case study of a successful entrepreneur named Heidi Roizen, only he changed the name to Howard in one section. The professor, Francis Flynn, recalls

> [b]efore class, I had the students go online and rate their impressions of "Roizen" on several dimensions. As you might expect, the results show that students were much harsher on Heidi than on Howard across the board. Although they think she's just as competent and effective as Howard, they don't like her, they wouldn't hire her, and they wouldn't want to work with her. As gender researchers would predict, this seems to be driven by how much they disliked Heidi's aggressive personality. The more assertive they thought Heidi was, the more harshly they judged her (but the same was not true for those who rated Howard).

The ultimate point here, of course, is not about names per se, but about the gendered double standard for workplace behavior. And yet the study is a stark reminder that names almost always convey our gender, and that gendered stereotyping and double standards often kick in on that basis alone.

In another recent study published in the *Proceedings of the National Academy of Sciences of the United States*, researchers asked natural sciences professors to rate the application materials of college students applying for a position as a laboratory manager. As with the Flynn study, the materials were identical in every way except for the name of the applicant: Jennifer or John. According to the study's authors, "[f]aculty participants rated the male applicant as significantly more competent and hirable than the (identical) female applicant. These participants also selected a higher starting salary and offered more career mentoring to the male applicant" (qtd. in Sharp). A final study shows how names are not only gendered but racialized. In this study, published by the Social Science Research Network, researchers sent an identical email to 6,500 professors across the United States. The researchers posed as prospective students asking to meet with the professor, with the only thing distinguishing the emails from one another being the names of those prospective students: Brad Anderson, Meredith Roberts, Lamar Washington, LaToya Brown, Juanita Martinez, Deepak Patel, Sonali

Desai, Chang Wong, and Mei Chen. The findings: "faculty ignored requests from women and minorities at a higher rate than requests from Caucasian males, particularly in higher-paying disciplines and private institutions" (Milkman, Akinola, and Chugh). In other words, professors were more likely to respond to the prospective students who, based on their name, were perceived to be white and male. These examples clearly reveal some of the workplace and education-related implications of gendered and racialized naming practices, and how social constructionism is at work in large and small ways in communicating gender and race, as well as social roles and status.

A different way that gender comes into play in relation to naming has to do with the use of first names, last names, and/or titles in social interactions. Henley and Freeman argue that status is often communicated and reproduced by the levels of intimacy allowed to be expressed between two people depending on their social or employment status. Subordinates and superordinates have varying levels of freedom to address each other by first or last names, with the superordinate granted greater levels of familiarity than the subordinate. On a related note, many women professors note the tendency of students to refer to them either by first name or as "Mrs.," but not by their title of Doctor or Professor. While campus culture varies greatly across the United States, anecdotal evidence suggests a gendered dimension to this, with female professors consistently experiencing this phenomenon to a greater degree than their male colleagues.

Perhaps one of the most notable gendered controversies around naming, and socially communicated messages about naming and status, is the issue of (typically) heterosexual women changing their last name upon marriage. As Scheuble, Johnson, and Johnson explain, "[t]he practice of married women taking their husband's last name originates from the patriarchal family system under which women were considered their husband's property" (282); yet, despite the many strides toward gender equity, this practice continues for the majority of women. Research and demographic information suggests that 80 percent to 90 percent or more of heterosexual women choose to take their husband's last name upon marriage, with women with greater levels of educational attainment and who marry at older ages less likely to adopt their husband's surname (Lockwood, Burton, and Boersma 827). As part of the social construction of gender roles, name changing remains a controversial practice among feminists, but a widely held cultural norm. One research study reported that women who change their surnames identified tradition and relationship bonding as key reasons for their decision, yet Lockwood, Burton, and Boersma concluded that concern for family dynamics—including upsetting extended family members with nontraditional naming choices—remained an important consideration for many women (837). That is, despite feminist critique of this patriarchal tradition, many women continue to adhere to traditional values. Some arguments suggest that with other strides in gender equity, taking a spouse's last name is not as meaningful now as in the past, such as Lynn Harris's argument in a 2003 *Salon* article, "Mrs. Feminist":

> [t]oday, a woman's decision to take her husband's name is not necessarily, or merely, "retro." When it comes to such political-slash-personal acts, the stakes have changed, and therefore so have the statements we're making with them. I would argue that we're not losing battles; we're choosing them. We're not retreating; we're showing, subtly, how far we've come.

Although a clear minority, some women keep their name upon marriage or take their husband's name without ditching their own, through hyphenation. An even smaller number of couples have gone further, by having the husband take his wife's name (either alone or through hyphenating with his last name), or by the couple legally declaring a new last name that is sometimes a combination of their two names. Whatever the decision and accompanying rationale, the argument seems to rest on the value attached to names and the weight ascribed to this practice within the context of cultural values around names and identity.

Bodies

Gender is inscribed *on* our bodies in terms of their shape, size, and appearance, and is also performed through how we use and move our bodies in the world. Our culture constructs masculine and feminine bodies in opposition to one another, with feminine bodies expected to be slender, soft, and hairless, and masculine bodies expected to be taller, broader, more muscular, and hairy. One way to explore and reveal how this works is to look at images that deliberately reverse these constructions.

As feminist sociologist Judith Lorber asserts, "[g]ender is such a familiar part of daily life that it usually takes a deliberate disruption of our expectations of how women and men are supposed to act to pay attention to how it is produced." Among fans of comic books, there are extensive and ongoing conversations about the gendering of comic book characters, with a vibrant feminist critique of the way that women characters are depicted and the storylines they are given. Below is an example of one artist, Aaron Clutter, who draws attention to how gender is constructed in this aspect of popular culture by depicting male superheroes in feminine clothing and poses. Note that the artist has separated out three distinct aspects of the social construction of gendered bodies: (1) the bodies themselves, in terms of their size and muscularity; (2) the clothing; and (3) bodily posture/presentation. The bodies themselves are still coded masculine, with broad shoulders, square jaws, and defined, bulging muscles, but the clothing and poses are distinctly feminine and sexualized.

Artist Hana Pesut's photographic series entitled "Switcheroo" explores similar terrain. The series consists of paired, side-by-side photographs; in the first, a couple poses together wearing their own clothing, whereas in the second the couple switches places and clothing, and also recreates the other's pose and posture.

In this example, we get a visual reminder and confirmation that in some ways, the boundaries of femininity are more elastic than the boundaries of masculinity when it comes to clothing. When the women in these photographs swap the clothes previously worn by the man, they are often oversized but not necessarily categorically different than clothing we would recognize as commonly seen worn by women, whereas the reverse is much less often true for the men in the photographs. At the same time, however, the postures and poses are often quite different, such that seeing the women mimic the men's posture and pose and vice

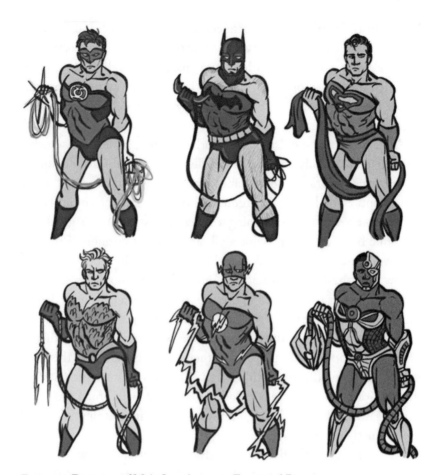

Figure 2.6 Depiction of Male Superheroes in Feminized Postures
Source: Aaron Clutter, Editor-in-Chief, *Comic Booked*, www.comicbooked.com

versa is startling and upsets expectations. Feminist philosopher Sandra Bartky has explored these gender differences in "gesture, posture,
movement, and general bodily comportment," noting that "[f]eminine
movement, gesture, and posture must exhibit not only constriction,
but grace and a certain eroticism restrained by modesty: all three" (81).
Henley and Freeman's early work in this area explores similar territory;
they note that

> [i]t is often considered "unladylike" for a woman to use her body
> too forcefully, to sprawl, to stand with her legs widely spread, to sit

with her feet up, or to cross the ankle of one leg over the knee of the other. Many of these positions are ones of strength and dominance.

(82)

They further note that differences in masculine and feminine clothing styles help reinforce these differences, as masculine clothing allows greater range of motion and more coverage. Bartky makes a similar point when noting that "women in short, low-cut dresses are told to avoid bending over at all, but if they must, great care must be taken to avoid an unseemly display of breast or rump" (83). While the increasing sexualization of women's bodies has meant that there are, for better or worse, fewer restrictions on exposing bare skin, we can see evidence of the continuation of this gender norm on websites devoted to celebrity gossip and entertainment "news"; these sites delight in posting paparazzi photos of so-called wardrobe malfunctions or inadvertent flashing, not only to titillate viewers but also to subtly or not-so-subtly shame said celebrities for lapses in ladylike presentation.

Yet another way that gender is inscribed on the body is through tattooing. The global history of tattooing is long and complex, and social norms related to tattoos have changed considerably in the past few decades. While historically it was considered to be a significant

Figure 2.7 Artist Hana Pesut draws attention to gender cues in her photographic series "Switcheroo"

Source: Photography by Hana Pesut, www.sincerelyhana.com

transgression of feminine gender norms for women to be tattooed, the norms are much more nuanced today, and there is no longer a significant gap between the number of men and women who get tattooed. Hawkes, Senn, and Thorn (2004) cite a study that estimates that "women currently acquire half of all tattoos, a rate that has quadrupled since the 1970s" (594). In spite of the relatively equal numbers of men and women getting tattooed, however, studies seem to suggest that there are gendered differences in perceptions of tattooed people.

In order to get at the nuanced ways that tattoos inscribe gender on the body, we need to consider a number of factors, including the placement, type, and size of those tattoos, as well as the race/ethnicity and social class of tattooed women. As we consider each of these factors, we are reminded of how women's bodies are a central site of social negotiation and struggle. On the one hand, many women get tattooed as a way to deliberately reject normative constructions of femininity, whereas other women do so with deliberate and conscious attention toward staying within the bounds of gendered social expectation. With regard to placement, there is first the question of whether a tattoo is visible or generally hidden from view while wearing clothing. Hawkes, Senn, and Thorn's (2004) study found that both men and women had a more negative attitude toward women whose tattoos were visible. For some women, this is precisely the point; they aim to defy expectations of feminine appearance. A 2013 study in the journal *Archives of Sexual Behavior* found that tattooed women were more likely to be viewed as sexually promiscuous and were quicker to be approached by men in the experiments conducted, while their level of physical attractiveness was unaffected by the presence of the tattoo (Guéguen), suggesting that body modifications like tattooing become social indicators with particular symbolic, and gendered, functions.

Beyond visible versus hidden, however, is the question of where on the body the tattoo is placed. Some parts of the body are particularly laden with meaning when it comes to both gender and sexuality. Many young women get tattooed on the small of their back; in slang terms, these tattoos are frequently called "tramp stamps," language that is both gendered and sexualized, in that it is an aspect of slut shaming. Arguably, there are also classed associations with the "tramp stamp" label.

A tattoo in that location is often described as "trashy," as opposed to respectably middle-class. Research shows that the size of a woman's tattoo is also a factor in whether and to what extent it is seen as a violation of feminine gender norms, with smaller tattoos being seen as more feminine than larger ones. Color and type are also important factors; pastel or primary-colored tattoos of butterflies, hearts, roses, the names or footprints/handprints of children, and inspirational words or phrases are all generally considered feminine.

A final point here is that the consumer marketplace has responded to women's desire to navigate this tricky gender landscape and perhaps to try to have it both ways, so to speak, as evidenced by the cosmetic company Sephora's tattoo concealer makeup, which carries the name of Kat Von D, celebrity tattoo artist, star of reality television show *LA Ink*, herself heavily tattooed. From the Sephora website:

> Kat says, "If you wanna hide a tattoo just for one day, the proper concealer can make that happen! No one has to see what you don't want them to see!" Take it from the tattoo pro: "I think just as much as people have the choice to be tattooed, they should also have the liberty to look whatever way they want whenever they want." This is your ticket to tattoo freedom!

Case Study

Gender Shifts in Professions

Clerical and Secretarial Work

In today's labor force, clerical work generally and secretary or receptionist positions specifically are female-dominated; however, clerical work up through the late 19th century was an exclusively male profession. As England notes, prior to the 20th century, few women engaged in paid work; less than one-fifth of women worked outside the home, and they were typically employed in the areas of domestic work, agriculture, and factory work (particularly textiles). In 1871, according to England and Boyer,

> clerical work accounted for a tiny proportion of all workers, less than one percent in the US in 1870 and Canada in 1871. Clerical

work in the US grew by over 450 percent between 1900 and 1903, at which point 9 percent of the labor force held clerical jobs.

(310)

Workers performing clerical functions were almost exclusively male, and the clerical occupation was "high status work, offered good job security and for those men in senior positions was a most prestigious job of the sort associated with middle management today" (310). With the development of technologies like typewriters and stenography, in 1880, cultural attitudes about women's stereotypical traits like compliance and fine motor coordination/dexterity led to occupational shifts, although these were visions of femininity typically connected to white women; over time (through various media imagery and advertising campaigns, an increase in demand for clerical workers that accompanied technological and industrial shifts from agricultural to urban industries), the demand and rewards for this type of work changed. England notes, "[i]n the popular imaginary, clerical work was promoted as a desirable job for young, educated white women to do for a few years prior to marriage" (313); race and ethnic bias accompanied this shift as office work was believed to be "reserved only for young, white protestant women" (314). Feminist scholars have examined the way that secretarial work offered some women opportunities to enter the labor market, while simultaneously positioning the work as low status, even as the technology aptitude and literacy required to do the work effectively was high. For example, Liz Rohan has challenged the class bias that has framed salaried professional work as higher skilled than the hourly wage work done by secretaries and clerical staff, even when the "amount of technological skill [and] . . . the amount of training and literacy the secretaries need to proofread technical documents" is substantial (Rohan 242).

In today's economy, secretarial work is almost exclusively performed by women and yet the tasks associated with this occupation have not substantially changed. An occupation once assumed to be high status and requiring traditional masculine traits has become dramatically female-dominated with no accompanying change in duties. This transformation highlights the way that social institutions can shift and adapt our understanding of gender over time.

Veterinary and Pharmaceutical Medicine

A contemporary example of the feminization of a profession comes from veterinary medicine, which went from being male-dominated to being female-dominated over a relatively short span of time. In 1960, only 2 percent of veterinarians were women, but as of 2015, according to the American Veterinary Medicine Association, women comprised 55.2 percent of veterinarians in private practice, and 52.2 percent of veterinarians in public or corporate settings ("Market Research Statistics"). Women's numbers in the profession may grow even larger in the decades to come, because women now constitute almost 80 percent of all students studying veterinary medicine. Sociologist Anne E. Lincoln studied the feminization of veterinary education and found that

> what's really driving feminization of the field is what I call "preemptive flight"—men not applying because of women's increasing enrollment. Also, fewer men than women are graduating with a Bachelor's degree, so they aren't applying because they don't have the prerequisites.

Lincoln's research challenged the belief that women's entry into veterinary medicine was an expression of caretaking, as well as the belief that women are less concerned than men with high earnings (Lincoln, 2010). It should be noted that Lincoln's research comes from outside the field itself (as noted above, she is a sociologist), and that professionals and professional organizations within the field have struggled to go beyond offering guesses as to why the gender composition of the profession has changed so rapidly and thoroughly in recent decades. A final note is that though women have represented the majority of veterinarians in the U.S. for several years, leadership in the field's professional organizations, as well as leadership in schools of veterinary medicine, is still largely male. The Women's Veterinary Leadership Initiative is focused on eliminating this leadership gap in the profession.

Though the first two examples of the feminization of a profession discussed here resulted in declining prestige and pay, feminization does not of necessity have that result, as can be seen in the case of pharmaceutical medicine, which was dubbed "The Most Egalitarian of All Professions" in a 2012 report by two Harvard University economists, Claudia Goldin and Lawrence Katz. According to Goldin and Katz, only 8 percent of pharmacists were women in 1960, but that number had risen to over 55 percent by 2012. Unlike veterinary medicine, however, in which women's entry both coincided with and resulted in a decline in pay and status, the earnings of pharmacists continue to be strong, the status of the profession has not fallen, and women pharmacists earn 92 cents for every dollar earned by men in the field, the smallest wage gap in health care fields, and a lower wage gap than in most other high-paying professions, according to the National Bureau of Economic Research. What sets the profession apart from the others discussed here is that women began entering the field at the same time that it was undergoing many structural changes; the number of jobs available for pharmacists has remained strong, and there has been a decline in small-business owners running their own pharmacies. Today, there are far more available positions for pharmacists in the pharmacies of chain drugstores (Walgreens and CVS, for example) and big box stores (Target, Wal-Mart, etc.). Significantly, these types of positions offer more flexible schedules and fewer responsibilities than being a pharmacist who is also a small-business owner. Goldin and Katz also report that "[p]harmacy earnings appear to be highly linear in hours and in that sense pharmacy has a relatively low 'career cost of family.'" For a number of reasons, and for better or worse, the market for pharmaceuticals has expanded in recent decades in ways that have positively impacted women's entry into and experience of the field.

End of Chapter Elements

Evaluating Prior Knowledge

1. Think about your own exposure to gender identity and gender awareness. Do you remember when you first became aware (or were made aware) of your gender? What moment or moments in your

life have you experienced a sense of what it means to be a boy or a girl? What cues did you get that led you to that awareness? How was your awareness of your gender intertwined with other aspects of your identity, such as your social class, your race/ethnicity, and/or your sexual identity?

2. Have there been moments in your life that you've felt limited or empowered by your gender identity? In what settings did you have those experiences?

3. This chapter briefly discusses several of the sites or arenas where gender socialization takes place. What do you recall about your experiences with those institutions when you were growing up? And today?

4. Prior to reading this chapter, had you ever encountered the word "cisgender" or "cissexual"? If so, where? If you had not encountered these terms before, what do you make of them? If you identify as cisgender, how does it feel to have a label to describe that identity?

Application Exercises

1. Occupational segregation by gender is one explanation for the gender pay gap. See Tables 2.3 and 2.4, which document the occupational segregation of labor, and examine the dominance of each gender in particular occupations. Select one female-dominated field and explain what qualities are typically associated with the responsibilities of that work environment. Do the same for a male-dominated occupation. How might a biological determinist explain this occupational clustering? What would a social constructionist focus on?

2. Choose a favorite film genre, and screen at least three films in that genre. Take note of the number and type of women characters and relevant identity factors—marital status, educational attainment, race, class, **sexual orientation**. What conclusions can you draw about "women in X genre" of film based on your analysis? What messages about gender would you draw as a viewer just paying attention to norms, values, and behaviors exhibited by female characters in that genre?

3. Take a field trip to a local department store like Wal-Mart or Target and peruse the toy aisles. Jot down what you observe about the messages, implications, and subtext communicated by the arrangement of the toys; how they are divided, marketed, packaged, and directed; and what they communicate about gender.

4. While the kind of dress codes discussed above in the gender socialization section are not nearly as widespread at the collegiate level as they are in middle schools and high schools, this is not to say that the explicit and/or implicit gender policing of clothing does not occur on college campuses. For example, investigate whether the recreation and wellness center on your campus has a dress code; if so, analyze it for gendered messages. Also, what are the tacit rules on your campus for classroom attire, and how are those rules gendered?

Skills Assessment

1. View the 2016 science fiction film *Passengers*, paying careful attention to the gendered identities of the two main characters, played by Jennifer Lawrence and Chris Pratt. Analyze the film's plot using chapter concepts.

2. Two of the academic fields with the smallest percentage of women earning doctorates are engineering[1] (22 percent) and philosophy[2] (21.9 percent). Explore your impressions and associations with these two fields of academic study; are they "gendered masculine" in ways that explain this disparity? If so, are they gendered masculine in similar or different ways?

3. Gender reveal parties are becoming more popular in the United States. Here's a description of a typical gender reveal party:

    The house was filled with balloons and confetti, and the guests were decked out in team colors, ready to cheer. Minutes before the party kicked off, they eagerly cast votes on the outcome. But this festive gathering was not a Super Bowl celebration. The decorations were all in pinks and powder blues, and the sides involved were "Team Boy" and "Team Girl." This was a gender-reveal party, during which expectant parents share the moment they discover their baby's sex, unveiling results of the ultrasound test among loved ones.

Write a two to four paragraph analysis of the gender reveal party as a cultural phenomenon. Using concepts from this chapter, how can you complicate our understanding of these parties and what they signify about our culture?

Discussion Questions

1. Why do you think that biological explanations for gender roles and expectations are so powerful and common sense? In what ways do biological explanations fail to account for human experiences broadly or your own experience specifically?
2. In what ways can you observe race, class, and sexuality operating in definitions of masculinity and femininity?
3. Review the chapter sections on institutions as agents of gender socialization. In what ways do you see institutions operating not just independently but in overlapping ways? Explore how different pairs of institutions operate together to reinforce gender socialization. For example, organized religion and the family are interconnected both because of theological beliefs about gender roles and family responsibilities and because religious involvement can be a significant source of support and community for families.
4. Read Charlotte Alter's article in *Time*, "Seeing Sexism from Both Sides: What Trans Men Experience" (http://time.com/4371196/seeing-sexism-from-both-sides-what-trans-men-experience/). How might trans men be uniquely poised to shed light on how gender is socially constructed in our society?

Writing Prompts

1. Describe a gender norm that you regularly perform and that, for the purposes of this assignment, you are willing to break for a set period of time. Describe how you broke the norm and who saw you break it. What reactions did you receive? How does your experiment support and/or challenge the arguments contained in this chapter? How does your experiment illustrate this chapter's key concepts?

2. Screen the documentary *Tough Guise 2: Violence, Manhood, and American Culture* or *The Bro Code: How Contemporary Culture Creates Sexist Men.* Then do some Internet research into some of the school shootings that most traumatized Americans: the Columbine shooting in 1999 and the Newtown shootings in 2012. Write an essay in which you examine the phenomenon of school shootings through a social constructionist lens that considers the formation of masculine identities in the United States.

3. Select two of the following comedic films targeting young male viewers. What vision of masculinity do they construct? *Van Wilder, Old School, Pineapple Express, Caddyshack, The Big Lebowski, Tropic Thunder, The Royal Tenenbaums, Swingers, Harold and Kumar Go to White Castle.*

4. Take a brief tour through a department store or big box store like Target or Wal-Mart (or their websites), looking carefully at the newborn, baby, and toddler sections of clothing and accessories (e.g., bibs and pacifiers). Make a list of all the gendered messages that are communicated through text, images, colors, styles, and so forth. What conclusions can you draw about how gender is "framed" even as early as infancy? What qualities, activities, and characteristics are emphasized for girls versus boys?

5. Watch the following commercial, entitled "Pretty" for Droid phones: (www.youtube.com/watch?v=w83UQkiuNZQ). Here is the text of the voiceover in the commercial:

    > Droid. Should a phone be pretty? Should it be a tiara-wearing digitally clueless beauty pageant queen? Or should it be fast? Racehorse duct-taped to a Scud missile fast. We say the latter. So we built the phone that does. Does rip through the Web like a circular saw through a ripe banana. Is it a precious porcelain figurine of a phone? In truth? No. It's not a princess. It's a robot. A phone that trades hair-do for can-do.

    How does this ad illustrate several key concepts from this chapter? Write a three- to five-paragraph essay that analyzes the cultural messages that this commercial reinforces.

Notes

1 www.insidehighered.com/news/2010/09/14/doctorates#sthash.1uZBi8e6.dpbs; see also Yoder.
2 http://opinionator.blogs.nytimes.com/2013/09/02/women-in-philosophy-do-the-math/?_php=true&_type=blogs&_php=true&_type=blogs&_php=true&_type=blogs&_r=2&

Works Cited

Bartky, Sandra. "Foucault, Femininity, and the Modernization of Patriarchal Power." In *The Politics of Women's Bodies: Sexuality, Appearance, and Behavior*. Ed. Rose Weitz. 3rd edition. Oxford University Press, 2010, pp. 76–97.

Bates, Karen Grigsby. "Study: Black Girls are Being Pushed Out of School." NPR News. 13 February 2015. www.npr.org/sections/codeswitch/2015/02/13/384005652/study-black-girls-are-being-pushed-out-of-school. Accessed 5 July 2017.

Bettis, Pamela, and Natalie Guice Adams. "Short Skirts and Breast Juts: Cheerleading, Eroticism, and Schools." *Sex Education*, vol. 6, no. 2, 2006, pp. 121–133.

Bian, Lin, Sarah-Jane Leslie, and Andrei Cimpian. "Gender Stereotypes about Intellectual Ability Emerge Early and Influence Children's Interests." *Science*, vol. 355, no. 6323, 2017, pp. 389–391. http://science.sciencemag.org/content/355/6323/389. Accessed 5 July 2017.

Bielanko, Monica. "Boy or Girl? 4-Month-Old Being Raised Genderless." Yahoo Shine. www.babble.com/baby/boy-or-girl-4-month-old-being-raised-genderless/. Accessed 24 May 2011.

Boyer, Kate. "Place and the Politics of Virtue: Clerical Work, Corporate Anxiety, and Changing Meanings of Public Womanhood in Early Twentieth Century Montreal." *Gender, Place, and Culture*, vol. 5, no. 3, 1998, pp. 261–276.

Bureau of Labor Statistics. "May 2016 National Occupational Employment and Wage Estimates United States." US Department of Labor. Accessed 5 July 2017.

Burn, Shawn Meghan. *Women Across Cultures: A Global Perspective*. McGraw-Hill, 2010.

Center for American Women and Politics. Rutgers University. 25 May 2014. www.cawp.rutgers.edu/. Accessed 5 July 2017.

Connell, Raewyn. "The Social Organization of Masculinity." In *Feminist Theory Reader: Local and Global Perspectives*. Eds. Carole McCann and Seung-kyung Kim. Routledge, 2013, pp. 252–265.

"Couple Finally Reveals Child's Gender, Five Years After Birth." Yahoo Shine. January 2012. https://ca.style.yahoo.com/couple-finally-reveals-child-s-gender—five-years-after-birth-20120123.html. Accessed 5 July 2017.

Crenshaw, Kimberlé, Priscilla Ocen, and Jyoti Nanda. "Black Girls Matter: Pushed Out, Overpoliced, and Underprotected." *African American Policy Forum*. 2015. www.aapf.org/recent/2014/12/coming-soon-blackgirlsmatter-pushed-out-overpoliced-and-underprotected. Accessed 5 July 2017.

Department of Labor. "Highlights of Women's Earnings in 2015." Bureau of Labor Statistics. November 2016. www.bls.gov/opub/reports/womens-earnings/2015/home.htm. Accessed 6 July 2017.

Diehm, Jan. "How Women Win Best Actress Oscars, All In One Chart." *Huffington Post.* 16 January 2014. www.huffingtonpost.com/2014/01/16/best-actress-winners_n_4596033.html. Accessed 5 July 2017.

Duberman, Amanda. "Why Women CEOs Are Fired More Than Men." *Huffington Post.* 7 May 2014. www.huffingtonpost.com/2014/05/07/women-ceos-fired-more-than-men_n_5249226.html. Accessed 5 July 2017.

Dusenbery, Maya. "Why the Gender Gap in Children's Allowances Matters." *Feministing.* 24 April 2014. http://feministing.com/2014/04/24/why-the-gender-gap-in-childrens-allowances-matters/. Accessed 5 July 2017.

England, Kim, and Kate Boyer. "Women's Work: The Feminization and Shifting Meanings of Clerical Work." *Journal of Social History,* vol. 43, no. 2, 2009, pp. 307–340.

Fausto-Sterling, Anne. *Sexing the Body.* Basic Books, 2000.

Fortini, Amanda. "The 'Bitch' and the 'Ditz.'" *New York Magazine.* 16 November 2008. http://nymag.com/news/politics/nationalinterest/52184/. Accessed 5 July 2017.

Gabriel, Paul, and Susanne Schmitz. "Gender Differences in Occupational Distributions among Workers." *Monthly Labor Review,* 2007, pp. 19–24. www.bls.gov/opub/mlr/2007/06/art2full.pdf. Accessed 5 July 2017.

Gilligan, Carol. *In a Different Voice: Psychological Theory and Women's Development.* Harvard University Press, 2012.

Girl Scouts of America. "Frequently Asked Questions: Social Issues." 28 May 2014. www.gsgcf.org/content/dam/girlscouts-gsgcf/documents/GSGCF%20FAQ%20 2%2015%2012.pdf. Accessed 5 July 2017.

Goldin, Claudia and Lawrence Katz. "The Most Egalitarian of All Professions: Pharmacy and the Evolution of a Family-Friendly Occupation." National Bureau of Economic Research. Working Paper 18410. 2012. www.nber.org/papers/w18410.pdf.

Gomez, Carlos Andres. *Man Up: Reimagining Modern Manhood.* Avery, 2013.

Gould, Lois. "X: A Fabulous Child's Story." *Polare,* February 1998. https://gendercentre.org.au/resources/support-resources/gender-queer?download=817:x-a-fabulous-childs-story&start=15. Accessed 5 July 2017.

Goulette, Natalie, John Wooldredge, James Frank, and Lawrence Travis III. "From Initial Appearance to Sentencing: Do Female Defendants Experience Disparate Treatment?" *Journal of Criminal Justice,* vol. 43, 2015, pp. 406–417.

Grant, Adam, and Sheryl Sandberg. "Madam C.E.O., Get Me a Coffee." *New York Times.* 6 February 2015. https://mobile.nytimes.com/2015/02/08/opinion/sunday/sheryl-sandberg-and-adam-grant-on-women-doing-office-housework.html. Accessed 5 July 2017.

——. "When Talking About Bias Backfires." *New York Times.* 6 December 2014. www.nytimes.com/2014/12/07/opinion/sunday/adam-grant-and-sheryl-sandberg-on-discrimination-at-work.html. Accessed 5 July 2017.

Guante. "10 Responses to the Phrase 'Man Up.'" *Guante.* www.guante.info/2012/02/10-responses-to-phrase-man-up-spoken.html. Accessed 5 July 2017.

Guéguen, Nicolas. "Effects of a Tattoo on Men's Behavior and Attitudes Towards Women: An Experimental Field Study." *Archives of Sexual Behavior,* vol. 2, no. 8, 2013, pp. 1517–1524.

Harris, Lynn. "Mrs. Feminist." *Salon.* 14 October 2003. www.salon.com/2003/10/16/names_2/. Accessed 5 July 2017.

Hawkes, Daina, Charlene Y. Senn, and Chantal Thorn. "Factors that Influence Atti-
    tudes Toward Women with Tattoos." *Sex Roles*, vol. 50, 2004, pp. 593–604.

Henley, Nancy, and Jo Freeman. "The Sexual Politics of Interpersonal Behavior." In
    Women: Images and Realities. Eds. Suzanne Kelly, Gowri Parameswaran, and Nancy
    Schniedewind. 5th edition. McGraw Hill, 2012, pp. 82–88.

Henn, Steve. "Facebook Gives Users New Options to Identify Gender." *All Tech Consid-
    ered*. National Public Radio. 13 February 2014.

Hetter, Katia. "Girl Scouts Accepts Transgender Kid, Provokes Cookie Boycott." *CNN*.
    13 January 2012. www.cnn.com/2012/01/13/living/girl-scout-boycott/index.html.
    Accessed 5 July 2017.

Hill, Catherine. "Barriers and Bias: The Status of Women in Leadership." *American
    Association of University Women*. 2016. www.aauw.org/research/barriers-and-bias/.
    Accessed 5 July 2017.

"Hours Spent Doing Unpaid Household Work by Age and Sex, 2003–2007." Bureau of
    Labor Statistics. 6 August 2009. www.bls.gov/opub/ted/2009/ted_20090806.htm.
    Accessed 5 July 2017.

International Cheer Union. "History of Cheerleading." 24 February 2014. http://
    cheerunion.org/history/cheerleading/. Accessed 5 July 2017.

Johnson, Allan. *The Gender Knot: Unraveling Our Patriarchal Legacy*. Temple University
    Press, 1997.

Johnson, Jenna. "On College Campuses, a Gender Gap in Student Government." *The
    Washington Post*. 16 March 2011. www.washingtonpost.com/local/education/on-
    college-campuses-a-gender-gap-in-student-government/2011/03/10/ABim1Bf_
    story.html?utm_term=.1d0084cc0ff4. Accessed 5 July 2017.

Junior Achievement USA and the Allstate Foundation. "Teens and Personal Finance
    Survey." 10 April 2014. www.juniorachievement.org/documents/20009/20652/20
    15+Teens+and+Personal+Finance+Survey. Accessed 5 July 2017.

Kawashima-Ginsberg, Kei, and Nancy Thomas. "Civic Engagement and Political Lead-
    ership among Women—A Call for Solutions." CIRCLE Fact Sheet. May 2013.
    www.civicyouth.org/wp-content/uploads/2013/05/Gender-and-Political-Leader
    ship-Fact-Sheet-3.pdf. Accessed 5 July 2017.

Kimmel, Michael. "Solving the 'Boy Crisis' in Schools." *Huffington Post*. 30 April 2013.
    www.huffingtonpost.com/michael-kimmel/solving-the-boy-crisis-in_b_3126379.
    html. Accessed 5 July 2017.

Kivel, Paul. "The 'Act-Like-A-Man' Box." In *Men's Lives*. Ed. Michael S. Kimmel and
    Michael A. Messner. 7th edition. Pearson, 2007, pp. 148–150.

Kliff, Sarah, and Soo Oh. "Why Aren't There More Women in Congress?" *Vox*. 4
    November 2016. www.vox.com/a/women-in-congress. Accessed 5 July 2017.

Levin, Sam. "First US Person to Have 'Intersex' on Birth Certificate: 'There's Power in
    Knowing Who You Are.'" *The Guardian*. 11 January 2017. www.theguardian.com/
    world/2017/jan/11/intersex-rights-gender-sara-kelly-keenan-birth-certificate.
    Accessed 5 July 2017.

Lincoln, Anne E. "The Shifting Supply of Men and Women to Occupations: Feminiza-
    tion in Veterinary Education." *Social Forces*, vol. 88, 2010, pp. 1969–1998.

Lockwood, Penelope, Caitlin Burton, and Katelyn Boersma. "Tampering with Tradi-
    tion: Rationales Concerning Women's Married Names and Children's Surnames."
    Sex Roles, vol. 65, 2011, pp. 827–839.

Lorber, Judith. *Paradoxes of Gender*. Yale University Press, 1994.

"Market Research Statistics: U.S. Veterinarians 2015." American Veterinary Medicine Association. www.avma.org/KB/Resources/Statistics/Pages/Market-research-sta tistics-US-veterinarians.aspx. Accessed 25 January 2017.

Milkman, Katherine, Modupe Akinola, and Dolly Chugh. "What Happens Before? A Field Experiment Exploring How Pay and Representation Differentially Shape Bias on the Pathway into Organizations." *Journal of Applied Psychology*, vol. 100, no. 6, 2015, pp. 1678–1712.

Mills, C. Wright. *The Sociological Imagination*. Oxford University Press, 1959.

Parker, Sydney. "The Mormon Feminists Fighting for Women's Right to Join the Priest-hood." *Broadly*. 1 March 2016. https://broadly.vice.com/en_us/article/kb4dwy/the-mormon-feminists-fighting-for-womens-right-to-join-the-priesthood, Accessed 5 July 2017.

Pesut, Hana. *Switcheroo*. Schapco, 2013.

Reilly, Katie. "Sesame Street Reaches Out to 2.7 Million American Children With an Incarcerated Parent." *Pew Research Center*. 21 June 2013. www.pewresearch.org/fact-tank/2013/06/21/sesame-street-reaches-out-to-2–7-million-american-chil dren-with-an-incarcerated-parent/. Accessed 5 July 2017.

Richardson, Sarah. "Y All the Hype?" *Slate.com*. 5 May 2014. www.slate.com/articles/double_x/doublex/2014/05/sex_difference_findings_in_human_genome_stud ies_be_very_skeptical.html. Accessed 5 July 2017.

Rohan, Liz. "Reveal Codes: A New Lens for Examining and Historicizing the Work of Secretaries." *Computers and Composition*, vol. 20, no. 3, 2003, pp. 237–253.

Sadker, David, and Karen R. Zittleman. "Gender Inequity in School: Not a Thing of the Past." In *Women: Images and Realities, A Multicultural Anthology*. Eds. Amy Kessel-man, Lily D. McNair, and Nancy Schniedewind. McGraw Hill, 2011.

Sandberg, Sheryl. "Why We Have Too Few Women Leaders." TED Talk. December 2010. www.ted.com/talks/sheryl_sandberg_why_we_have_too_few_women_leaders? language=en. Accessed 6 July 2017.

Sandberg, Sheryl. *Lean In: Women, Work, and the Will to Lead*. Knopf, 2013.

Scheuble, Laurie, David R. Johnson, and Katherine M. Johnson. "Marital Name Chang-ing Attitudes and Plans of College Students: Comparing Change over Time and across Regions." *Sex Roles*, vol. 66, 2012, pp. 282–292.

Seelye, Katharine Q. "School Vote Stirs Debate on Girls as Leaders." *New York Times*. 11 April 2013. www.nytimes.com/2013/04/12/education/phillips-andover-girls-leadership-debated.html. Accessed 5 July 2017.

The Sentencing Project. "Fact Sheet: Incarcerated Women and Girls." 2015. www. sentencingproject.org/wp-content/uploads/2016/02/Incarcerated-Women-and-Girls.pdf. Accessed 5 July 2017.

Serano, Julia. "Trans Woman Manifesto." In *Feminist Theory: A Reader*. Eds. Wendy Kolmar and Frances Bartkowski. McGraw Hill, 2013, pp. 547–550.

Sharp, Gwen. "We Like You a Lot, Ms. Scientist, But We'd Rather Hire the Guy." Weblog entry. *Ms. Magazine Blog*. 26 September 2012. http://msmagazine.com/blog/2012/09/26/we-like-you-a-lot-ms-scientist-but-wed-rather-hire-the-guy/. Accessed 5 July 2017.

Smith, Stacy. "Research Informs and Empowers." Geena Davis Institute on Gender and Media. https://seejane.org/research-informs-empowers/. Accessed 5 July 2017.

Stryker, Susan. *Transgender History*. Seal Press, 2008.

Tanenbaum, Leora. *Slut! Growing Up Female with a Bad Reputation*. Seven Stories Press, 1999.

UN Women. "Facts and Figures: Leadership and Political Participation." UN Women. www.unwomen.org/en/what-we-do/leadership-and-political-participation/facts-and-figures. Accessed 1 March 2017.

"Unisex Names: Toward a Gender-Free Ideal?" *Nameberry*. 22 August 2012. https://nameberry.com/blog/unisex-names-toward-a-gender-free-ideal. Accessed 5 July 2017.

University of Michigan Institute for Social Research. "Time, Money, and Who Does the Laundry." *University of Michigan*, no. 7, 2007. http://ns.umich.edu/podcast/img/ISR_Update1–07.pdf. Accessed July 5 2017.

Valenti, Jessica. *Full Frontal Feminism: A Young Woman's Guide to Why Feminism Matters*. Seal Press, 2007.

Wade, Lisa. "American Men's Hidden Crisis: They Need More Friends!" *Slate*. 7 December 2013. www.salon.com/2013/12/08/american_mens_hidden_crisis_they_need_more_friends/. Accessed 5 July 2017.

Wade, Lisa and Myra Marx Ferree. *Gender: Ideas, Interactions, Institutions*. WW Norton, 2014.

Weil, Elizabeth. "What if It's (Sort of) a Boy and (Sort of) a Girl?" *New York Times*. 24 September 2006. www.nytimes.com/2006/09/24/magazine/24intersexkids.html. Accessed 5 July 2017.

"What Is Intersex?" *Intersex Society of North America*. www.isna.org/faq/what_is_intersex. Accessed 5 July 2017.

Williams, Joan, and Rachel Dempsey. *What Works for Women at Work: Four Patterns Working Women Need to Know*. New York University Press, 2014.

Women's Ordination Conference. www.womensordination.org/. Accessed 5 July 2017.

Yoder, Brian. "Engineering by the Numbers." American Society for Engineering Education. 2011–2012. www.asee.org/papers-and-publications/publications/college-profiles/15EngineeringbytheNumbersPart1.pdf. Accessed 5 July 2017.

Zettel, Jen. "Appleton School Dress Code Draws Debate." *Appleton Post-Crescent*. 30 May 2015. www.postcrescent.com/story/news/local/2015/05/31/appleton-school-dress-code-draws-debate/28204303/. Accessed July 5 2017.

Suggested Readings and Videos

Alter, Charlotte. "Seeing Sexism From Both Sides: What Trans Men Experience." *Time*. 27 June 2016. http://time.com/4371196/seeing-sexism-from-both-sides-what-trans-men-experience/. Accessed 6 July 2017.

Angier, Natalie. *Woman: An Intimate Geography*. Anchor, 2000.

Bornstein, Kate. *Gender Outlaw: On Men, Women, and the Rest of Us*. Vintage Books, 1995.

Brumberg, Joan Jacobs. *The Body Project: An Intimate History of American Girls*. Vintage Books, 1997.

Butler, Judith. *Gender Trouble: Feminism and the Subversion of Identity*. Routledge, 1990.

Crittenden, Ann. *The Price of Motherhood: Why the Most Important Job in the World Is Still the Least Valued*. Picador, 2010.

Davis, Angela Y. *Women, Race, and Class*. Vintage Books, 1983.

Davis, Georgiann. "5 Things I Wish You Knew About Intersex People." UNLV News Center. www.unlv.edu/news/article/5-things-i-wish-you-knew-about-intersex-people#.VhWCfg5OtLo.twitter. Accessed 6 July 2017.

Fausto-Sterling, Anne. *Sex/Gender: Biology in a Social World.* Routledge, 2012.

Grose, Jessica. "Cleaning: The Final Feminist Frontier." *New Republic.* 19 March 2013. https://newrepublic.com/article/112693/112693. Accessed 5 July 2017.

Halberstam, Judith. *Female Masculinity.* Duke University Press, 1998.

hooks, bell. *Feminism Is for Everybody: Passionate Politics.* Pluto P, 2000.

Hurt, Byron. "Why I Am a Male Feminist." *The Root.* 16 March 2011. www.theroot.com/why-i-am-a-male-feminist-1790863150. Accessed 6 July 17.

Ingraham, Chrys. *White Weddings: Romancing Heterosexuality in Popular Culture.* Routledge, 1999.

Katz, Jackson. *Tough Guise 2: Violence, Manhood and American Culture.* Media Education Foundation, 2013.

Kimmel, Michael. *Manhood in America: A Cultural History.* 3rd edition. Oxford University Press, 2011.

Kliff, Sarah, and Soo Oh. "Why Aren't There More Women in Congress?" *Vox.* 4 November 2016. www.vox.com/a/women-in-congress. Accessed 6 July 2017.

Lawless, Jennifer, and Richard L. Fox. "Girls Just Wanna Not Run: The Gender Gap in Young American's Political Ambition." March 2013. Women and Politics Institute. www.american.edu/spa/wpi/upload/Girls-Just-Wanna-Not-Run_Policy-Report.pdf. Accessed 6 July 2017.

Mifflin, Margot. *Bodies of Subversion: A Secret History of Women and Tattoo.* 3rd edition. powerHouse Books, 2013.

Moss-Racusin, Corrine, John F. Dovidio, Victoria L. Brescoll, Mark J. Graham, and Jo Handelsman. "Science Faculty's Subtle Gender Biases Favor Male Students." *PNAS*, vol. 109, no. 41, pp. 16474–16479.

Stolakis, Kristine. *Where We Stand.* Video 2016. http://kristinestolakis.com/portfolio-item/where-we-stand/. Accessed 6 July 2017.

Thomas, Katie. "Born on Sideline, Cheering Clamors to be a Sport." *New York Times.* 22 May 2011.

"What It's Like to Be Intersex." BuzzFeedYellow. 28 March 2015. www.youtube.com/watch?v=cAUDKEI4QKI. Accessed 6 July 2017.

Yogachandra, Natascha. "Teaching Positive Masculinity." *The Atlantic.* 14 May 2014. www.theatlantic.com/health/archive/2014/05/becoming-men-teaching-opositive-masculinity/361739/. Accessed 6 July 2017.

Zhou, Li. "The Sexism of School Dress Codes." *The Atlantic.* 20 October 2015. www.theatlantic.com/education/archive/2015/10/school-dress-codes-are-problematic/410962/. Accessed 6 July 2017.

3

PRIVILEGE AND OPPRESSION

Figure 3.1 Kathrine Switzer runs the Boston Marathon in 1967

Source: Getty Images/*Boston Globe*

Opening Illustration

In 1967, the idea of women participating in a long-distance race as grueling as the Boston Marathon was so farfetched that no official document stated that women were prohibited. Kathrine Switzer, a 19-year old Syracuse student, loved running and had been training with her coach Arnie Briggs to do long-distance races; she even completed a 30-miler to prepare herself to compete in the flagship race in the United States. Registering as K.V. Switzer, Kathrine started the race with Briggs and her boyfriend, Tom Miller. Two miles in, race officials attempted to eject her from the race, with race director Jock Semple lunging at her, attempting to pull her from the course and tear off her race number (see Figure 3.1). Miller and Briggs deflected Semple, allowing Kathrine to finish the 26.2 mile race in a respectable 4 hours and 20 minutes. The experience was a life-changing one for Switzer, as her experience inspired her to become a lifelong advocate for equal opportunity for women in athletics and beyond (Butler). More broadly, Switzer's historic run helped propel a sea change in women's sports, marked in 1972 by women's official inclusion in the Boston Marathon and the passage of Title IX legislation, which prohibited discrimination in education, including athletic programs. Change came a bit more slowly to the Olympics, however; it was not until 1984 that the women's marathon was first included as an event.

We open the chapter with this story because it illustrates the chapter's threshold concepts, privilege and oppression, particularly institutional structures that shape our individual experiences, and how activism, agency, and advocacy—as well as the action of feminist allies—can challenge and ultimately change those structures. As you read this chapter, consider how the key concepts outlined are at work in Switzer's historical action as part of completing the end of chapter Application Exercise.

A feminist stance posits that systems of privilege and oppression profoundly shape individual lives. These systems play out via **ideology** and societal institutions and are internalized by individuals.

Why a Threshold Concept?

Now that you have started to develop an understanding of the concept of a socially constructed sex/gender system, the next step is to broaden our inquiry, or widen our lens, to use a visual metaphor. Imagine a film that opens with a close-up shot and then quickly pans out to show the viewer the bigger picture. That's precisely the move we'll be making in this chapter. Although we began this textbook by focusing on the power dynamics that are at play in the gender system, when we widen our lens we are able to see that similar dynamics structure many other systems of difference and inequality. Sexism, the system of oppression and privilege based in gender, is but one type of oppression. What's more, these additional structures of oppression and privilege are interconnected and mutually reinforcing (a point that will be developed more fully in Chapter 4 on intersectionality).

Definitions

Oppression

The concepts of privilege and oppression provide a fundamental framework for understanding how power operates in society. This framework helps explain people's experiences in the world, and it provides us with tools to name and describe our social location. *Oppression* can be defined as prejudice and discrimination directed toward a group and perpetuated by the ideologies and practices of multiple social institutions. A number of scholars and activists have explored the ways of thinking and the mechanisms through which these systems are created and perpetuated. For example, legal scholar Mari Matsuda notes that "[a]ll forms of oppression involve taking a trait X, which often carries with it a cultural meaning, and using X to make some group the 'other' and to reduce their entitlements and power." This terminology of privilege and oppression, then, gives us the tools to name and describe not just sexism but the whole "-ism family," as Gloria Yamato calls it; for example, **racism, classism, heterosexism**, and **ableism**.

Type of Oppression	Corresponding Type of Privilege
Racism	White privilege
Sexism	Male privilege
Classism	Middle-class privilege
Heterosexism/homophobia	Heterosexual privilege
Ableism	Able-bodied privilege
Cissexism/transphobia	Cisgender privilege

Within each system of privilege and oppression, we can see that there is a dominant group and a marginalized group, one group who is considered to be the norm, with their counterpart being the "other." Audre Lorde calls it a **mythical norm**, "usually defined as white, thin, male, young, heterosexual, christian, and financially secure," and goes on to argue that "[i]t is with this mythical norm that the trappings of power reside within this society" (116). Those who are outside the mythical norm in one or more ways are seen as lesser as a result of being judged in relation to it. As discussed in Chapter 2, masculinity is the default norm in our culture, and it is valued more highly than femininity. The same can be said for being able-bodied, young, white, and so forth. Audre Lorde argues that

> we have *all* been programmed to respond to the human differences between us with fear and loathing and to handle that difference in one of three ways: ignore it, and if that is not possible, copy it if we think it is dominant, or destroy it if we think it is subordinate.

> (115)

As we will discuss in this chapter, idealization of the mythical norm manifests in many ways, both material and ideological.

In addition to the scholarship that has explored the ways of thinking that create and perpetuate systems of privilege and oppression, many scholars have also explored in depth how these systems manifest, that is, what forms they take. Oppression can take *cultural and symbolic* forms (discussed in the Ideologies section), such as images of beauty and success, and *material* forms (discussed in the Institutions section), such as structured forms of failure that disproportionately impact some groups more than others.

For members of marginalized groups, as Marilyn Frye notes, the experience is

> that the living of one's life is confined and shaped by forces and barriers which are not accidental or occasional and hence avoidable, but are systematically related to each other in such a way as

to catch one between and among them and restrict or penalize motion in any direction.

(43)

Labeling one's experience with oppression, framed through the "wide lens" that we described previously, means using the sociological imagination discussed in Chapter 2, and situating one's experience within a broader framework; often, this means revising a personal understanding of successes, failures, and circumstances from narratives of individual action and personal will to a paradigm that considers how those experiences fit in with social, material, and economic forces. In order to fully understand the concept of oppression, we have to be willing to think on a "macro level," which is not particularly easy to do. In our experiences of talking about and teaching about this concept (as well as the concept of privilege, discussed below), we have found that some misconceptions and misunderstandings crop up over and over again. We detail a few of them in this chapter.

Misconception Alert

Racism, sexism, and other forms of oppression happen only on an individual level. One of the most challenging concepts to understand in many sociologically based disciplines and in Women's and Gender Studies specifically are the differences between what feminist scholar Beverly Daniel Tatum identifies as bigotry, prejudice, and racism. It's important to distinguish between these three ideas, because whereas the first two happen on a practical and potentially individual level, the last is structural and systemic. As with patriarchy, racism is not the product or conduct of an individual person but what Tatum defines as "a system involving cultural messages and institutional policies and practices as well as the beliefs and actions of individuals" (362). Some people use "prejudice" and "bigotry" as interchangeable with "racism"; bigotry is a personal belief system that may manifest in acts of meanness or hostility on an individual level. Prejudice is a preconception about an individual on the basis of a racial identity. Racism differs from either of these because it involves what David Wellman has called a "system of advantage based on race" and means prejudice plus bigotry plus power, or the ability to grant privileges to groups and withhold them from others (qtd. in Tatum).

The critical elements differentiating oppression from simple prejudice and discrimination are that it is a group phenomenon and that institutional power and authority are used to support prejudices and enforce discriminatory behaviors in systematic ways. Everyone is socialized to participate in oppressive practices, either as direct and indirect perpetrators or passive beneficiaries, or—as with some oppressed peoples—by directing discriminatory behaviors at members of one's own group.

Internalized Oppression and Horizontal Hostility

Institutional and ideological manifestations of privilege and oppression are internalized by members of both dominant and marginalized groups. In other words, it is often the case that members of marginalized groups come to internalize the dominant group's characterizations of them as lesser and inferior. This phenomenon is called **internalized oppression**, and can be seen as a marker of the "success" of the dominant group's use of ideology. For example, when working-class and poor people internalize classism, they come to believe that their class position is deserved, that their failure to succeed economically is the result of their failure to work hard enough and exert enough effort to achieve class mobility. Gay men and lesbians internalize heterosexism if they accept the belief that they are unfit to parent or are undeserving of protection from discrimination. Women internalize sexism if they come to believe that they are less capable in mathematics and the natural sciences.

A related concept is that of *horizontal hostility*, introduced in Chapter 2, whereby members of marginalized groups police each other's behavior and/or appearance. Horizontal hostility happens when a member of a marginalized group identifies with the values of the dominant group. The phenomenon of women slut shaming other women is an example of horizontal hostility, as it entails women internalizing the sexual double standard, and monitoring and casting judgment on other women's appearance and behaviors. "Respectability politics," or the politics of respectability, is a term used to describe horizontal hostility and internalized oppression in a racial context. Members of marginalized racial groups who engage in respectability politics police the language, behavior, and appearance of other members of their same group, out of the belief that conforming to norms of the dominant group is a key component of combating racial oppression.

Oppression is internalized by individuals, then, and as such, has a psychological dimension that must be addressed when working to dismantle it. As Audre Lorde writes,

> [f]or we have, built into all of us, old blueprints of expectation and response, old structures of oppression, and these must be altered at the same time as we alter the living conditions which are a result of those structures.
>
> (123)

Privilege

Privilege can be defined as benefits, advantages, and power that accrue to members of a dominant group as a result of the oppression of the marginalized group; individuals and groups may be privileged without realizing, recognizing, or even wanting it. A key point here is that oppression and privilege are inextricably linked; they are opposite sides of the same coin. For every type of oppression, a corresponding set of privileges exists. That is, the flip side of sexism is male privilege; of racism, white privilege; of heterosexism, heterosexual privilege; of transphobia, cisgender privilege, and so forth.

One of the best known essays on the topic of white privilege is Peggy Mcintosh's "White Privilege: Unpacking the Invisible Knapsack," where she writes: "I was taught to see racism only in individual acts of meanness, not in invisible systems conferring dominance on my group" and

> I have come to see white privilege as an invisible package of unearned assets that I can count on cashing in each day, but about which I was "meant" to remain oblivious. White privilege is like an invisible weightless knapsack of special provisions, maps, passports, codebooks, visas, clothes, tools, and blank checks.

Mcintosh's essay is now a classic because of its trenchant enumeration of all the (mostly unconscious) assumptions that white people make on a day-to-day basis about their social location and role in the world. Some of the clearest include her notes on "Daily Effects of White Privilege":

7. When I am told about our national heritage or about "civilization," I am shown that people of my color made it what it is.

8. I can be sure that my children will be given curricular materials that testify to the existence of their race.

13. Whether I use checks, credit cards or cash, I can count on my skin color not to work against the appearance of financial reliability.

16. I can be pretty sure that my children's teachers and employers will tolerate them if they fit school and workplace norms; my chief worries about them do not concern others' attitudes toward their race.

20. I can do well in a challenging situation without being called a credit to my race.

21. I am never asked to speak for all the people of my racial group.

22. I can remain oblivious of the language and customs of persons of color who constitute the world's majority without feeling in my culture any penalty for such oblivion.

25. If a traffic cop pulls me over or if the IRS audits my tax return, I can be sure I haven't been singled out because of my race.

34. I can worry about racism without being seen as self-interested or self-seeking.

36. If my day, week or year is going badly, I need not ask of each negative episode or situation whether it had racial overtones.

46. I can choose blemish cover or bandages in "flesh" color and have them more or less match my skin.

What Mcintosh's ideas call attention to are the specific ways that privilege operates in daily life. She argues that, although whites may have experiences that feel like discrimination, those experiences are generally not attributable to their racial identity. Further, McIntosh's examples show individual experience within the context of larger structures and institutions: law enforcement, government agencies, educational institutions, and so forth.

The Black Lives Matter movement was created in 2012 by a group of activists in response to the acquittal of George Zimmerman in the shooting of African American teenager Trayvon Martin. Subsequent police shootings or deaths of African American people while in police custody strengthened the movement, and unrest in Ferguson, MO in August of 2014 after teenager Michael Brown was shot by a white police officer brought the movement into greater public visibility. The online and media discourse around the #blacklivesmatter hashtag and the subsequent "counter-hashtags," #alllivesmatter and #bluelivesmatter, shows the tension that emerges around the recognition of privilege and oppression, particularly how both are woven into individual experience of institutions like law enforcement and the justice system. In this instance, a documented pattern of police militarization, racial profiling, systematic racism, and questions about the use of force in encounters with people of color are clearly interrelated with the power and social authority of police. The experiences of people of color as they interact with police are differently inflected by systemic racism than whites; the #alllivesmatter hashtag reflects white privilege in that it fails to account for the documented violence and brutality disproportionately experienced by people of color in the justice system.

Many writers and activists have been inspired by Mcintosh's list to generate similar lists to name other types of privilege; this strategy of explicitly enumerating instances of privilege continues to be powerful in raising awareness and provoking reflection among members of the group who experience it. There are many lists that explore able-bodied privileges and cisgender privileges, for example. Interestingly, a point of confluence on these lists is around the issue of bathroom access. Sam Dylan Finch's list, published on the Everyday Feminism website, includes the following cisgender privilege: "You can be sure that when you go out, you will be able to find a restroom or locker room that corresponds with your gender identity"; another list, which uses first person perspective, asserts, "I do not have to worry about whether I will be able to find a bathroom to use or whether I will be safe changing in a locker room" ("Daily Effects"). Many lists of able-bodied privilege mention that able-bodied people don't have to give thought to how and where they can find a restroom that accommodates their needs. More generally, the experience of being able-bodied is one of not having to give thought to how one will enter, exit, and navigate through public buildings, including opening and closing doors, operating light switches, moving through hallways and around corners, etc. If you would like to explore issues of accessibility on your campus, consider using one of the checklists created to gauge public facilities' compliance with the Americans with Disabilities Act. The suggested readings section at the end of the chapter includes several of these lists and checklists; we recommend exploring a variety of them.

Antiracist activist Tim Wise has used his own experience to illustrate the concept of white, male privilege. Wise argues that

> to be white [in the US] not only means that one will typically inherit certain advantages from the past but also means that one will continue to reap the benefits of ongoing racial privilege, which itself is the flipside of discrimination against persons of color.
>
> (xi)

Here he details the historical and legal circumstances of his family that ultimately allowed him, as a white man, to benefit from those injustices and advance socially and educationally. For example, as the child of a middle-income household with relatively modest standardized test scores, Wise found himself a not particularly competitive applicant to the selective Tulane University. Wise traces back his mother's ability (even as a woman who had never owned a piece of property) to take out a loan to help him pay tuition, with his grandmother as a cosigner. His grandmother also had never worked outside the home, and her ability to cosign was inextricably linked to her marriage to a white man whose financial fortunes rested on his racial whiteness—working in the military and government in an era when people of color were systematically denied such opportunities, and buying a house in a neighborhood where, due to a lack of legal structures to prevent housing discrimination, people of color did not live (Wise 12–13). As Wise concludes,

[a]lthough not every white person's story is the same as mine, the simple truth is that any white person born before 1964, at least, was legally elevated above any person of color, and as such received directly the privileges, the head start, the advantages of whiteness as a matter of course.

(13)

Learning Roadblock

Defensiveness and denial of privilege: Research on learning has shown that a learner's existing understanding strongly influences how that learner absorbs new information. The use of "privilege" in this discipline-specific context requires some rethinking of the common-sense use of the term "privilege," or the way we refer to it in everyday life. Most frequently, we think of a privilege as something like a "gift" or "honor," an opportunity of some kind. What differentiates privilege as a kind of term used in Women's and Gender Studies is the notion that privilege refers not just to individual opportunity but to *structured and social opportunities*, particularly those that are systematically granted on the basis of a social category of identity rather than merit or individual will and that become woven into the fabric of institutions. Examinations of structural forms of privilege seek to help people situate themselves within these larger contexts and cultivate self and cultural awareness of how privilege and oppression operate, as well as strategies for challenging them.

But it's not just that our commonsense understanding of privilege gets in the way of grasping how we use that term here. Another more fundamental kind of misunderstanding can come from the fact that this framework of privilege and oppression runs counter to the values and assumptions of many people in our culture. Several examples illustrate this point. At Delavan-Darien High School in Wisconsin, a parent complained about a teacher's use of materials on white privilege in an "American Diversity" course. After looking at the course materials, which drew on the work of Tim Wise and Peggy McIntosh, the parent drew the conclusion that the materials were divisive, and that they had the intention of inducing "white guilt." It seems clear that the parent rejected the overall premise that society is structured into systems of oppression and privilege, and she was quoted as saying that, in her understanding of them, the course materials were saying, "If you're white, you're oppressing. If you're non white, you've been a victim" (Starnes). The parent seems to have been thinking only in individual terms, as opposed to structural, macro-level terms. Michael Kimmel, a sociologist who has written extensively about privilege, argues that statements like these "are as revealing as they are irrelevant." He notes the strong impulse in our culture to "individualize and personalize processes that are social and structural" (2), and goes on to point out that this type of response is a way to dodge and avoid taking these issues seriously. Such misunderstandings can extend even into the political landscape; for example, a proposed January 2017 bill in Arizona, HB120, called for the prohibition of many courses that the bill interpreted as causing "division, resentment or social justice toward a race, gender, religion, political affiliation, social class or other class of people" (Flaherty), a bill proposed in response to a course called "Whiteness and Race Theory." A similar case emerged in Wisconsin that same year, where representative Dave Murphy called for state funding ramifications to be imposed on the University of Wisconsin–Madison for offering a course entitled "The Problem of Whiteness."

Learning Roadblock

"If I don't see it, it must not exist." One of the biggest barriers many students experience in understanding the "big picture" or structural contexts of privilege and oppression is the temptation to use one's own experience as a "measuring stick." For example, it may be hard to grasp the enormity of rates of violence against women if it is an issue that has not touched one's life personally. Julie Zeilinger calls this the "If I don't see it, it must not exist" mentality, and she argues that this mentality is often a product of being unaware of our privileges. The important point to remember here is that although personal experience is a critical source of knowledge in Women's and Gender Studies, it also has to be measured against other kinds of knowledge that can provide a framework within which to place one's personal experience and compare

it with the experiences of others. Students who are learning to think, know, and see like Women's and Gender Studies practitioners learn to position their own experiences and awareness of the world alongside the statistical, demographic, and theoretical knowledge gained by systematic evidence collection by researchers, as well as the varying perspectives that their classmates and conversation partners can bring to their understanding. What this means is that new students of Women's and Gender Studies should think about how their own personal experience is reflective of others' gendered experiences of the world, and how it departs from others' experiences.

Institutions

In Chapter 2, we introduced the concept of gender socialization. As a part of that discussion, we asked you to consider both where and how we are socialized into our gender, that is, where we learn what it means to be a boy or a girl, a man or a woman, in our society. Those sites of gender socialization are our society's institutions, and as we mentioned there, they consist of marriage, family, the educational system, the health care system, religion, mass media, the military, the political system, the legal and criminal justice systems, sports, and the economy. We return to a discussion of institutions in the context of this chapter on oppression and privilege because systems of oppression and privilege are embedded within and are played out through these societal institutions.

In Chapter 2, we focused on how societal institutions are patriarchal in nature; that is, as Allan Johnson explains, male-dominated, male-identified, male-centered, and obsessed with control, particularly of women. Here we go one step further by stating that (1) societal institutions also structure oppression and privilege based on race, class, and sexual identity, as well as other categories of identity; and (2) these systems of oppression and privilege overlap with and reinforce one another. In other words, these systems cannot be understood in isolation from one another.

The terms "institutions" and "institutional or structural" forms of oppression are used frequently to highlight the way that systems function to grant resources and privileges to some groups and withhold them from others. Institutions can be formal, organized structures like law and policy-making groups (the House of Representatives and Senate, the Food and Drug Administration, or the medical profession and its related professional organizations), or they can be less formal but still an agreed-upon way of organizing and reproducing social norms (e.g., mass media and popular culture). In other ways, institutions can have a combination of formal and informal structural elements. For example, "marriage" as an institution is governed by formal laws that dictate who can marry and under what conditions; it is simultaneously shaped by formal religious organizations that grant benefits to certain couples and not others, and that enact doctrine that participants in that faith are expected to comply with in order to remain in good standing. Social norms about marriage are promulgated via other informal institutions such as mass media and other aspects of popular culture (think, for example, of the number of magazines, television shows, and websites that are devoted to wedding culture). The example of marriage also illustrates the points made in the previous paragraph, in that not only is the institution of marriage historically patriarchal but it is also heterosexist. And in the 21st century, marriage is increasingly becoming a middle-class institution that consolidates and protects the privileges of those with economic means and serves to further marginalize working-class and poor people. This point will be explored more fully in the Anchoring Topics section below.

Ideologies

The concept of ideology might be one that you have heard before, as academics tend to use it *a lot*, but you might not really know what it means or why it's used so much. We are introducing it in the context of this chapter on privilege and oppression, along with institutions, because it is the other primary means or method through which those systems of oppression and privilege manifest and are played out.

Quite simply, ideologies are sets of ideas or beliefs. Just as there are dominant and marginalized groups in society, so there are dominant ideologies. Ideologies always represent the attitudes, interests, and values of a particular group. Lynn Weber defines dominant ideologies as "pervasive societal beliefs that reflect the dominant culture's vision about what is right and proper. Controlling images (stereotypes) are dominant-culture ideologies about subordinate groups that serve to restrict their options, to constrain them" (117). Legal scholar Mari Matsuda asserts that "[l]anguage, including the language of science, law, rights, necessity, free markets, neutrality, and objectivity can make subordination seem natural and inevitable, justifying material deprivation" (336). What we invite you to do is to develop a heightened awareness of the ways that ideologies operate in culture at large as well as in your own life and thinking. This involves developing *metacognition*—or thinking about one's own thinking or thinking processes. Understanding ideologies means being able to (1) identify patterns of thinking, (2) monitor one's own thinking for those patterns of belief, and (3) critically reflect on how one's ideas and attitudes are shaped by those beliefs.

Health Care

Privilege and oppression play out in the institution of health care in the United States, where the amount and quality of health care people have access to is shaped by economic resources or the lack thereof, as well as racism. The U.S. Department of Health and Human Services Office of Minority Health, for example, has documented significant disparities in the health outcomes of marginalized racial and ethnic groups. Their action plan to reduce health disparities notes

> [i]ndividuals, families and communities that have systematically experienced social and economic disadvantage face greater obstacles to optimal health. Characteristics such as race or ethnicity, religion, SES, gender, age, mental health, disability, sexual orientation or gender identity, geographic location, or other characteristics historically linked to exclusion or discrimination are known to influence health status.
>
> (Office)

The report notes that these health disparities are not only about lack of access to care, but about the kind of care that people of color receive when seeking it. More specifically, they note that "[r]acial and ethnic minorities are more likely than non-Hispanic Whites to report experiencing poorer quality patient–provider interactions." These patient–provider interactions are often of poor quality because providers may bring stereotypical understandings of patients into their treatment. In other words, ideology also plays a role in shaping people's experiences of the institution of health care. We will return to this topic in Chapter 4.

A related example focuses on gender in health care. While women obtain health care in equal if not greater numbers than men, their experiences may be negatively shaped on a number of levels by gender stereotypes. As we discussed in Chapter 2, in a binary sex/gender system, masculinity is associated with the mind and rationality, and femininity with the body and irrationality. These characteristics have made their way into gender stereotypes of women as hysterical, with their physical complaints not being taken seriously by their health care practitioner. As Laurie Edwards notes in "The Gender Gap in Pain," the Institute of Medicine's 2011 report "Relieving Pain in America" "found that not only did women appear to suffer more from pain, but that women's reports of pain were more likely to be dismissed." Instead, Edwards observes, women's pain is often characterized as "'emotional,' 'psychogenic' and therefore 'not real.'"

Anchoring Topics through the Lens of Privilege and Oppression
Work and Family

Two societal institutions through which women experience varying degrees of privilege and oppression are the workplace and the family. For example, workplaces are governed and authorized by a variety of laws, acts, and policies regarding labor, safety, and leave for illness or family obligation. And as discussed in Chapter 2, gendered ideas and images of work and leadership deeply impact women's experiences of the workplace. Family structure is also subject to laws, acts, or policies, particularly in relation to marriage, and particular family structures may be reinforced, acknowledged, or ignored by those policies and laws. For example, even though the U.S. Supreme Court's 2015 ruling in

Obergefell had the effect of legalizing same-sex marriage in this country, as of 2017, some state and county courts and vital records offices continue to refuse legal recognition to the families of same-sex lesbian couples in the form of parentage orders and birth certificates. Ideology surrounding the family is also especially strong, and many of us have internalized these ideas and images about what constitutes a family and what a "normal" family looks like, as well as how families function in terms of assumed roles and responsibilities.

Among these internalized ideas and images of a "normal" family is that it is nuclear in structure, with a married (heterosexual) couple at its center. This image, however, is deeply out of touch with reality, as evidenced by data from the 2010 Census, which revealed that married couples now constitute a minority of households (48%). By contrast, in 1950, married couples represented 78 percent of households; this significant decrease has been attributed to a number of factors, including later ages for first marriage and cohabitation for longer periods before marriage. In addition, while divorce rates have stabilized overall, a growing number of people are choosing not to marry, or not to remarry after getting divorced or being widowed. There is a particularly striking change evident among middle-aged Americans. Reporting on a study that appeared in *The Gerontologist*, Rachel Swarns notes that "[a]bout a third of adults ages 46 through 64 were divorced, separated or had never been married in 2010, compared with 13 percent in 1970."

These changes to rates of marriage and family form in the last several decades stand in complex relationship to women's rates of participation in the paid labor market. In some segments of society, women's increasing participation in the labor market has contributed to delaying the age of first marriage, and sometimes shaped women's choices around whether to stay married and/or to remarry after divorce. On the flip side of this is the reality that more and more families rely on women's earnings, whether as the primary or sole income. In 1948, only 17 percent of married mothers were in the paid labor force; as of 2015, according to the Bureau of Labor Statistics, 69.9 percent of all mothers with children under the age of 18 participated in the labor force, a substantial increase over the span of slightly less than 80 years. The participation rate for married mothers with a spouse present was slightly lower (67.6%) than those who were single, divorced, or separated (74.8%). Further, although women were less likely to be in the labor force when their children were not yet of school age, almost two-thirds of women with children under the age of 6 participated in the labor force (64.2%), and even a majority of married women with infants less than 1 year old worked outside the home (57.6%). The importance of women's paid work is underscored by the finding that, as of 2015, "42% of mothers were sole or primary breadwinners, bringing in at least half of family earnings" (Glynn). One key point, then, is that a majority of women (regardless of marital status) in the U.S. want and/or need to combine childbearing and childrearing with paid work, and their earnings are an indispensable part of their household's income.

When discussing women's rates of marriage and participation in paid work (and the relationship between the two), we also must pull back and look at how economic forces shape both. Women's rates of marriage vary widely by economic class in ways that suggest that marriage is itself becoming a marker of class privilege. While rates of marriage are declining across the board, the decline is sharper among people with lower incomes and levels of education. More specifically, the decline in rates of marriage for women is both a cause and a consequence of economic inequality. It is a cause of economic inequality because single women who are heads of household bear the brunt of the gender wage gap even more sharply than do their married heterosexual counterparts. It is a consequence of economic inequality because studies are finding that marriage feels increasingly out of reach for women in lower income brackets. The results of a 2014 Pew Research survey, for example, reported that "never-married [heterosexual] women place a high premium on finding a spouse with a steady job. However, the changes in the labor market have contributed to a shrinking pool of available employed young men." When faced with a potential spouse who has experienced significant under- or unemployment, many women choose instead to remain single, out of a fear that, as Stephanie Coontz puts it, "legally hitching yourself to a man who might lose his job or misuse your resources can leave you worse off than if you stayed single." The divorce rate also differs quite dramatically by income and education, with rates of divorce significantly lower for those with more education and income. One study cited by the Bureau of Labor Statistics, for example, showed a gap of 20 percentage points in the rates of divorce for those with less than a high school degree (50% divorce rate) and those with a college degree (30% divorce rate). While there are many factors that contribute to the difference in divorce rates by income and education, one key factor that increases a couple's chance of divorce is instability caused by under/unemployment and the resulting financial stresses and worries.

Policy Implications

U.S. social policy reflects the dominant ideology idealizing the heterosexual two-parent nuclear married family in several key ways that conflict with the reality of the family lives of most U.S. women. For example, looking at the statistical and demographic realities of women, marriage, and motherhood reveals how misaligned the relationship between family structures and responsibilities is with workplace and public policies, structures that subsequently oppress women—poor women and women of color most of all. That is to say, in spite of the fact that a majority of women (regardless of marital status) in the U.S. want and/or need to combine childbearing and childrearing with paid work, and their earnings are an indispensable part of their household's income, our societal institutions and many of our governmental policies have not kept pace with this reality. In some cases this gap or mismatch can be characterized in terms of a time lag; that is, we can expect that our institutions and policies haven't caught up with the pace of change (but they eventually will), but in other instances the gap or mismatch represents deliberate efforts to stem the tide of changes to family structure based on the belief that these changes are problematic and even destructive.

Relevant policies are the **Family and Medical Leave Act (FMLA)** of 1993, the Personal Responsibility and Work Opportunity Reconciliation Act of 1996, and the provision in the Affordable Care Act of 2010 regarding the rights of breastfeeding workers. An analysis of these policies shows how these realities of family structure and labor force participation by women are misaligned with current public policies that support work–life balance, that allow women to fully participate in the workplace, and that promote particular sorts of economic dependence for women while discouraging and stigmatizing others, resulting in privilege for some women and oppression for others.

The FMLA illustrates how public policy has not kept pace with changes in women's roles and women's workforce participation—and the resistance to establishing the policy shows how ideologies can determine material realities. Pregnancy, lactation, and child care are a regular part of many women's life course, but it wasn't until 1993 under President Clinton that the United States adopted the FMLA, the first step toward ensuring that women could retain the right to return to their jobs after any leave to accommodate family needs. Although the passage of the FMLA represented a positive first step toward creating policy that would help make workplaces more accommodating of the needs of women workers, this Act has several limitations. First, FMLA provides a good example of something that privileges certain women but does not serve others: workers may only avail themselves of its benefits if they have worked a certain number of hours within a year and if they work for an employer with more than 50 employees. The Act may not protect their right to return to their exact position, only a similar one within that workplace. For professional women who work full time and who have access to a second wage in their household, FMLA may cover their needs. However, FMLA provides only unpaid leave, and unless a specific workplace complements this leave with paid leave, most women who are not partnered with a second wage earner (and even many who are) may not be able to take the full twelve weeks of unpaid leave.

In these regards, the current legislative protection for women lags far behind that of other countries. As the Project on Global Working Families has documented in its report, *The Work, Family, and Equity Index*, of 173 countries studied, 168 offer guaranteed leave with some associated income in connection with childbirth; 98 countries offer fourteen weeks or more of paid leave. The United States offers none (Heymann, Earle, and Hayes, see Figure 3.2). For a variety of reasons, it seems unlikely that significant federal-level paid family leave legislation will be passed in the next few years, though Rep. Rosa DeLauro and Sen. Kirsten Gillibrand have proposed what they call the FAMILY Act,

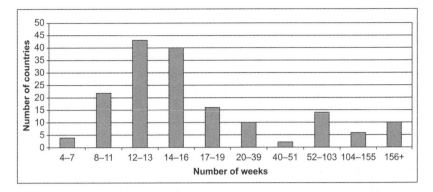

Figure 3.2 Maximum Paid Leave (Maternity & Parental) Available to Mothers in Countries Providing Paid Leave

Source: *New York Times*

which stands for the Family and Medical Insurance Leave Act. Their proposed legislation would provide workers with up to twelve weeks of partial income, and would cover workers in all companies no matter their size. In the meantime, a small number of states (California, New Jersey, Rhode Island, and New York) have created family and medical leave insurance programs in recent years.

Further, despite overwhelming scientific evidence in support of breastfeeding infants, the United States only minimally supports and protects breastfeeding mothers legislatively. As the Centers for Disease Control reports, mothers are the "fastest-growing segment of the U.S. Labor Force." With the passage of the 2010 Affordable Healthcare Act, employers are now required to "provide reasonable break time and a private, non-bathroom place for nursing mothers to express breast milk during the workday, for one year after the child's birth" (United States Breastfeeding Committee). Although this is a welcome policy, not all workplaces are covered under the law (the law contains an exemption for workplaces with fewer than 50 employees), and there is a long way to go in terms of raising awareness and ensuring compliance. Furthermore, as of 2017, the fate of the Affordable Care Act is unknown, as Congress and President Trump attempt to repeal it in part or in full.

Additionally, as of 2016, 49 states, as well as the District of Columbia and the Virgin Islands, have legislation protecting women's right to breastfeed in public, though just twelve have a protective law with an enforcement provision. As we discuss in Chapter 4, breastfeeding support and resources are also particularly tied to social class and the types of work environments that are amenable to promoting a climate friendly for lactating mothers. Women working in salaried, professional positions are more likely to have access to unmonitored breaks and private working spaces that will allow them to pump or breastfeed. What this means is that these laws and policies offer protection to women with class privilege, often in stable work environments with greater levels of autonomy, whereas other women will be disempowered by their workplaces. Overall, the difficulties many women face when attempting to maintain their supply of breast milk upon returning to work after the birth of a child reveal U.S. society's continued ambivalence about working mothers. Facing barriers to combining work with parenthood, some women feel pushed out of the workplace. Other women are not in a position to leave the workforce, even if they would like to, but instead may have to stop breastfeeding, because their employer is not accommodating.

A different dimension of ambivalence about combining paid work and mothering can be discovered through a discussion of the 1996 Personal Responsibility and Work Opportunity Reconciliation Act (PRWORA), which replaced Aid to Families with Dependent Children (which provided cash benefits to recipients) with the new program Temporary Assistance for Needy Families (TANF). Generally referred to as "welfare reform," the Act made some significant revisions to support benefits available to recipients, including placing a lifetime limit of 60 months on recipients, mandating work outside the home or work-seeking behaviors, and more stringent consequences for failure to comply with the program requirements.

The ideological assumptions underpinning welfare reform reflect the threshold concept of privilege and oppression around gender, class, and race. There is a classed double standard; whereas married mothers with class privilege are seen as good mothers for prioritizing family over paid work, poor unmarried mothers, within the rhetoric of welfare reform, are seen as bad mothers for wanting to do the same thing. In truth, poor mothers experience not just a double standard but a double bind, being judged bad mothers whether they stay at home or work. Because they are poor, they are often seen, by definition, as unfit parents.

The mandate that women seeking TANF funds must look for and find jobs does not account for the individual circumstances and social location of those who are in need of and seek government assistance. For example, many TANF recipients face significant barriers to employment. As the Office of Public Affairs notes, 42 percent of welfare recipients did not have a high school diploma or its equivalent; another one-third had serious health issues; and about one-third did not have recent work experience that would make them employable. Recipients often faced additional challenges to paid employment including young infants at home, language barriers, or care responsibilities for family members/children with disabilities.

Under TANF, poor unmarried mothers are required to seek work, but they also often receive explicit encouragement to marry as a way to lift themselves and their children out of poverty. In her 2008 study of low-income mothers, Marcella Gemelli notes the tension in this approach: "advocating for independence and self-sufficiency through working for wages, yet encouraging marriage seems contradictory" (102). More specifically, PRWORA included "Marriage Promotion" policies and funding—a set of policies and allocated resources dedicated toward promoting marriage, particularly out of concern from social conservatives that providing financial support to poor women created a disincentive to marry. Provisions of the bill supported public advertising campaigns on the value of marriage, the support of high school curricula promoting marriage, premarital education and training, marriage workshops, and divorce reduction programs focused on relationship skills (Dailard). The privileging of the heteronormative family—and the consequent structural oppression that results from the imposition of one ideological perspective on family configuration, particularly on poor women—present clear evidence that race, class, and gender are central in determining social location and status. The policy changes brought about by PRWORA reinforce the notion that particular forms of dependence—dependence on a male breadwinner—are acceptable forms (and the nuclear family is an ideal to which all families with children should aspire) while reflecting a prevailing assumption that financial dependence on government benefits should be curbed. Policies aimed at marriage promotion also discount the personal autonomy of women with multiple responsibilities by channeling resources into the promotion of an ideological ideal that is based on male dominance and **compulsory heterosexuality**.

An analysis of a range of marriage promotion programs around the U.S. has shown that they have not worked in promoting marriage or preventing divorce, much less in lifting women out of poverty, in spite of the fact that nearly a billion dollars has been spent on them (Covert). Marriage, then, is not a panacea for poverty, for reasons that have already been touched on in this section. In a 2014 report for the Council on Contemporary Families, Dr. Kristi Williams makes the case that social and economic family supports, rather than the promotion of marriage, are keys to improving the circumstances of single mothers and their children. She cites a study showing the impact of three specific policies on rates of poverty in single parent households: "(1) family allowances (direct payments to parents of dependent children), (2) paid parental leave, and (3) publicly funded childcare for children under age 3." She continues,

> [p]aid parental leave and publicly funded childcare for children under age three appear especially advantageous in reducing poverty among single mothers, largely by increasing their employment rates—a primary goal of the 1996 welfare reform legislation. Such policies benefit all families and are likely to be more effective than marriage promotion in reducing poverty and improving the lives of the growing number of single mothers and their children.

As our discussion above shows, social policies such as these would benefit not only single mothers living in poverty, but working- and middle-class women, married and unmarried.

Overall, the institutions of work and family profoundly impact women's lives. In the arenas of work and family—which have perhaps some of the most significant impacts on an individual's quality of life—macro-level and micro-level forms of privilege and oppression intersect at multiple levels. Women's ability to combine paid labor with reproductive labor; the choices they have with regard to partners, their personal finances, and their occupational trajectories; and the quality of their health and relationships are shaped by policies affecting the workplace at local and national levels.

Language, Images, and Symbols

Privilege and oppression manifest in symbolic ways as well as material ways (for example, language and images versus material conditions such as institutions like work and education). Three key examples illustrate how privilege and oppression play out through language, images, and symbols:

Language, Voice, and Power: "Mansplaining" and "Whitesplaining"

One way that privilege and oppression play out in language is through whose words are (and are not) listened to and granted authority. In 2008, author Rebecca Solnit published the piece "Men Explain Things to Me," a more cerebral and socially conscious meditation of the phenomenon subsequently coined **mansplaining**. As stated in a "Words We're Watching" blog post on the Merriam-Webster site, mansplaining "occurs when a man talks condescendingly to someone (especially a woman) about something he has incomplete knowledge of, with the mistaken assumption that he knows more about it than the person he's talking to does." Use of the term has subsequently gone mainstream. In her short essay, Solnit originally described a dinner party experience where a male guest insisted on describing a new book he had read a review of, summarizing its thesis and holding forth on the topic until being made to realize, only after several interruptions by another party guest, that Solnit herself was the author of the book under discussion. What Solnit ultimately tries to show is that, although for some women mansplaining may be a minor "social misery," for others she argues, "[a]t the heart of the struggle of feminism to give rape, date rape, marital rape, domestic violence, and workplace sexual harassment legal standing as crimes has been the necessity of making women credible and audible." That is, the power dynamic at play in mansplaining illustrates a key aspect of male privilege, which is the assumption of the right to speak, the assumption that one is knowing and has something to say worth listening to, and the expectation that one's words will be listened to. Conversely, the phenomenon of mansplaining reveals the extent to which many women still struggle to be heard. As Solnit explains, mansplaining is a phenomenon that

> keeps women from speaking up and from being heard when they dare; that crushes young women into silence by indicating, the way harassment on the street does, that this is not their world. It trains us in self-doubt and self-limitation just as it exercises men's unsupported overconfidence.

Solnit's point about the feminist struggle to make violence against women a crime speaks to the difficulty that members of all marginalized groups have when it comes to being heard when they describe their experiences of oppression. A pernicious manifestation of privilege is the belief that members of dominant groups are the best judges of what does and doesn't count as oppression. The term whitesplaining was coined to describe the phenomenon of white people explaining to people of color how they should feel about issues of race and racism, and offering their unsolicited judgment about whether those experiences could be considered legitimate examples of racism. A recent example

Rob Schneider ✔
@RobSchneider

                       👤• Follow   ⌄

Rep. Lewis. You are a great person. But Dr. King didn't give in to his anger or his hurt. That is how he accomplished & won Civil Rights.

RETWEETS   LIKES
2,955   7,930

12:00 PM - 16 Jan 2017

Figure 3.3 Tweet from Rob Schneider

Source: Twitter, www.dailymail.co.uk/news/article-4126906/Rob-Schneider-fire-MLK-Day-tweet-John-Lewis.html

made social media headlines when 1980s celebrity Rob Schneider tweeted comments to Georgia congressman John Lewis in response to Lewis's critiques of then-presidential candidate Donald Trump (Figure 3.3).

Extensive online and media commentary pegged this as an example of whitesplaining because of John Lewis's role as a close collaborator with Martin Luther King and one member of the group that organized the 1963 Civil Rights March on Washington, a group that included Dr. King.

On a related note, whitesplaining can also entail derailing and tone policing. The site Everyday Feminism provides a visual definition of this term:

Figure 3.4 Definition of Tone Policing

Source: http://everydayfeminism.com/2015/12/tone-policing-and-privilege/

The phrase captures the challenges of dialogue around issues that bear emotional weight for oppressed groups whose lived reality is dismissed or made invisible by demands for a particular type of communication preferred by a dominant group. This is sometimes an unintentional silencing, while in other scenarios it could be viewed as a strategy to shut down public resistance to oppression. For example, as the Black Lives Matter movement gained momentum, the types of public protest that individuals and groups engaged in frequently came under scrutiny. San Francisco 49ers quarterback Colin Kaepernick made headlines when he knelt rather than stood with his hand to his heart during the national anthem at professional football games. Other athletes, professional or otherwise, subsequently used this same strategy to register opposition to police violence against people of color. Backlash against this method of protest—as well as the range of protest strategies from marches to sit-ins to other demonstrations—led activists to critique these efforts to control the conversation and set terms for dialogue in ways that reinforce and derive from race, class, and gender privilege.

Online Presence and Wikipedia

As the increasingly ubiquitous source of information for online users, Wikipedia is an important part of the construction of knowledge and popular access to knowledge on the widest range of topics of practically any compendium, print or online. A number of new studies (and subsequent activist work) have centered on the gender disparity in the type and quality of contributions and edits made to Wikipedia, as well as the virtual environment experienced by Wikipedia contributors.

Research published by the Association of Computing Machinery and cosponsored by Yahoo showed that women editors of Wikipedia made fewer revisions in numbers to entries but made qualitatively more robust and fuller revisions, even though they make up an overall total of just 18 percent of Wikipedia editors. Other research estimates female contributions at 9–15 percent of editors. Research from the University of Minnesota's GroupLens Research Lab offered three key findings in their 2011 examination of over 110,000 Wikipedia editors: in terms of sheer numbers, just 16 percent of editors identified as women. They observed that women editors were more likely than men to leave or cease editing, particularly when, as newcomers, their edits were challenged or "reverted." In 2014, the Isla Vista, California shooting tragedy became the subject of a social media and Wikipedia battle illustrating this online tension. Shooter Elliot Rodger killed six people, and investigations revealed his self-reported motivation to fulfill what he himself called his "war on women" (Covarrubias, Mather, and Stevens). Harnessing the power of social media in response to the tragedy, women took to **Twitter** with the hashtag **#yesallwomen** to call out violence and sexism; this hashtag served as a counterpoint and challenge to the previously existing tag, **#notallmen**, which was created by men's rights activists to contradict the effort to make visible and to critique sexism and violence. A battle for control over the message around the shooting became visible in the Wikipedia page over how the shooting and subsequent social media coverage was presented. One draft of the entry specifically identified Rodger's misogyny as his motivation for the shootings, while a counter-edit charged that such claims reflected "feminist propaganda" and "misandry" (Dries). The Wikipedia entries for "#YesAllWomen" and "Isla Vista Shootings" saw heated disagreement on the discussion page about how this tragic event could be discussed in terms that critiqued male privilege and made women's oppression visible.

More recently, there have been intense editing conflicts over Gamergate, a term applied to a series of controversies within gaming culture and gaming communities centered on a game created by Zoe Quinn, and subsequent video game publication coverage of the game. Heated online battles—often rooted in misogyny and using tactics like "doxxing"—publicly posting the home addresses and contact information of individuals as a way of making them vulnerable—culminated in a review at the highest levels of Wikipedia's organizational review body that banned some editors from making changes to the Wikipedia Gamergate entry. Feminist media critic Anita Sarkeesian faced similar online harassment after producing a series of YouTube videos called "Tropes vs. Women in Video Games" which critically analyzed depictions of women in video games—for example the "damsel in distress," "women as background decoration," and "the lady sidekick"; partway through the series debut she received death threats and had to vacate her home.

A second area of investigation concluded that topics traditionally of greater interest to women received less attention than those that have been historically of interest to men. For example, discussions of films aimed at female audiences were shorter or of lower quality than those with primarily male audiences, leading researchers to conclude "Wikipedia seems to be growing in a way that is biased toward topics of interest to males" (Zurn).

Finally, in terms of the community and culture of Wikipedia editing, the researchers observed, in conflicts among editors, entries by women were more likely to be "undone" than those of men, and female editors were more likely than male editors to be "indefinitely blocked." Sue Gardner, Executive Director of the Wikimedia Foundation, explains in her blog that women's contributions to Wikipedia are inhibited or discouraged for a variety of reasons, ranging from hostile editing tactics (for example, editing wars over the difference between identifying a rape scene in a film as a "sex scene" and meeting the standards of "neutrality"), to the unfriendly interface, to men's greater level of self-confidence and willingness to speak with authority, to the conflict-heavy culture. The "Gender Gap Manifesto" appears on the Wikimedia Foundation and aims to "foster an environment where people can express their thoughts, feelings, and solutions regarding the gender gap on Wikipedia. The goal is to collaboratively find solutions to improve the presence of women on Wikipedia and its sister projects."

As part of actualizing these goals, several initiatives have emerged. For example, the FembotCollective hosts annual "Edit-A-Thons" at the offices of *Ms.* Magazine to generate content that will narrow the gender gap. Large-scale efforts such as the partnership between the Wikipedia Education Program and the National Women's Studies Association support Wikipedia article content creation, expansion, or revision by integrating it with teaching and learning in the college classroom. Instructional modules and support for instructors is housed at the NWSA Wikipedia Initiative website. This kind of activism is sometimes referred to as **crowdsourcing**. Through these strategies, contributors from a variety of positions are aiming to change the culture of online contributions to Wikipedia to make it a more welcoming space for women to contribute and to challenge an online culture that is exclusionary, adversarial, or belittling. In this way, privilege and oppression are demonstrated by the ways that women's voices are more systematically closed off whereas men's voices are dominant, whereas the efforts to correct the situation show how marginalized groups resist their oppression.

Marked vs. Unmarked in Language

In the early days of second-wave feminism, much attention was paid to the ways in which sexism was embedded in language. This feminist critique of language took many forms, including a critique of the default use of masculine pronouns in English and the default use of masculine gendered occupational titles like "mailman," "fireman," "chairman," and "congressman." While these critiques resulted in widespread change, it is also clear that there are significant ways in which oppression and privilege continue to play out in language.

One of the markers of privilege is invisibility, and one of the ways this invisibility manifests is through identity terms and labels. In other words, dominant groups that are a part of the mythical norm have the privilege of being unmarked and unremarkable because of their presumed neutrality and normality. To return to the term transgender that was introduced in Chapter 2, for example, current usage of the term refers to people whose gender identity is at odds with their birth-assigned gender, but until very recently there was no term to describe people whose gender identity is consistent with their birth-assigned gender. The term *cisgender* was coined to fill this vacuum, and arguably to draw attention to, and make visible, the privilege of the dominant group. In *Transgender History*, Susan Stryker explains that the term cisgendered "names the usually unstated assumption of nontransgender status contained in the words 'man' and 'woman'" (22). Another example comes from politicized groups within the autism community; they have coined the term *neurotypical* to describe people who are not on the autism spectrum. To be in the unmarked group is to be considered the default norm.

A slight variation on this point comes from considering when we do and don't attach qualifiers to our descriptions of and references to people and institutions; for example, it is still fairly common practice to specify race only when referring to a person of color, to specify gender when referring to women, to specify sexual identity when referring to someone who is gay, lesbian, or bisexual, and so forth. As Gloria Steinem wryly points out, "adjectives are mostly required of the less powerful. . . . As has been true forever, the person with the power takes the noun— and the norm—while the less powerful requires an adjective." Similarly, marriage is frequently modified with the word "gay" when referring to same-sex couples. As GLAAD's "Ally's Guide to Terminology" points out, however, "[j]ust as it would be inappropriate to call the marriage of two older adults 'elder marriage,' it is inappropriate to call the marriage of a same-sex couple 'gay marriage' or 'same-sex marriage.' Simply talk

Figure 3.5 Marked and Unmarked T-Ball Sets

Source: Image, Jane George

about *marriage* instead." The argument here is that marriage is marriage regardless of the sex of the couple. To do otherwise, whether with regard to people or institutions, is to reinforce the mythical norm and the notion that those outside the mythical norm are both "other" and lesser-than.

Contributors to the blog Sociological Images have documented this phenomenon of **marked and unmarked** language as it plays out in public signage, as well as in product packaging and products themselves; new examples of this phenomenon continue to be added to the Pinterest site as they are discovered. For example, one posted photo shows an end-of-aisle sign in the health and beauty section of a big box store that describes what customers will find in that aisle; it lists "Deodorant" and "Women's Deodorant." Figure 3.5 shows an example of this phenomenon in children's toy packaging. In the examples they document, maleness is an unmarked, invisible category, and only girls/women have a gender.

This illustrates how the mythical norm and unearned privilege manifest in language, although the example about the coinage of new terms to name dominant groups that are a part of the mythical norm shows that language can also be harnessed to bring previously invisible privilege to light.

Bodies

The threshold concept of privilege and oppression (as well as the social construction of gender) is illustrated through the operation of **rape culture**, which Lynn Phillips defines as "a culture in which dominant cultural ideologies, media images, social practices, and societal institutions support and condone sexual abuse by normalizing, trivializing and eroticizing violence against women and blaming victims for their own abuse" (Kacmarek and Geffre). The term was coined and is used to neatly capture and describe the fact that sexual violence is socially tolerated and woven into the fabric of our society. Phillips' definition echoes the overall focus in this chapter of asserting that privilege and oppression play out through institutions and ideology; examples of both will be explored in this section.

It is also important to note in this context that rape culture is an aspect of multiple forms of oppression, not just or only sexism. Put slightly differently, violence, or the threat of violence, is a mechanism that helps maintain many types of oppression, including sexism, but also racism, heterosexism, and transphobia, to name a few. Given that reality, queer men, trans and non-binary people, and men and women of color all experience high rates of violence, and often fear for their safety and security. Chapter 4, which focuses on the threshold concept of intersectionality, will delve more deeply into how and why systems of oppression intersect.

Rates of violence in the U.S. (both intimate partner violence and sexual violence) are consistent with the existence of a rape culture. Data from the CDC's National Intimate Partner and Sexual Violence Survey shows that nearly 1 in 5 (18.3%) women reported experiencing rape at some time in their lives. This survey data is further broken out by race and ethnicity, and reveals that many groups of women of color experience violence at even higher rates. For example, in a survey of 2,000 Native American and Alaskan Native women, 56 percent have experienced sexual violence. Transgender people, especially trans women, also experience significantly higher rates of sexual violence; according to the Office for Victims of Crime, one in two transgender people are sexually abused or assaulted at some point in their lives.

In a rape culture, sexual violence is normalized, and when perpetrated by members of the dominant group, their behavior is more often than not excused and minimized and/or made to seem inevitable. The normalization of sexual violence among young girls and women that is a characteristic of rape culture was documented by sociologist Heather Hlavka in a 2014 research study that concluded that many young women view sexual violence and accompanying behaviors such as objectification, abuse, and harassment by boys and men as a normal part of daily life. One young woman quoted in the study says, of young men's sexually aggressive behaviors, "It just happens" and, "They're boys—that's what they do" (344). The study focused on explaining why few girls and women report sexual violence, offering "normalization" as one explanation, as well as the lack of confidence young women have in authority and the lack of support from other girls and women. The "naturalization" of violent masculinity also played a role. The lack of support from other girls and women is a good example of how oppression is internalized.

The lack of confidence in authority figures (including the police and courts) documented in Hlavka's study is often warranted, as seen in the high-profile rape case of Brock Turner, who was convicted in 2016 of three felony charges: intent to commit rape, sexual penetration with a foreign object of an intoxicated person, and sexual penetration with a foreign object of an unconscious person. In spite of the jury finding him guilty on all three counts, judge Aaron Persky issued what many considered to be an extremely lenient sentence of only six months in county jail (he was released after three months). Prosecutors had recommended that he serve six years. Persky was seen as diminishing or downplaying Turner's culpability in the crimes, and many argued that Turner's privileged status as an affluent, white male athlete factored into Persky's decision. Indeed, in his sentencing decision, Persky noted that a longer sentence would have "a severe impact" and "adverse collateral consequences" on Turner. Public outrage was further fueled by Turner's father's statement, in which he argued for leniency in sentencing, that his son had "paid a steep price" for "20 minutes of action." The Brock Turner rape case illustrates how privilege and oppression manifest through societal institutions, and both the judge's decision and Turner's father's statement constitute evidence that we live in a rape culture.

Rape culture is also often perpetuated through how news media (another example of a societal institution) choose to write about and frame their reporting of sexual assault cases. Analysis of news coverage of the outcome of the 2012 Steubenville rape case, in which two young men were convicted of assaulting a young woman, revealed that many media outlets framed the case in a way that engaged in victim-blaming. As Annie-Rose Strasser and Tara Culp-Ressler write in a piece on *Think Progress*, "[b]y emphasizing the boys' good grades and bright futures, as well as by describing the victim as 'drunk' without clarifying that the defendants were also drinking, many mainstream media outlets became active participants in furthering victim-blaming rape culture." Their analysis focuses on news coverage by CNN, ABC News, NBC News, The Associated Press, USA Today, and Yahoo News.

An ideological manifestation of rape culture can be seen in the prevalence of rape jokes in American culture. The film *The Bro Code: How Contemporary Culture Creates Sexist Men* highlights the ubiquity of humorous treatments of rape and sexual assault in popular culture and mass media; one only has to peruse a newspaper, news magazine, or Internet news site to identify many daily examples of rape and sexual assault, including gang rape. As *The Bro Code* notes, 99 percent of rapists are men, and popular shows such as *Family Guy* and comedians such as Daniel Tosh of the show *Tosh* routinely take comic approaches to rape that, instead of deconstructing or critiquing rape culture, endorse or embrace it. The "Rape Joke Supercut"[1] short at the Women's Media Center highlights the difference between these two types of rape jokes: See also Jessica Valenti's "Anatomy of a Successful Rape Joke"[2]; and Lindy West's "How To Make a Rape Joke"[3] for trenchant critiques of this element of rape culture.

Another characteristic of rape culture is that the burden for preventing sexual violence is carried primarily by members of marginalized groups who are expected to limit their behavior, actions, dress, and other aspects of their daily life to try to minimize the likelihood that they will be victimized. These internalized and routinized behaviors and habits are referred to as a "rape schedule." In his essay "Why I Am a Male Feminist," filmmaker Byron Hurt recalls an experience that raised his consciousness about this phenomenon. In a workshop about preventing gender violence, the facilitator

> posed a question to all of the men in the room: "Men, what things do you do to protect yourself from being raped or sexually assaulted?" Not one man, including myself, could quickly answer the question. Finally, one man raised his hand and said, "Nothing."

By contrast, when the facilitator asked the women in the room the same question, nearly all of them raised their hands to offer examples. Hurt continues, "[t]he women went on for several minutes, until their side of the blackboard was completely filled with responses. The men's side of the blackboard was blank. I was stunned." Women's oppression, then, is illustrated by the mental self-monitoring that many must continually do to assess themselves, their surroundings, and their conduct for threats of violence or "gender-based miscommunications," whereas male privilege is illustrated by the fact that men are typically not expected to monitor themselves or their conduct for safety and security and freedom from sexual violence.

A marker of privilege is the ability *not* to have to live one's life according to a rape schedule; as such, feminist activism focused on eliminating rape culture works to shift responsibility for preventing sexual violence off of victims and onto potential perpetrators. An alternative model, then, places primary responsibility on members of dominant groups to engage in conduct that creates safe communities, workplaces, and homes, and calls out practices and messages that perpetuate victim-blaming. Feminist activist groups on many college campuses, for example, have criticized the messages directed at women by administrators and campus police that perpetuate the idea that preventing sexual violence is their responsibility alone by only mentioning what they should or shouldn't do in order to lower their chances of being raped. Many of these groups have then worked with campus leadership to change the messaging in ways that attempt to change the campus culture and climate.

In a rape culture, the bodies of people in marginalized groups are vulnerable and subject to violation. The perpetuation of rape culture shores up the privilege of dominant groups and is a mechanism through which marginalized groups experience oppression.

Case Study

The role of both institutions and ideology in maintaining systems of privilege and oppression can be seen through an examination of the **bootstraps myth**, which is the idea that upward class mobility is not only possible but probable, and that individual will and hard work are the only requisites for moving out of poverty and into the middle class. One of the consequences or implications of this myth is that poor people are then blamed for their continued poverty. Within the logic of the bootstraps myth, if individual will and hard work are the only requisites for moving out of poverty and into the middle class, then poverty can be explained by a *lack* of will and hard work on the part of poor people.

The ideology of upward class mobility has its roots in the long history of the United States as a colony, but was popularized by a series of novels in the 1890s written by Horatio Alger, novels about hardworking boys whose work elevated them from a hardscrabble life to one of success and luxury. So-called Cinderella or rags-to-riches stories continue to be popular and have been continually updated over the past century in such movies as *Pretty Woman, Maid in Manhattan, The Blind Side*, and *Slumdog Millionaire*. Rags-to-riches stories are also a frequent premise of reality television shows. These narratives have the effect of reinforcing belief in the possibility of dramatic upward mobility. This ideology is also buttressed by the language we use to talk (or avoid talking) about class in the United States. Politicians, for example, almost always use the term "middle-class Americans" to refer to the broad mainstream and rarely use class labels that reflect the reality that a full majority of Americans are in fact working-class. The bootstraps myth has great explanatory and persuasive power because it builds upon a cultural belief in *self-determination* that resonates with many U.S. residents, the idea that we are each the captain of our own destiny, as it were.

However, data on the realities of social mobility demonstrate that, in fact, movement from one class to a higher or lower one, particularly from the lowest rungs of the American economic ladder to a higher one, is uncommon and difficult, as data from a *New York Times* special feature on social class reveal. In covering the topic of "How Class Works," the *New York Times* tracked American families by income quintile (breaking down family income by quintile) and examining how, over time, people in those income brackets moved up or down the "economic ladder."

As these data illustrate, social class is fairly immutable; that is, the bottom fifth of the U.S. population in 1988 largely remained in that economic quintile, with relatively few people born into poverty rising up even a single income quintile. The same immutability is demonstrated for those in the top income quintile. In sum, the class a person is born into greatly shapes life experiences and has a huge impact over the life course. Gregory Mantsios puts it even more bluntly: "[c]lass standing, and consequently life chances, are largely determined at birth," a reality that frames our discussion of the institutions and the various experiences of them.

Table 3.1 Economic Mobility in the U.S.

Top 20%	Of those in the top quintile, 52% remained there a decade later.	Just 5% had dropped to the bottom quintile.
Upper Middle 20%	Those in the upper middle quintile largely remained there, with 30% in the same income bracket.	Seven percent of the upper middle had dropped to the bottom quintile, while 25% had moved up to the top, and 27% had dropped to the middle.
Bottom 20%	Most notably, those who occupied the bottom quintile generally remained there. The same number of bottom 20 percenters remained poor as top 20 percenters remained rich: 52%.	Similarly, just 5% of bottom quintile earners had reached the top 20%, and a small number had reached the upper middle income bracket: 7.5%.

Many questions follow: why is it that the class structure in the United States is fairly static? And how can we account for the persistence of the belief in widespread class mobility given the data that disproves it? There are many answers to these questions, but one key factor is the societal institution of education, an institution that reinforces privilege and that some can experience as oppressive. We'll start by looking at the relationship between baccalaureate degree attainment and social class.

As the chart below shows, income quartile has enormous predictive power in attainment of four-year degrees, and this disparity between fourth-quartile (the poorest) families and first-quartile (the wealthiest) families has grown in the last 40 years. Eighty-two percent of those individuals in the top quartile of the economic spectrum earned a four-year degree, a rate that has doubled in the last four decades to result in the majority of wealthy families producing college graduates; by contrast, the very small percentage of degree-earners from the bottom quartile in 1970 (just 6.2%) has barely budged, up to 8.3 percent; that is, children raised in wealthy households are ten times as likely to earn a baccalaureate degree—essentially, entrance into stable employment and household security as well as the starting point for most professional occupations—as those from the poorest families (see Figure 3.6).

Further, the profound interrelationships between nearly all measures of academic achievement and **socioeconomic status (SES)** reveal the

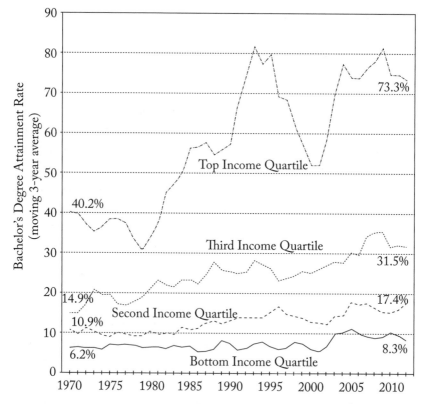

Figure 3.6 Estimated Baccalaureate Degree Attainment by Age 24 by Family Income Quartile, from 1970 to 2012

Source: Tom Mortensen, PEO Newsletter

deep roots of privilege and oppression, particularly how social strata reproduce and maintain inequality despite the efforts of individuals to navigate them—or to transform them. As Rebecca Zwick reports in "Is the SAT a Wealth Test?," the connections between social class and academic achievement are demonstrated by both the major standardized tests, the SAT and ACT. When comparing student achievement of the benchmark score for admission to selective colleges, a combined verbal and math score of 1100 (in 2001), students from high socioeconomic status (SES) were three and a half times more likely to meet the benchmark (32%) compared with low-SES students (9%). The average SAT score for low-income students was 887, according to Zwick's findings, while scores steadily increase, with the average score for students with family income above $100,000 reaching 1126 (307). Research shows a similar gap on the ACT score, as well as many other standard measures of academic achievement including completion of a rigorous, college-preparation curriculum and high school grades. This is largely attributable to the differential access to resources both at home and in their educational systems including variation in teacher preparation (more teachers with advanced training and credentials teach at schools with lower percentages of students receiving free and reduced lunch). In this way, privilege and oppression in the forms of access to the cultural capital that produce social mobility are structured into a system that reproduces itself with each generation.

This is *not* to say that working-class and poverty-class people cannot do well in school, but that their chances of academic success are lower than their more affluent peers. A 2014 *New York Times* story highlights the gap between high-income and low-income students' rates of graduation:

> [a]bout a quarter of college freshmen born into the bottom half of the income distribution will manage to collect a bachelor's degree by age 24, while almost 90 percent of freshmen born into families in the top income quartile will go on to finish their degree.
>
> (Tough)

Further, even nonacademic experiences at college can be framed by social class. A 2013 Harvard University book by Armstrong and Hamilton, *Paying for the Party: How College Maintains Inequality*, traced the ways that university and social structures facilitate upward class mobility for affluent students whose class background influenced their social groups, majors, and extracurricular activities, preserving what the authors call a "pathway to privilege," while low-income students lacked the benefits provided by college-educated and high-income parents. Jessica Valenti summarizes the intersection of class and gender, emphasizing from Armstrong and Hamilton's study that

> [r]egardless of the success, class impacted almost every aspect of the college women's lives—even sexual assault. Female students who had parents who went to college were able to warn their daughters about the tactics of fraternity predators, and were

actually less likely to be targeted because, as Armstrong and Hamilton write, 'insulting a highly ranked woman in a top sorority was akin to affronting her whole sorority.' Lower-income students—especially those women who were perceived as garish—were more likely to be assaulted and less likely to be believed.

(Valenti, "How to End")

Another important point is that working-class and poverty-class students who *do* manage to succeed are often pointed to as proof that structural inequality does not exist, which is not only a mistake but cruel when an individual's success is used to berate those who, because of structural inequality, are unable to follow suit. Neither is our point to diminish or dismiss the success that middle- and upper-class students achieve through hard work; rather, the point is to acknowledge the enabling conditions that provided a context for those students' hard work in the first place.

Further complicating the relationship between educational access, social mobility, and identity is the role of race. Disaggregating and pinpointing racially disparate outcomes in education adds another layer to and understanding of privilege and oppression. Research from the Community College Research Center documents that, four years after graduation, black college graduates have nearly twice the student loan debt as white students ($52,726 vs. $28,006); and black students are more likely to take out student loans and more likely to leave college without completing a degree (Goldrick-Rab, Kelchen, and Houle). Also notable is the increase in enrollment by black students at for-profit universities, which, as the same report notes, "can account for all of the differential growth in black graduate school enrollment between 2004 and 2012: at public and private not-for-profit institutions, black students have remained a roughly constant percentage of the graduate population," with 28 percent of black students enrolling in a for-profit graduate university program compared with 10 percent of white students. With traditionally much higher tuition rates, for-profit colleges have been criticized for preying on students to take advantage of a 2005 piece of federal legislation that increased the amount of borrowing allowed for students (Deruy).

One final point: the class-based structural barriers to educational achievement are buttressed by controlling images of working-class and poverty-class people as dumb and buffoonish. These images and characterizations appear both in the news media and in popular culture, from Homer Simpson to MTV's short-lived reality TV series "Buckwild." In other words, ideology purports to show that working-class and poverty-class people of all races and ethnicities are poor as a result of both poor choices and lesser innate intelligence.

As the previous illustrations suggest, the bootstraps myth serves an important function in suggesting that certain kinds of privilege and oppression (namely, economic) are irrelevant to social and educational achievement even though there is strong statistical and demographic data to suggest that those social indicators have a great deal of power over who achieves traditional markers of success in the United States.

End of Chapter Elements

Evaluating Prior Knowledge

1. Write briefly about how and in what context you have heard the terms "privilege" and "oppression" before. Generate some examples of how the terms are typically used (for example, in childrearing, in educational contexts, or other settings). Then discuss how your understanding has changed after reading Chapter 3 as well as any lingering questions you have about these key terms.

2. Reflect on how you have, historically, conceptualized or would describe your class background. What aspects of your identity, family context, or life experiences have factored into this conceptualization?

Application Exercise

1. Consider the opening illustration about Kathrine Switzer's entry in the Boston Marathon in 1967. In conversation with a partner or in an informal writing activity, think about how the key concepts from this chapter are illustrated by Switzer's story:
   a. Privilege
   b. Oppression

    c. Institutions

    d. Ideologies

2. Visit the website, the Americans with Disabilities Act Checklist for Readily Achievable Barrier Removal: www.ada.gov/racheck.pdf. Identify a location where you spend significant amounts of time and assess it using the checklist for accessibility.

Skills Assessment

1. Review this bar graph from the *Washington Post* story "Poor Kids Who Do Everything Right Don't Do Better than Rich Kids Who Do Everything Wrong," with specific attention to socioeconomic and educational privilege and oppression. In what ways do you see chapter concepts demonstrated by the data?

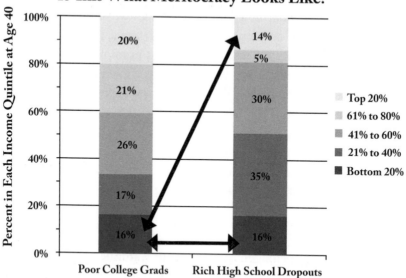

Figure 3.7 Poor Kids Who Do Everything Right Don't Do Better than Rich Kids Who Do Everything Wrong

Source: www.washingtonpost.com/news/wonk/wp/2014/10/18/poor-kids-who-do-everything-right-dont-do-better-than-rich-kids-who-do-everything-wrong/?utm_term=.7e6326328ed0

2. Using concepts from Chapter 2 and Chapter 3, discuss how access
    to and support for participation in athletics demonstrates the social
    construction of gender as well as privilege and oppression.

**"Son, you throw like a girl raised in a patriarchal society
that discourages women from participating in sports."**

Figure 3.8 You Throw Like a Girl

Source: https://medium.com/matt-bors/you-throw-like-a-girl-c5cc1d098b6c

3. Select a term or concept from the chapter that seems "muddy" to
    you. With a partner, talk through the muddiness. What is creating
    a learning block? Why is it difficult? What would clarify it for you?
    Use a strategy called a "difficulty log" to map out the parts of the
    idea that are challenging you, including background knowledge you
    wish you had, challenging or confusing vocabulary, unclear relation-
    ships to other chapter concepts or other chapters, or unfamiliarity
    from your experience. As an additional activity, once you've had a
    chance to work through a muddy/difficult concept, try your hand at
    writing a "Misconception Alert" or "Learning Roadblock" like those

featured in the chapter in order to spell out (a) what the learning challenge is and (b) how other students can overcome it.

Discussion Questions

1. Which concepts from this chapter are the most challenging for you and why? Which seem intuitively easy to grasp?
2. With particular attention to the case study on the bootstraps myth, consider why this concept has such explanatory power, specifically within the context of the United States. Are there examples not provided in the chapter that you can think of that reflect this ideology?
3. Building on your understanding of rape culture from the Bodies Anchoring Topics section, think about how and where you see examples of rape culture around you. Conversely, how and where have you seen rape culture being challenged?

Writing Prompts

1. Navigate to Harvard University's Implicit Bias Test (https://implicit. harvard.edu/implicit/takeatest.html) and take one or more of the available tests. Write about your results and include reflection analysis of the ways in which the results help you understand concepts from the chapter including privilege, oppression, horizontal hostility, internalized oppression, or others.
2. Select a topic of personal interest to you (a band, recreational activity, intellectual interest, book or TV show) and that you know a lot about. Next, search for related entries on Wikipedia. First, read over the entry and do your own independent assessment of neutrality standards—is the topic presented in accurate and objective ways? Are there aspects that you believe reflect a specific bias or slant? Second, click on the "Talk" tab at the top of the page. What kinds of discussions are Wikipedia editors having about the information presented and does it match with your own assessment? In what ways, if any, do you see particular beliefs or perceptions being privileged (or underrepresented, or misrepresented) in the conversation?

Notes

1 www.womensmediacenter.com/blog/entry/rape-joke-supercut-i-cant-believe-you-clapped-for-that
2 www.thenation.com/blog/168856/anatomy-successful-rape-joke
3 http://jezebel.com/5925186/how-to-make-a-rape-joke

Works Cited

Americans with Disabilities Act. www.ada.gov/racheck.pdf. Accessed 6 July 2017.

Armstrong, Elizabeth, and Laura Hamilton. *Paying for the Party: How College Maintains Inequality.* Harvard University Press, 2013.

The Bro Code: How Contemporary Culture Creates Sexist Men. Media Education Foundation. 2011.

Bureau of Labor Statistics. "News Release: Employment Characteristics of Families—2015." 6 March 2017. www.bls.gov/news.release/famee.htm. Accessed 6 July 2017.

Butler, Sarah Lorge. "How Kathrine Switzer Paved the Way." *ESPN.* 12 April 2012. www.espn.com/espnw/news-commentary/article/7803502/2012-boston-marathon-how-kathrine-switzer-paved-way-female-runners. Accessed 6 July 2017.

Centers for Disease Control and Prevention. "Findings from the National Intimate Partner and Sexual Violence Survey: 2010–2012 State Report." www.cdc.gov/violenceprevention/pdf/nisvs_report2010-a.pdf. Accessed 26 May 2017.

Coontz, Stephanie. "Why Gender Equality Stalled." *New York Times.* 16 February 2013.

Covarrubias, Amanda, Kate Mather, and Matt Stevens. "Isla Vista Shooting Suspect Targeted Sorority, Neighbors, Strangers." *Los Angeles Times.* 24 May 2014.

Covert, Bryce. "Nearly a Billion Dollars Spent on Marriage Promotion Programs Have Achieved Next to Nothing." *Think Progress.* https://thinkprogress.org/nearly-a-billion-dollars-spent-on-marriage-promotion-programs-have-achieved-next-to-nothing-e675f0d9b6. Accessed 6 July 2017.

Dailard, Cynthia. "Reproductive Health Advocates and Marriage Promotion: Asserting a Stake in the Debate." *The Guttmacher Report on Public Policy*, vol. 8, no. 1, 2005. www.guttmacher.org/gpr/2005/02/reproductive-health-advocates-and-marriage-promotion-asserting-stake-debate.

"Daily Effects of Cisgender Privilege." University of Texas Gender and Sexuality Center. http://diversity.utexas.edu/genderandsexuality/wp-content/uploads/2016/03/Handout-Cisgender-and-Heterosexual-Privilege-2016.pdf. Accessed 6 July 2017.

Deruy, Emily. "The Racial Disparity of the Student-Loan Crisis." *The Atlantic.* 24 October 2016.

Dries, Kate. "There's a Battle Going on over the Wikipedia Page for #YesAllWomen." *Jezebel.* 6 June 2014. http://jezebel.com/theres-a-battle-going-on-over-the-wikipedia-page-for-y-1586704111. Accessed 6 July 2017.

Edwards, Laurie. "The Gender Gap in Pain." *New York Times.* 16 March 2013.

Finch, Sam Dylan. "130+ Examples of Cis Privilege in All Areas of Life for You to Reflect On and Address." *Everyday Feminism.* 29 February 2016. http://everydayfeminism.com/2016/02/130-examples-cis-privilege/. Accessed 6 July 2017.

Flaherty, Colleen. "White Is the Word." *Inside Higher Ed.* 18 January 2017. www.inside highered.com/news/2017/01/18/arizona-lawmakers-failed-ban-divisive-college-courses-highlights-new-criticism-white. Accessed 6 July 2017.

Frye, Marilyn. "Oppression." In *The Feminist Philosophy Reader.* Eds. Alison Bailey and Chris Cuomo. McGraw Hill, 2008, pp. 41–49.

Gardner, Sue. "Nine Reasons Women Don't Edit Wikipedia (In Their Own Words)." *Sue Gardner's Blog.* 19 February 2011. https://suegardner.org/2011/02/19/nine-reasons-why-women-dont-edit-wikipedia-in-their-own-words/. Accessed 6 July 2017.

Gemelli, Marcella. "Understanding the Complexity of Attitudes of Low-Income Single Mothers Toward Work and Family in the Age of Welfare Reform." *Gender Issues,* vol. 25, no. 101, 2008, pp. 101–113.

"Gender Gap Manifesto." 27 March 2011. https://meta.wikimedia.org/wiki/Gender_Gap_Manifesto. Accessed 6 July 2017.

GLAAD. "Ally's Guide to Terminology." 2012. www.glaad.org/sites/default/files/allys-guide-to-terminology_1.pdf. Accessed 6 July 2017.

Glynn, Sarah Jane. "Breadwinning Mothers Are Increasingly the U.S. Norm." Center for American Progress. 19 December 2016. www.americanprogress.org/issues/women/reports/2016/12/19/295203/breadwinning-mothers-are-increasingly-the-u-s-norm/. Accessed 6 July 2017.

Goldrick-Rab, Sara, Robert Kelchen, and Jason Houle. "The Color of Student Debt: Implications of Federal Loan Program Reforms for Black Students and Historically Black Colleges and Universities." Wisconsin Hope Lab. 2 September 2014. https://news.education.wisc.edu/docs/WebDispenser/news-connections-pdf/thecolorofstudentdebt-draft.pdf?sfvrsn=4. Accessed 6 July 2017.

Heymann, Jody, Alison Earle, and Jeffrey Hayes. *The Work, Family, and Equity Index: How Does the US Measure Up?* The Project on Global Working Families and the Institute for Health and Social Policy. www.worldpolicycenter.org/sites/default/files/Work%20Family%20and%20Equity%20Index-How%20does%20the%20US%20measure%20up-Jan%202007.pdf. Accessed 6 July 2017.

Hlavka, Heather. "Normalizing Sexual Violence: Young Women Account for Harassment and Abuse." *Gender and Society,* vol. 28, no. 3, 2014, pp. 337–358.

"How Class Works." Interactive Graphic. *New York Times.* 2005. www.nytimes.com/packages/html/national/20050515_CLASS_GRAPHIC/index_04.html. Accessed 6 July 2017.

Hurt, Byron. "Why I Am a Male Feminist." *The Root.* 16 March 2011. www.theroot.com/why-i-am-a-male-feminist-1790863150. Accessed 6 July 2017.

Johnson, Allan. *The Gender Knot: Unraveling Our Patriarchal Legacy.* Temple University Press, 2005.

Kacmarek, Julia, and Elizabeth Geffre. "Rape Culture Is: Know It When You See It." *Huffington Post Blog.* 1 June 2013. www.huffingtonpost.com/julia-kacmarek/rape-culture-is_b_3368577.html. Accessed 7 July 2017.

Kimmel, Michael S. "Introduction: Toward a Pedagogy of the Oppressor." In *Privilege: A Reader.* Eds. Michael S. Kimmel and Abby Ferber. 1st edition. Westview, 2003, pp. 1–10.

Lorde, Audre. "Age, Race, Class, and Sex: Women Redefining Difference." In *Sister Outsider.* Crossing Press, 1984.

Mantsios, Gregory. "Class in America—2006." In *Race, Class, and Gender in the United States*. Ed. Paula Rothenberg. 7th edition. Worth, 2007, pp. 182–197.

Matsuda, Mari. "Beside My Sister, Facing the Enemy: Legal Theory Out of Coalition." In *Feminist Theory Reader: Local and Global Perspectives*. Ed. Carole R. McCann and Seung-Kyung Kim. 3rd edition. Routledge, 2013, pp. 332–342.

Mcintosh, Peggy. "White Privilege: Unpacking the Invisible Knapsack." 1989. https://nationalseedproject.org/white-privilege-unpacking-the-invisible-knapsack. Accessed 6 July 2017.

Merriam-Webster Dictionary. "Mansplaining: Words We're Watching." www.merriam-webster.com/words-at-play/mansplaining-definition-history. Accessed 16 March 2017.

Mortensen, Tom. "Estimated Baccalaureate Degree Attainment by Age 24 by Family Income Quartile 1970 to 2012." *Postsecondary Education Opportunity*. November 2010.

National Women's Studies Association. "NWSA Wikipedia Initiative." www.nwsa.org/wikiedu. Accessed 6 July 2017.

O'Brien, Matt. "Poor Kids Who Do Everything Right Don't Do Better Than Rich Kids Who Do Everything Wrong." *The Washington Post*. 18 October 2014.

Office of Disease Prevention and Health Promotion. "Disparities." U.S. Department of Health and Human Services. www.healthypeople.gov/2020/about/foundation-health-measures/Disparities. Accessed 7 July 2017.

Office for Victims of Crime. "Responding to Transgender Victims of Sexual Assault." June 2014. www.ovc.gov/pubs/forge/. Accessed 6 July 2017.

Solnit, Rebecca. "Men Explain Things to Me." *TomDispatch.com*. 13 April 2008.

Starnes, Todd. "Public School Teaches 'White Privilege' Class." *Fox News*. 2013. http://radio.foxnews.com/toddstarnes/top-stories/public-school-teaches-white-privilege-class.html. Accessed 6 July 2017.

Steinem, Gloria. "Women Have 'Chick Flicks.' What About Men?" *New York Times*. 2 March 2017.

Strasser, Annie-Rose, and Tara Culp-Ressler. "How the Media Took Sides in the Steubenville Rape Case." *Think Progress*. 18 March 2013. https://thinkprogress.org/how-the-media-took-sides-in-the-steubenville-rape-case-e92589afbadf. Accessed 6 July 2017.

Stryker, Susan. *Transgender History*. Seal Press, 2008.

Sun, Feifei. "What MTV's *Teen Mom* Doesn't Deliver." *Time Magazine*. 14 July 2011.

Swarns, Rachel. "More Americans Rejecting Marriage in 50s and Beyond." *New York Times*. 1 March 2012.

Tatum, Beverly Daniel. "Defining Racism: Can We Talk?" *Women, Images and Realities: A Multicultural Anthology*. Eds. Amy Kesselman, Lily McNair, and Nancy Schniedewind. 3rd edition. McGraw-Hill, 2003.

Tough, Paul. "Who Gets to Graduate?" *New York Times Magazine*. 15 May 2014.

United States Breastfeeding Committee. "Existing Laws." 2013. www.usbreastfeeding.org/laws. Accessed 6 July 2017.

Valenti, Jessica. "How to End the College Class War." *Guardian*. 27 May 2014. www.theguardian.com/commentisfree/2014/may/27/how-to-end-college-class-war. Accessed 6 July 2017.

Weber, Lynn. *Understanding Race, Class, Gender, and Sexuality.* 2nd ed. Oxford University Press, 2009.

Williams, Kristi. "Promoting Marriage among Single Mothers: An Ineffective Weapon in the War on Poverty?" *Council on Contemporary Families.* 6 January 2014. https://contemporaryfamilies.org/marriage-ineffective-in-war-on-poverty-report/. Accessed 6 July 2017.

Wise, Tim. *White Like Me: Reflections on Race from a Privileged Son.* Soft Skull Press, 2005.

Yamato, Gloria. "Something about the Subject Makes It Hard to Name." In *Making Face, Making Soul.* Ed. Gloria Anzaldua. Aunt Lute Books, 1990, pp. 25–30.

Zeilinger, Julie. *A Little F'd Up: Why Feminism is Not a Dirty Word.* Seal Press, 2012.

Zurn, Rhonda. "University of Minnesota Researchers Reveal Wikipedia Gender Biases." 11 August 2011. https://cse.umn.edu/news-release/university-of-minnesota-researchers-reveal-wikipedia-gender-biases/. Accessed 6 July 2017.

Zwick, Rebecca. "Is the SAT a Wealth Test?" *Phi Delta Kappan*, vol. 84, no. 4, 2002, pp. 307–311.

Suggested Readings and Videos

"Able-Bodied Privilege Checklist." MIT School of Architecture and Planning. www.sap.mit.edu/content/pdf/able_bodied_privilege.pdf.

Antin, Judd, et al. "Gender Differences in Wikipedia Editing." *Wikisym.* October 2011.

Aughinbaugh, Alison, Omar Robles, and Hugette Sun. "Marriage and Divorce: Patterns by Gender, Race, and Educational Attainment." *Bureau of Labor Statistics Monthly Labor Review.* October 2013.

Braun, Nicole. "Taken-for-Granted Social Class Privileges." *Classism Exposed.* Class Action. 19 January 2015. http://www.classism.org/taken-granted-social-class-privileges/.

"Breastfeeding State Laws." *National Conference of State Legislatures.* www.ncsl.org/research/health/breastfeeding-state-laws.aspx#State. Accessed 6 July 2017.

Carbone, June, and Naomi Cahn. "Family Values? Conservative Economics Have Shredded Marriage Rates." Next New Deal: The Blog of the Roosevelt Institute. 9 August 2011. http://rooseveltinstitute.org/family-values-conservative-economics-have-shredded-marriage-rates/.

——. *Marriage Markets: How Inequality Is Remaking the American Family.* Oxford University Press, 2014.

Coontz, Stephanie. "Why Gender Equality Stalled." *New York Times.* 16 February 2013.

Crittenden, Ann. *The Price of Motherhood: Why the Most Important Job in the World Is the Least Valued.* Holt, 2002.

"Daily Effects of Cisgender Privilege." University of Texas Gender and Sexuality Center. http://diversity.utexas.edu/genderandsexuality/wp-content/uploads/2016/03/Handout-Cisgender-and-Heterosexual-Privilege-2016.pdf. Accessed 1 March 2017.

Edwards, Laurie. "The Gender Gap in Pain." *New York Times.* 16 March 2013.

"Fact Sheet." *National Partnership for Women and Families.* February 2017. www.nationalpartnership.org/research-library/work-family/paid-leave/family-act-fact-sheet.pdf. Accessed 6 July 2017.

"Family Income and Educational Attainment 1970–2009." *Postsecondary Education Opportunity: Public Policy Analysis of Opportunity for Postsecondary Education*. November 2010.

Ferber, Abby, and Michael Kimmel. *Privilege: A Reader*. 2nd edition. Westview Press, 2010.

Finch, Sam Dylan. "130+ Examples of Cis Privilege in All Areas of Life For You to Reflect On and Address." *Everyday Feminism*. 29 February 2016.

Heldke, Lisa, and Peg O'Connor, eds. *Oppression, Privilege, and Resistance: Theoretical Perspectives on Racism, Sexism, and Heterosexism*. McGraw Hill, 2004.

Hess, Amanda. "Are You a Slut? That Depends. Are You Rich?" *Slate.com*. 28 May 2014.

Jacobi, Tonja, and Dylan Schweers. "Justice, Interrupted: Gender, Ideology, and Seniority on the Supreme Court." *SCOTUSblog*. 5 April 2017.

Johnson, Allan. *Privilege, Power, and Difference*. Mayfield, 2001.

Kacmarek, Julia, and Elizabeth Geffre. "Rape Culture Is: Know It When You See It." *Huffington Post Blog*. 1 June 2013.

Konnikova, Maria. "Lean Out: The Dangers for Women Who Negotiate." *The New Yorker*. 10 June 2014.

Leistyna, Pepi. *Television and Working Class Identity: Intersecting Differences*. Palgrave Macmillan, 2014.

McDonough, Katie. "Report: Many Girls View Sexual Assault as Normal Behavior." *Salon*. 14 April 2014.

Mcintosh, Peggy. "White Privilege: Unpacking the Invisible Knapsack." *Peace and Freedom Magazine*, July/August, 1989, pp. 10–12.

Miller, Claire Cain. "The Motherhood Penalty vs. The Fatherhood Bonus." *New York Times*. 6 September 2014.

Office of Justice Programs. U.S. Department of Justice. 26 May 2017. https://ojp.gov/.

Peralta, Katherine. "Marriage Gap Widens with Income Inequality." *U.S. News & World Report*. 16 December 2014.

Pharr, Suzanne. *Homophobia: A Weapon of Sexism*. Chardon Press, 1997.

Ridgway, Shannon. "19 Examples of Ability Privilege." *Everyday Feminism*. 5 March 2013. Web.

Rooks, Noliwe. "The Myth of Bootstrapping." *Time Magazine*. 7 September 2012.

Scott, Judith Clayton, and Jing Li. "Black-White Disparity in Student Loan Debt More Than Triples After Graduation." Economics Studies. Brookings Institute. 20 October 2016. http://ccrc.tc.columbia.edu/publications/black-white-disparity-in-student-loan-debt-more-than-triples-after-graduation.html. Accessed 6 July 2017.

Solnit, Rebecca. "A Rape a Minute, A Thousand Corpses a Year." *Mother Jones*. 25 January 2013.

——. "Men Explain Things to Me." *GuernicaMag*. 20 August 2012. https://www.guernicamag.com/rebecca-solnit-men-explain-things-to-me/. Accessed 20 October 2017.

Tatum, Beverly Daniel. "Defining Racism: Can We Talk?" In *Women, Images and Realities: A Multicultural Anthology*. Eds. Amy Kesselman, Lily McNair, and Nancy Schniedewind. 3rd edition. McGraw-Hill, 2003.

Unslut. Dir. Emily Lindin. The Unslut Project, 2015. Film.

Urban Institute. "A Decade of Welfare Reform: Facts and Figures." Urban Institute. 26 July 2006. https://www.urban.org/research/publication/decade-welfare-reform-facts-and-figures.

Van Galen, Jane. "Middle Class Privilege." Education and Class: Exploring the Intersections of Social Class, Education, and Identity. 16 May 2008. https://education andclass.com/2008/05/16/middle-class-privilege/.

Wang, Wendy, and Kim Parker. "Record Share of Americans Have Never Married." *Pew Research Center.* 24 September 2014. www.pewsocialtrends.org/2014/09/24/record-share-of-americans-have-never-married/. Accessed 6 July 2017.

Yamato, Gloria. "Something about the Subject Makes It Hard to Name." *Making Face, Making Soul.* Ed. Gloria Anzaldua. Aunt Lute Books, 1990, pp. 25–30.

Zeilinger, Julie. "6 Forms of Ableism We Need to Retire Immediately." *Mic.* 7 July 2015. Web.

4

INTERSECTIONALITY

Table 4.1 Percent of Infants Exclusively Breastfed in the Past 7 Days (First Four Rows)

		Infant age in months								
	Neonatal	2	3	4	5	6	7	9	10	12
ALL(n)	3,002	2,546	2,381	2,232	2,178	2,092	2,017	1,942	1,804	1,802
(%)	38.8	38.1	36.0	27.7	14.0	4.3	1.0	0.2	0.3	0.0

Source: Centers for Disease Control and Prevention, Infant Feeding Practices Study II

www.cdc.gov/breastfeeding/pdf/ifps/data/ifps2_tables_ch3.pdf

Opening Illustration

Discussions of breastfeeding have increasingly been in the public eye for the last several years, in both news stories and social media memes. Part of what has fueled these discussions is the fact that rates of breastfeeding in the U.S. have risen in the last decade, as a result of public health campaigns. Recent news reports tout the increase in mothers breastfeeding their newborns, noting "[m]ore mothers in the United States are breastfeeding their babies, a practice that could potentially save billions in health care costs, the Centers for Disease Control said in a study released on Wednesday" (Abutaleb). Aggregate data from the Centers for Disease Control and Prevention (CDC) show, for example, that

> [w]hile 35 percent of babies were breastfed at six months in 2000, that figure climbed to 49 percent in 2010, and the 27 percent of

babies still breastfeeding at 12 months was up from 16 percent over that same decade.

(Abutaleb)

As these rates have increased, however, controversy has arisen in some quarters over whether women should breastfeed in public spaces. Many women have reported facing negative responses, being told that it is somehow inappropriate to breastfeed where others might see, and in other cases, being asked to move into a private space. As we discussed in Chapter 3, almost every state in the U.S. protects women's right to breastfeed in public, though this has not stopped disapproving individuals from expressing their opinions and attempting to shame women for doing so. Groups of people who believe strongly in women's right to breastfeed in public have pushed back against these attempts to constrict that right by engaging in "nurse-ins" and pressuring offending businesses to issue apologies and create or clarify their policies regarding the accommodation of nursing parents.

But as a public health and social justice issue, discussions of breastfeeding that focus only on gender as a lens will not accurately capture or target the needs of diverse groups of women. A "single-lens" axis understanding of the data above, for example, might focus exclusively on the average overall percentage of infants who were receiving nutrition exclusively through breast milk, a practice endorsed by major medical and public health organizations as best for mothers and infants; in such an approach, the number under the "neonatal" category would show that about 39 percent of mothers of newborns are exclusively breastfeeding.

However, an *intersectional* analysis that examines breastfeeding will acknowledge that discussions of gender in relation to race, class, and age will result in a more nuanced picture of infant feeding practices, potential public health initiatives, and breastfeeding activism. As Sy Mukherjee notes, "there is a shifting but stubborn disparity between rich, white women's breastfeeding rates and those of low-income and minority mothers—disparities that are enshrined through policies in this area that disproportionately hurt the poor."

An intersectional analysis of breastfeeding asks and attempts to answer the question of *why* this disparity exists. Mukherjee posits that one major factor that accounts for the disparity can be traced back to where women give birth and the health care they receive in those settings. More specifically, many hospitals that serve large numbers of low-income women have experienced budget cuts that have eliminated positions for lactation consultants, trained professionals who help new mothers establish breastfeeding. Mukherjee notes that many of these hospitals are "overburdened and understaffed, making it easier for doctors and nurses to hand out formula milk rather than engage in the time-consuming process of preparing a first-time mom for the challenges of breastfeeding." Kiran Saluja also notes that women's experiences in these health care settings also contribute to this stubborn disparity:

> [d]isempowerment is pervasive among poor women of color; even when they know why and how they should breastfeed exclusively, they are often unable to advocate for their rights in health care facilities with practices that systematically override the mother's verbalized desire to breastfeed. This simultaneously erodes her ability to produce breast milk.
>
> (Geraghty, Saluja, and Merchant 207)

Other factors include how much family and social support a new mother has for nursing; how much financial support and time away from paid labor she has access to; and cultural norms influencing infant feeding decisions.

Knowledge about what causes and perpetuates the disparity should of course be brought to bear on efforts to eradicate the disparity. Public health interventions that attempt to increase the number of women who are able to and choose to breastfeed that *only* consider gender would miss important information about other identity factors that may influence women's choices and affect their ability to breastfeed when they desire to do so. More fundamentally, an intersectional approach to public health initiatives and activism around breastfeeding understands breastfeeding as a social justice issue. In other words, increasing rates of breastfeeding for all women entails not only tackling the sexism nursing parents face from employers or from strangers in public, but also racism and income inequality. This is not to say that "nurse-ins" are not a viable form of activism, but rather to say that the struggles faced by low-income women and women of color when it comes to breastfeeding differ from the struggles of white, middle-class women. Chapter 5, Feminist Praxis, will explore some of the organizations and initiatives that are tackling this issue through an intersectional lens.

A feminist stance explores how systems of privilege and oppression intersect.

Table 4.2 Percent of Babies Exclusively Breastfed in Past 7 Days by Infant Age and Selected Demographics

		Infant age in months								
	Neonatal	2	3	4	5	6	7	9	10	12
ALL(n)	3,002	2,546	2,381	2,232	2,178	2,092	2,017	1,942	1,804	1,802
(0/0)	38.8	38.1	36.0	27.7	14.0	4.3	1.0	0.2	0.3	0.0
Age										
18–24	22.9	24.3	20.7	15.1	7.1	2.0	0.6	0.0	0.0	0.0
25–29	44.3	43.7	40.1	31.0	17.2	6.3	1.7	0.2	0.3	0.0
30–34	44.2	41.3	40.3	30.8	13.7	4.3	0.8	0.0	0.2	0.0
35+	41.0	39.4	39.3	30.7	15.5	3.3	0.5	0.6	0.9	0.0
		Infant age in months								
Education										
HS or less	24.6	24.0	22.4	14.9	7.0	1.8	0.3	0.0	0.3	0.0
Some college	36.5	35.0	32.5	24.7	12.3	4.2	1.0	0.3	0.5	0.0
College graduate	53.5	51.7	48.7	38.6	19.7	6.0	1.2	0.1	0.3	0.0
Income (% of poverty)										
< 185%	33.5	33.1	32.3	25.3	13.1	4.3	0.9	0.1	0.7	0.0
185– < 350%	41.2	41.5	39.0	31.6	15.2	4.3	1.1	0.3	0.2	0.0
>=350%	44.7	41.6	37.7	26.0	13.6	4.6	1.0	0.0	0.0	0.0
Race										
White	41.4	39.7	38.2	30.0	14.7	5.1	1.1	0.2	0.4	0.0
Black	13.6	24.5	16.3	8.0	5.1	0.0	0.0	0.0	0.0	0.0
Hispanic	29.7	30.6	25.0	12.5	7.1	0.0	0.0	0.0	0.0	0.0

Source: Centers for Disease Control and Prevention, Infant Feeding Practices Study II

www.cdc.gov/breastfeeding/pdf/ifps/data/ifps2_tables_ch3.pdf

Why a Threshold Concept?

As previous chapters have asserted, in order to understand how individual social locations are shaped, it's important to see how systems of privilege and oppression intersect. This notion of "intersectionality" is at the heart of feminist analysis. As this chapter will explore, different groups benefit from or are disadvantaged by institutional structures, and this chapter will review how overlapping categories of identity profoundly shape our experiences within institutions. You should build on the learning you have done to this point about social constructionism and privilege and oppression in order to gain a greater understanding of those threshold concepts by applying an intersectional lens to your thinking. Although gender as a category of analysis is useful, it is incomplete without understanding that other categories of identity (race, sexuality, class, age, etc.) are equally as important in gaining accurate knowledge about people's lives and experiences. As Estelle Freedman asserts in *No Turning Back: The History of Feminism and the Future of Women*, "[f]eminists must continually criticize two kinds of false universals. We must always ask not only, 'What about women?' (what difference does gender make?) but also 'Which women?' (what difference do race, class, or nationality make?)" (8).

Definitions, Key Terms, and Illustrations

We begin here by returning to and expanding on the point that intersectionality is at the heart of feminist analysis, or what Patrick Grzanka calls a "leading paradigm" and an "indispensible tool" (xiii). This fact has a history that is important to recount here, at least briefly. Early models of intersectional analyses of race and gender have been offered by African American women writers dating back to the 19th century (see, e.g., Beverly Guy-Sheftall's collection, *Words of Fire*). Sojourner Truth's powerful and foundational 1851 speech to the Women's Convention in Ohio, for example, is suggestive of an intersectional approach:

> That man over there says that women need to be helped into carriages, and lifted over ditches, and to have the best place everywhere. Nobody ever helps me into carriages, or over mud-puddles, or gives me any best place! And ain't I a woman? Look at me!

Look at my arm! I have ploughed and planted, and gathered into barns, and no man could head me! And ain't I a woman? I could work as much and eat as much as a man—when I could get it—and bear the lash as well! And ain't I a woman? I have borne thirteen children, and seen most all sold off to slavery, and when I cried out with my mother's grief, none but Jesus heard me! And ain't I a woman?

What Truth aimed to critique were assumptions about womanhood and femininity, and what her speech gets at is the ways that, in the mid-19th century as in contemporary society, womanhood has no single, monolithic definition; race, class, sexuality, and other identities are profound influences on an individual woman's experience, and all of these rich identities are equally valid forms of womanhood. Intersectionality must be an important consideration when attempting to define, understand, and advocate for the needs of "women."

Intersectionality as a central, formal, and scholarly concern of the field of Women's and Gender Studies did not come about until the late 20th century, and was a result of the powerful critiques leveled by U.S. women of color against some elements of second-wave feminism. Many of these critiques had their origins in the experiences of women who struggled to reconcile their involvement in both antiracist and feminist activism. Latina women, for example, decried the sexism they experienced from Latino men, even as they themselves experienced racism when organizing with white women against sexism. This double bind was succinctly captured by the title of a classic anthology, *All the Women Are White, All the Blacks Are Men, But Some of Us Are Brave: Black Women's Studies*. Many Black and Chicana women, personally faced with both racism and sexism, carved out a middle ground in which they maintained the importance of working in solidarity with men of their racial group. As Elizabeth Martinez writes in "La Chicana,"

We will not win our liberation struggle unless the women move together with the men rather than against them. We must work to convince the men that our struggle will become stronger if women are not limited to a few, special roles. We also have the right to expect that our most enlightened men will join the fight against sexism; it should not be our battle alone.

(115)

On a similar note, the Combahee River Collective writes, "[w]e struggle together with black men against racism, while we also struggle with black men about sexism" (118). What these sources did, along with other texts like *This Bridge Called My Back: Writings by Radical Women of Color*, edited by feminists of color Cherie Moraga and Gloria Anzaldua, as well as work by Patricia Hill Collins, including "Toward a New Vision: Race, Class and Gender as Categories of Analysis and Connection," was articulate what ultimately became a pillar of social justice and scholarship that supports such work.

In addition to sometimes facing overt discrimination, a variety of women, including women of color, lesbians, and working-class women, found that their experiences and perspectives were not always reflected in the agendas of feminist organizations, nor reflected in early feminist theorizing. For example, working-class women (both white women and women of color) rightly critiqued the liberal feminist assumption that working outside the home was a key to women's liberation; these women countered that women of their economic class had been working outside the home for generations in ways that had not transformed their experience of sexism, nor had it alleviated their economic struggles. In short, these women revealed the implicit classed assumptions of some liberal feminist agendas, and they challenged feminists to incorporate the perspectives of poor and working-class women into their work. As bell hooks writes in "Rethinking the Nature of Work," some white middle-class feminists in the early second wave

> were so blinded by their own experiences that they ignored the fact that a vast majority of women were . . . already working outside the home, working in jobs that neither liberated them from dependence on men nor made them economically self-sufficient.
>
> (95)

Some conceptions of second-wave feminism, for example, consider Betty Friedan's *The **Feminine Mystique*** to be a touchstone text that relaunched feminist critique of women's social roles. Friedan's illustration of the frustrated ambitions of educated, middle-class women, however, while driving some feminist movement, did not reflect or speak to women who already worked in factories, as domestics, or in service positions, and who felt neither liberated nor empowered by wage work.

Women of color, working-class women, and lesbians were critiquing what Chela Sandoval has called **hegemonic feminism**: that is, a feminism that was "white led, marginalize[d] the activism and world views of women of color, focuse[d] mainly on the United States, and treat[ed] sexism as the ultimate oppression" (Thompson 56). Rather than abandoning feminism, however, women of color, working-class women, and lesbians asserted their right to claim and expand its focus. Barbara Smith, an African American lesbian feminist from a working-class background, coined an expanded, reconfigured definition of feminism that succinctly articulates this critique of and challenge to hegemonic feminism:

> [f]eminism is the political theory and practice to free all women: women of color, working-class women, poor women, physically challenged women, lesbians, old women—as well as white economically privileged heterosexual women. Anything less than this is not feminism, but merely female self-aggrandizement.
>
> (48)

In this way, intersectionality can be seen as part of the evolution of feminist thinking and action; as the social and political activities surrounding feminist movement matured and gained more ground, so, too, did the focus of feminist theory, and a greater level of alignment between feminist ideals and feminist practice developed.

One way to better understand intersectionality is by exploring what it is *not*, that is, what it stands in contrast to. As a theoretical framework and an analytical approach, intersectionality stands in contrast to a single-lens or single-axis approach. Going back to our opening illustration about breastfeeding, a single-lens approach doesn't look beyond gender by considering *which* women breastfeed and why or why not. Grzanka writes, "[s]ingle-axis" is the term used in intersectional research to denote those perspectives, methods, and modes of analysis that privilege one dimension of inequality (e.g., race *or* gender *or* class) and which derive ideas, knowledge, and policy from that single dimension such that all members of a racial, gender, or class group are thought to have essentially the same experiences of race, gender, or class.

(xv)

But acknowledging that a single lens is insufficient doesn't just mean adding in another separate lens, what Elizabeth Spelman calls an "additive" approach to understanding multiple social categories. In an additive approach, sex and race and class are treated as separate categories, as opposed to intersecting. The Combahee River Collective make this point succinctly when they use the term "simultaneity" to capture the interconnectedness of their identities and oppressions. They write, "[w]e know that there is such a thing as racial-sexual oppression which is neither solely racial nor solely sexual, e.g., the history of rape of Black women by white men as a weapon of political repression" (118). As Richard Delgado and Jean Stefancic concur in their primer, *Critical Race Theory*,

> [t]hese categories . . . can be separate disadvantaging factors. What happens when an individual occupies more than one of these categories, for example, is both gay and Native American, or both female and Black? Individuals like these operate at an intersection of recognized sites of oppression. Do such cases require that each disadvantaging factors be considered separately, additively, or in some other fashion?
>
> (57)

By now we hope it is clear that an intersectional approach requires us to consider them as overlapping, and that without that perspective, we can't fully understand how multiple identities overlap to shape women's experiences on the individual (micro) and institutional (macro) level.

Having given a sense of why and how intersectionality as a framework and tool came about and what it stands in contrast to, it is also important to say more about what it *is* and what it can *do*, or rather what can be seen and understood when adopting it as a lens or category of analysis.

Intersectionality is a theoretical framework that posits that multiple social categories (e.g., race, ethnicity, gender, sexual orientation, socio-economic status) intersect at the **micro** level of individual experience to reflect multiple interlocking systems of privilege and oppression at the **macro**, social-structural level (e.g., racism, sexism, heterosexism, compulsory heterosexuality, **heteronormativity**, ableism).

When introducing the concept of intersectionality to undergraduate students, one place to start is with the micro level of individual identities and experiences. Generally speaking, it is relatively easy to grasp the notion that the experiences and perspectives of women differ in relation to various additional aspects of identity. For many students, they need look no further than to their fellow classmates to understand this. For example, trans women know beyond a shadow of a doubt that they don't experience the privilege of cis women; lesbian students immediately grasp that their experience of navigating their social world differs from that of their straight peers; upon reflection, white students can acknowledge that the experiences of students of color differ dramatically from theirs; and students from impoverished and working-class backgrounds know from the start that their lives have differed from their middle-class peers in fundamental ways that shape their perspectives on a wide number of issues. In other words, it is relatively easy for students to "get" that it is inaccurate to assume that there is some monolithic set of experiences that are shared by all women.

Learning Roadblocks

"We're all different but equal" and *"Intersectionality is just or only about personal identity."* Starting a consideration of intersectionality with a focus on micro-level identities can become a roadblock to learning, however, when students don't integrate the lessons learned about privilege and oppression; namely, that identities outside the mythical norm have less power than those inside it. In this scenario, students might be able to recognize differences among them, but be thinking in terms of being "different but equal," i.e., acknowledging differences, but not acknowledging that society ranks these differences hierarchically in

ways that privilege dominant groups and oppress marginalized groups. This wrong but ostensibly well-meaning tactic can be seen, for example, when white students embrace the belief that they "don't see color" or are "color blind." To be clear, this is not what it means to take an intersectional approach. Ignoring or not acknowledging racial identity can erase important features of a person of color's identity and simultaneously close off opportunities for much-needed critical thinking and discussion about racism and anti-racism efforts. Overall, the challenge is to name and recognize differences of identity, *and* think about those differences among women in the context of systems of privilege and oppression (see Chapter 3). Otherwise, we lapse into relativism and lose sight of the significance or implications of those differences in terms of power and privilege.

On a related note, Kimberlé Crenshaw points out that some people mistakenly believe that intersectionality is *only* about micro-level personal identity. As she writes in "Why Intersectionality Can't Wait," "intersectionality is not just about identities but about the institutions that use identity to exclude and privilege." In a similar vein, Patrick Grzanka points out, "[w]hile intersectionality helps us to explore social and personal identities in complex and nuanced ways, intersectional analyses direct their critical attention to categories, structures, and systems that produce and support multiple *dimensions of difference*" (xv). A feminist stance offers us macro-level and critical perspectives on how institutions and other social structures create and maintain these differences—with varying impacts on people affected by them, which is to say, all of us.

Focusing on the macro level allows us to see and consider how systems of oppression intersect and are interlocking. One clear example is the connection between class oppression and ableism. As Rebecca Vallas and Shawn Fremstad succinctly put it, "[d]isability is a cause and consequence of poverty." In other words, disability can and does cause poverty, and poverty can and does cause disability. As Vallas and Fremstad point out, poverty as a consequence of disability can be seen in the fact that "the poverty rate for working-age people with disabilities is nearly two and a half times higher than that for people without disabilities." Likewise, the experience of living in poverty increases the likelihood of becoming disabled, as "poverty can limit access to health care and preventive services, and increases the likelihood that a person lives and works in an environment that may adversely affect health." In her work on the social construction of disability, Susan Wendell broadens this point even further when she points out that "[t]he social factors that can damage people's bodies [resulting in disability] almost always affect some groups in a society more than others because of racism, sexism, heterosexism, ageism, and advantages of class background, wealth, and education." Some forms of oppression, then, are frequently linked.

The intersecting and interlocking nature of oppressions can also be seen through the issue of gendered violence. One of the pioneering texts on the topic of intersectionality is legal scholar Kimberlé Crenshaw's essay "Mapping the Margins: Intersectionality, Identity Politics, and Violence against Women of Color." What she illustrates is how an intersectional approach to the issue of gendered violence can support social justice by acknowledging that "woman" is not an essential, stable category, and all women who are in violent situations do not face the same challenges or have the same resources. Recognizing, for example, that the role of social class and access to economic resources is of profound importance for women seeking to leave a violent situation, or that national status/immigration status shapes the needs of immigrant women who experience violence, Crenshaw's analysis points to the ways that institutions, as they intersect with individual women's needs, must be examined if we hope to have a full understanding of how to combat racism, sexism, or other forms of social oppression.

Crenshaw observes that the provisions in the Immigration Act of 1990 allowed for exceptions to the standard "marriage fraud rules," requiring that immigrant women be married for two years before being considered for permanent citizenship; this made immigrant women particularly vulnerable to battering and abuse because they (a) fear deportation, (b) may possess limited language or literacy skills that would prevent them from accessing the resources and securing the documentation required to pursue the exemption process, and (c) face cultural barriers that might discourage women from proceeding with the process. In this case, intersecting institutions—government and legal agencies, family structures, cultural norms, employment status, legal status, marriage structures—all overlap to shape individual women's experiences; simultaneously, immigrant women's language status, age, class, and national identity make up "micro" categories that are also important in understanding—and interrogating—essentialist rhetorics around equality of choice and autonomy.

Thinking about the issue of combating gendered violence at the level of praxis, without an intersectional approach, a shelter for victims of violence might not consider the need to ensure that their facility was accessible via public transportation so that it could be reached by a wide range of people, not just those who had the economic means to own and/or have access to a car. Similarly, without an intersectional approach, the same shelter might not consider the need to provide their written materials in multiple languages, not just English. And finally, without an intersectional approach, a shelter might not consider that some women seeking their services might be in same-sex relationships, and that some people seeking their services might not be women. More discussion of intersectional praxis will be found in Chapter 5.

At the level of analysis, intersectionality is also an invaluable tool for making sense of the world around us and for complicating our thinking and understanding. For example, 1970s research about men's gender role expectations by David and Brannon (and popularized by Michael Kimmel) identified four dictates of masculinity: (1) No Sissy Stuff (i.e., a prohibition on expression of feminine characteristics); (2) Be a Big Wheel (i.e., strive for status and success); (3) Be a Sturdy Oak (i.e., be confident, stoic, and self-reliant); and (4) Give 'em Hell (i.e., take risks, be daring and aggressive). If we take a new look at these four dictates of masculinity from an intersectional perspective, we might ask the question of whether and how some of these dictates also have a basis in, or association with, men of different races or classes in ways that don't fully account for men's experiences of male gender socialization. The status and success associated with being a Big Wheel, for example, is clearly defined in terms of material goods and affluence, more typical of a middle-class and upper-middle-class masculinity grounded in **consumer capitalism**. In other words, we would not be content to think about masculinity exclusively in terms of gender but would ask how race and class, for example, shape its expression. We might also ask whether there are internal tensions or even contradictions in the performance of masculinity that are related to race and class.

One arena in which to try out these ideas would be in the media coverage of male heads of state. Arguably, male heads of state epitomize the second dictate of masculinity, the Big Wheel, but the activities, clothes, and mannerisms that go along with that aspect of masculinity run the risk of overshadowing or perhaps undermining the fourth dictate ("Give 'em Hell"), and also the first, "No Sissy Stuff." Thinking about masculinity in this way can help us understand why Vladimir Putin of Russia so frequently appears shirtless in rugged natural settings; why President George W. Bush was photographed so frequently during his presidency wearing Western-style clothing while engaged in manual labor on his ranch and grabbing a beer with constituents in rural bars; or why former President Obama felt compelled to respond publicly and repeatedly to journalists and critics who dubbed the pants he wore to the 2009 Major League Baseball All-Star game "mom jeans." Writing in the *Washington Post* about the "mom jeans" episode, Robin Givhan reflects on the difficulties faced by all campaigning politicians:

> [w]hen they're angling for votes, they know any hint of rarefied tastes or an aesthetic sensibility that is more Barneys New York than Macy's raises questions about whether they are fit for the job of representing all the regular folks. When it comes to clothes, the president must appear to be as mass market and main floor as possible.

Givhan's remarks hint at the class tensions in the president's appearance, but the gender dynamic evident in the descriptor of his jeans is evident as well. The ways that masculinity is classed and racialized will be discussed again in the Language, Images, and Symbols anchoring topic.

Closely related to the issue of what intersectionality, as a tool or lens, can *do*, then, are its goals, or what it aims to accomplish. Dill and Zambrana identify four main goals of intersectional scholarship:

> 1) reformulate the world of ideas so that it incorporates the many contradictory and overlapping ways that human life is experienced;

2) convey this knowledge by rethinking curricula and promoting institutional change in higher education institutions; 3) apply the knowledge in an effort to create a society in which all voices are heard; and 4) advocate for public policies that are responsive to multiple voices.

(177)

Anchoring Topics through the Lens of Intersectionality

Work and Family

In this section, we build upon Chapter 3's discussion of work and family by looking at three topics through an intersectional lens: 1) work–life balance; 2) the horizontal segregation of the labor market; and 3) the gendered division of household labor and child care.

Work–life balance refers to how working families attempt to balance the demands of paid labor with the demands of personal responsibilities, including children and eldercare. Different countries take different approaches to developing policies that will support this kind of balance—paid family leave to accommodate the birth or adoption of a child or care of a sick family member, for example—as well as policies to support breastfeeding, to accommodate family responsibilities, to care for sick children, or to limit maximum work hours per week. One way to take an intersectional approach to the issue of work–life balance is to explore how the experiences of working women differ depending on their social class.

As discussed in Chapter 3, social class is profoundly important in shaping women's experiences of the labor market and the various kinds of privileges and rights they are entitled to. Even within certain classes of employment—for example, professional work—there are varying levels of work–life balance and policies that guarantee those. Women working part time, for hourly wages, or in low-income occupations face particular challenges in securing paid leave and time off to accommodate family responsibilities, the birth of a child, or to cover sickness or the illness of a family member. The current FMLA eligibility policies, for example, disproportionately limit the access of part-time and low-income women to its provisions. As mentioned in Chapter 3, FMLA applies only to private employers with at least 50 employees, which excludes employees who work for small businesses. It also only applies to those employees who have been working close to full time (1,250 hours/ year) and for at least 12 months. For women whose caretaking responsibilities require them to work limited or part-time hours, federal policies are inadequate, such that policies aimed only at "working women" miss an important opportunity to carefully assess the diverse needs of women and make appropriate accommodations and interventions.

Professional women in the labor force with what Sylvia Ann Hewlett has called "extreme jobs" may face a double bind—although they may be salaried employees with a relatively greater degree of job security, corporate culture may dissuade such women (and men) from availing themselves of the policies that do exist to accommodate work–life balance. Marissa Mayer, CEO of online search engine Yahoo from 2012 until 2017, provides a case study of this dilemma. Mayer caused public controversy throughout her 2012 pregnancy and childbirth. Prior to giving birth, Mayer told *Fortune*, "'I like to stay in the rhythm of things,' she said. 'My maternity leave will be a few weeks long and I'll work throughout it.'" In response, Kara Nortman, a fellow woman tech entrepreneur and Senior Vice President of Consumer Businesses at CityGrid Media, wrote an impassioned blog post asking Mayer to "take a real maternity leave of some variety!" Nortman wrote:

> Whether Marissa realizes it or not, the way she treats maternity leave will serve as an example or an anti-example for all woman looking for a path, for those women who do not want "to gap" their ambition, but also want to enjoy *being a parent*.

Later, Mayer stated at a public event, "The thing that surprised me is that the job is really fun . . . and the baby's been easy. The baby's been way easier than everyone made it out to be. I've been really lucky that way" (Grose).

Mayer's decision to double available family leave for new mothers from 8 weeks to 16 weeks, but to prohibit telecommuting and working from home, also engendered public discussion when Yahoo's new policy was announced. The human resources department released a statement arguing "[s]peed and quality are often sacrificed when we work from home," and "[w]e need to be one Yahoo!, and that starts with physically being together" (Swisher). In Sylvia Hewlett's *Off-Ramps and On-Ramps,* she critiques the "male competitive model" that structures work expectations around extreme hours, office "face time," and relentless demands on the time of employees, along with what she calls "cumulative, lockstep careers and a continuous, linear employment history," a model that can derail women employees in their childbearing years without structural and institutional policies that allow for work–life balance, as the debate around Mayer's pregnancy and postpartum work schedule illustrates.

Benefitting from resources and institutional power, Marissa Mayer's array of choices in work–life/work–family balance stands in striking contrast with those women who do not hold jobs in the professional class. As *Working Mother* magazine reports, the majority of hourly employees (those who have less secure employment and are more likely to work part time) are women, with women making up 61 percent of the 75 million hourly employees and a median wage of $11.49 per hour (Working Mother). Simultaneously, the average cost of full-time child care for an infant ranges in 2016 from $9,484 per year in Mississippi to $29,878 in Massachusetts. Center-based child care fees for two children were greater than the cost of household expenditures for rent in all 50 states and average mortgage costs in 20 states (Childcare Aware).

The contrast between the experiences of the professional middle class and working-class people can be seen even more sharply by looking at one company's two-tiered benefits package. In 2015 Netflix made headlines when it announced that it would be providing twelve months of paid parental leave to its employees. The move was heralded as progressive and a good step toward helping the U.S. catch up with other countries. Praise for the policy was quickly tempered, however, as people realized the catch: the policy did not apply to *all* of their employees. The new policy pertained only to white-collar, salaried employees on the streaming side of the business, and *not* to the more blue-collar hourly workers in their DVD distribution centers. In his commentary on the Netflix policy, Robert Reich not only criticized the company for creating a two-tier policy that provided more generous benefits to a select few, but also noted that the select few were unlikely to take advantage of the policy, which echoes the discussion above about Marissa Mayer and Yahoo. As Reich noted of the elite, salaried workers at Netflix, "[f]orget work–life balance. It's work-as-life."

Petitions demanding that Netflix extend its generous benefits to all of its workers quickly circulated and gathered 100,000 signatures; in response, Netflix defended its two-tier policy, pointing out that the twelve weeks of paid leave offered to its hourly employees was more generous than most companies, many of whom offer *no* paid family leave. In a 2015 article about the controversy over the policy, Emily Peck notes that "only 12 percent of workers in the U.S. are offered paid family leave by their employers," and that "[a]bout 25 percent of women in the nation return to work just two weeks after giving birth." Peck and many others argue that two-tiered policies like Netflix's are the result of leaving family leave up to employers, as opposed to mandating paid family leave at the federal level. This argument echoes the point made in Chapter 3 that federal-level policies (or the lack thereof) have the effect of privileging some groups of women while oppressing others, and further illustrates how macro-level policy making reinforces privilege and oppression that is understood more effectively through an intersectional analysis (in this case, of gender and social class).

The second topic in this section returns us to the discussion, in Chapter 2, of the horizontal segregation of the labor market. To review, the horizontal segregation of labor refers to the fact that many occupations and professions are dominated by either men or by women. As discussed in that chapter, women tend to dominate in fields where the work is seen as feminine, while men tend to make up the majority in fields where the work is seen as masculine (and in both cases, it is important to remember that the traits and characteristics of masculinity and femininity are socially constructed). Given that masculinity is valued more highly in our culture, male-dominated occupations and professions tend to have higher status and pay than female-dominated ones. The case study in Chapter 2 looked at examples of how some professions have changed their gender composition over time, and to what effect; in those instances, the focus was on women entering previously male-dominated professions. If we take an intersectional approach to this topic and look at race and class in relation to gender, however, we can see a more nuanced picture of who does what kinds of work and why.

Claire Cain Miller recently reported on a research study that shows that in the last fifteen years, men have been as likely to move into previously female-dominated occupations as women have been to move into male-dominated occupations. Miller quickly follows up this assertion with a qualification that points to how the researchers, sociologists Patricia A. Roos and Lindsay M. Stevens, used an intersectional lens when conducting their research; as she puts it, men are now just as likely to move into previously female-dominated occupations as the other way around, "but not all men." The question to ask, then, is *which* men are moving into previously female-dominated jobs such as counter clerks and product promoters? Miller's answer

"[i]t's those who are already disadvantaged in the labor market: black, Hispanic, less educated, poor and immigrant men. While work done by women continues to be valued less, the study demonstrates, job opportunities divide not just along gender lines but also by race and class.

Referring back to Chapter 2's focus on women moving into previously male-dominated fields, we could ask a similar question: *which* women are moving into the higher paying, higher status previously male-dominated fields? According to the researchers, the women "are likely to be white, educated, native-born, and married." One of the takeaways of this research is that if we only focus on gender when looking at the labor market, we fail to fully understand how and why the gender composition of occupations changes over time. As Raewyn Connell puts it, in order to understand gender "we must constantly go beyond gender."

The final topic in this section brings an intersectional focus to the division of labor within families; more specifically, non-heterosexual families. Discussions of the gendered division of labor in heterosexual families are a staple of Women's and Gender Studies courses.

A significant body of feminist scholarship focuses on who does what kind of work and how much of it within the home, in terms of housework and childcare in particular, as a way of charting whether and how men's and women's expectations and societal roles have changed over time. While data show that, within heterosexual families, men do markedly more household work than they did in the past (an average of 12.5 hours a week in 2005, compared to about six hours a week in 1976), overall, women still perform more household labor than men (16.5 hours per week in 2005). Likewise, according to Bianchi et al. (2012), married heterosexual men have increased the amount of time spent in caring for children over the last several decades (from 2.4 hours per week in 1975 to 7.2 hours per week in 2009/10), but the gap between the time married heterosexual men and women spend in childcare is even more pronounced than the gap in housework, with women spending 13.7 hours. In this body of research, the explicit focus is on gender inequality, but what is often not named explicitly or taken for granted is the sexual identity of the couples. What happens when the lens is expanded to look at families other than heterosexual ones?

Until relatively recently, there was very little research done on families with same-sex couples. As such, the 2015 survey "Modern Families: Same- and Different-Sex Couples Negotiating at Home" is interesting for many reasons, but especially because it includes both same-sex and different-sex couples. Including same-sex couples in the survey along with different-sex couples allows for comparisons to be made across the two groups, comparisons that can shed light on the extent to which traditional gender roles shape contemporary family life for heterosexual couples, and how same-sex couples negotiate the division of labor in their homes in the relative absence of those gender role expectations. One of the more striking findings of the survey is that the same-sex couples surveyed reported sharing childcare more equally than the different-sex couples. And even when household work was not equally shared by same-sex couples, it seemed to be for different reasons than in different-sex couples. More specifically, according to the report, "[a]mong different-sex, dual-earner couples, gender, income, and work hours are predictive of how responsibilities are divided," whereas in same-sex, dual-earner couples, "relative income and work hours are not reliable predictors for how they do divide responsibilities." Research like this that goes beyond a single-axis lens is more inclusive and sheds light on a previously under-researched group (same-sex couples), but as significantly, in doing so, it also sheds light on the dominant group.

But research on the division of labor within same-sex couples could go even further in adopting an intersectional approach, as pointed out by Abbie E. Goldberg in her 2013 article, "'Doing' and 'Undoing' Gender: The Meaning and Division of Housework in Same-Sex Couples." Goldberg points out that most research on same-sex couples and housework has focused on middle-class couples, and she posits that "[r]esearch on working-class same-sex couples' experiences of dividing labor may more fully reveal how both structural and attitudinal factors associated with social class affect the negotiation and perception of housework." While this research has not yet been conducted, Goldberg imagines possible reasons why working-class same-sex couples may have either an easier or more difficult time equally sharing household chores than same-sex middle-class couples.

All three of these examples illustrate how intersectional approaches to issues of work and family help us see those issues more fully, deeply, and complexly.

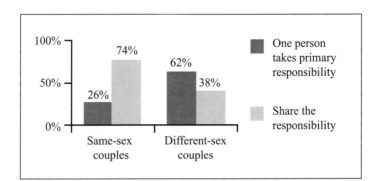

Figure 4.1 Division of Routine Childcare by Couple Type

Source: Modern Families: Same and Different Sex Couples Negotiating at Home, Families and Work Institute

Note: N = 52 couples with children where both members agree one or both of them takes responsibility for routine child care; p < .01

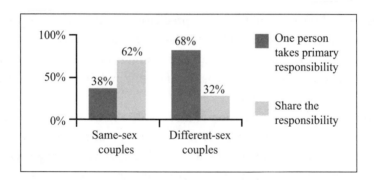

Figure 4.2 Division of Sick Child Care by Couple Type

Source: Modern Families: Same and Different Sex Couples Negotiating at Home, Families and Work Institute

Note: N = 52 couples with children where both members agree one or both of them takes responsibility for routine child care; p < .05

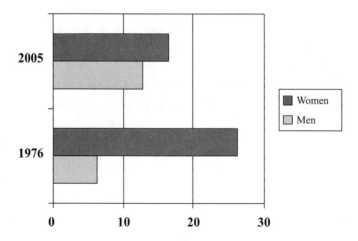

Figure 4.3 Weekly Hours of Basic Housework by Gender

Source: U of Michigan Institute for Social Research Panel Study of Income Dynamics

Language, Images, and Symbols

Chapter 3 presented the idea that systems of privilege and oppression play out through the arena of cultural images and representations. One of the ways that the power of a dominant group manifests is through its ability to produce and control images and representations not only of its own group but of marginalized groups, who by definition have less power. A substantial body of feminist scholarship has focused on the creation and perpetuation of feminine beauty ideals and masculine body ideals. This scholarship has focused on the fact that the cultural images and representations of feminine beauty ideals are often not created by women themselves. Feminist communication and media studies scholarship seeks to explain how the beauty and body ideal functions in the context of consumer capitalism for both men and women. A related focus of feminist scholarship has been the exploration of how people both internalize and resist these images and representations.

An intersectional approach to masculine and feminine norms of appearance emphasizes that those norms differ by race and class. That is, gendered norms of appearance are racialized and classed. Theorist R.W. Connell, for example, writes about "multiple masculinities: black as well as white, working-class as well as middle-class" (256). The popular and controversial reality television show *Duck Dynasty* provides a good example of how masculinity is classed, and more generally shows the socially constructed and performative aspects of masculinity. The hair and clothing of the men featured on the show have become iconic in American culture: consumer products everywhere feature the clan with long hair and beards, wearing camouflage clothing. Photos of the men surfaced in 2012, however, which revealed that prior to their show, they performed masculinity very differently, wearing polo shirts and khaki shorts, with short haircuts and clean cut faces. One photo features the men posed with golf clubs. The outrage some expressed after these photos surfaced came from a sense that the men on the show were attempting to appeal to their largely politically conservative, working-class, and male audience through being inauthentic, performing a working-class masculinity that drew from recreational activities (hunting, for example) and male-dominated institutions (military-inspired appearances) to create a hugely profitable popular culture product. At the very least, the two sets of images reveal that masculinity is not monolithic or one-size-fits-all, but rather co-constructed with other aspects of identity and that individuals or groups may and can choose to express those gender constructions differently. Complicating this point, however, is the notion that gender constructions can be wielded for commercial and/or political purposes.

Furthermore, Connell and others have emphasized that some forms of masculinity are valued more highly than others; this point builds on Chapter 2's discussion of gender ranking. Just as masculinity is valued more highly than femininity in our culture, so some forms of masculinity are valued more highly than others. For example, Connell asserts, "[g]ay men are subordinated to straight men by an array of quite material practices" (257). Paul Kivel makes a similar point when he asserts that while the act-like-a-man box (discussed in Chapter 2) "is a metaphor for the pressure all boys must respond to, the possibility that a boy will have control over the conditions of his life varies depending on his race, class, and culture" (149). Returning to the arena of images and symbols, working-class men and men of color are frequently pathologized in popular culture representations of them, and gay men are frequently represented in stereotypical and one-dimensional ways.

For example, men of color occupy central roles in particular types of popular culture—athletics, particularly football and basketball and to a lesser degree baseball—high status and well-compensated cultural venues that resonate with the "big wheel" and "no sissy stuff" dictates of masculinity. However, male athletes of color must simultaneously occupy a space in which this violent masculinity is particularly fraught because of the intersection of gender and race. For example, the 2014 controversy over remarks made by Seattle Seahawks cornerback Richard Sherman illustrates this dilemma. Following a game-winning play, Sherman conducted a post-game interview with white female sports reporter Erin Andrews, in which he offered comments filled with a range of emotion. Sherman's intense interview resulted in widespread Internet and media characterization of him as a "thug," a term Sherman astutely deconstructed in later interviews, observing "[t]he only reason it bothers me is because it seems like it's the accepted way of calling somebody the N-word nowadays. Because they know" (Petchesky). Although Sherman's remarks to Andrews used the typical athletic rhetoric of dominance (against an opposing team player), Sherman's "outburst" drew a heated public response in which an analysis of television discourse the following day revealed the term "thug" to have appeared three times as frequently as the day before (Wagner). Although Sherman's outburst was hardly more extreme than those that white players offer with regularity, the cultural response supports Greg Howard's claim that

> [t]oo many of us think that one ecstatic, triumphant black man showing honest, *human* emotion just seconds after making a play that very well could be written into the first appositive of his obituary, is not only offensive, but is also representative of the tens of millions of blacks in this country. And in two weeks time, in the year 2014, too many of us will be rooting for the Denver Broncos for no other reason than to knock Richard Sherman down a few notches, if only to put him back in his place.
>
> (Howard)

Many of those criticizing Sherman's behavior and calling him a thug seemed to do so because they perceived his words and actions to be an affront to Erin Andrews's white womanhood (in one highly publicized tweet, her reaction was described as "petrified"). In other words, an intersectional analysis of Sherman's racialized masculinity must be understood in relation to Andrews's racialized femininity.

An intersectional approach to representations of the feminine beauty ideal focuses on the fact that beauty, at least in mainstream, mass-market culture, continues to be defined primarily as white, able-bodied, young, and heterosexual. This means that older women, women of color, women with disabilities, and queer women are featured less often in advertisements, on television, in movies, and on magazine covers. In 1978, Tuchman and colleagues coined the term **symbolic annihilation** to describe the relative absence of marginalized groups in the mass media. This absence has the effect of sending the message that these marginalized groups are unimportant and beneath notice. With regard to beauty ideals, the message is that women who are not white, able-bodied, young, and heterosexual are not attractive or desirable. For example, in their 2006 study of bridal magazines, Frisby and Engstrom asked the question, "How often and in what roles are African American women represented as brides and bridesmaids in advertisements in national bridal magazines over the past five years?" (11–12). They looked at over 6,000 ads in 57 issues of three different bridal magazines and found that less than 2 percent of the ads featured an African American woman as a bride, and no issues featured an African American bride on its cover, although African Americans make up 13.1 percent of the U.S. population (U.S. Census). Feminist scholars engaged in this kind of inquiry pose and investigate these questions in order to make visible such gaps in mass media, popular culture, or other forms of symbolic representation.

Furthermore, when women whose identities place them de facto outside the feminine beauty ideal *are* represented in the media, those representations tend to be stereotypical and to reinforce the dominant culture's ideas about these marginalized groups. Women of color and poor women in particular tend to be represented in ways that reinforce their otherness. For example, Patricia Hill Collins has written about the "controlling images" of African American women; in *Black Feminist Thought* she writes, "[p]ortraying African-American women as stereo-typical mammies, matriarchs, welfare recipients, and hot mommas helps justify U.S. Black women's oppression. Challenging these controlling images has long been a core theme in Black feminist thought" (69). Vivyan Adair, a white, female professor of Women's Studies raised by a single mother on welfare, uses similar language. In "Branded with Infamy: Inscriptions of Poverty and Class in the United States," she writes, "[t]he bodies of poor women and children, scarred and mutilated by state-mandated material deprivation and public exhibition, work as spectacles, as patrolling images socializing and controlling bodies within the body politic" (461). Adair's claims are clearly shown in some of the most popular contemporary forms of television entertainment. For example, reality television is a genre where working-class women and women of color frequently appear, but often in negative and stereotypi-cal ways (think *Here Comes Honey Boo Boo*). One show, VH1's *Charm School* (itself an offshoot of *Flavor of Love* and *Rock of Love*, which are similar to *The Bachelor*), not only shows that the feminine beauty ideal is racialized and classed, but also reveals that there is a hierarchy of femi-ninity, with the femininity of working-class women of all races being characterized as deficient or pathologized. The premise of the show is that the feminine behavior and appearance of the women featured on the show is problematic and dysfunctional; the show offers to teach these women the proper, correct type of femininity, which is to say, a dominant culture (read: white and middle-class) femininity.

An intersectional approach to representations of the feminine beauty ideal not only focuses on whether and how diverse groups of women appear in the mass media; it also focuses on how diverse groups of women respond to and are affected by the mainstream culture's narrow construction of beauty. Lisa Duke, for example, notes "the interest media scholars and critics have shown in identifying the ways in which the mass media might be implicated in producing negative psychic effects in women and girls" (367). In her article "Black in a Blonde World: Race and Girls' Interpretations of the Feminine Ideal in Teen Magazines," she set out to explore how "race influence[s] girls' readings of teen magazines and the magazines' portrayals of the feminine ideal" (368).

Media critics interested in an audience's response to a text and whether and how they are affected by it have noted that responses range from accommodation to rejection and all points in between— what Stuart Hall referred to as dominant hegemonic, negotiated, and oppositional readings. In Duke's findings, based on interviews with middle-class white and African American teen girls, the African American girls invested less authority in the teen magazines' prescriptions about beauty and body image than the white girls did. When asked, the African American teens defined beauty more often in terms of personality than physical appearance, and valued a different body aesthetic (curvier and heavier) than the white girls did. This is not to say, however, that African American girls and women, as well as other women of color, do not experience self-doubt or lowered self-esteem as a result of their symbolic annihilation in the media, but rather that their relative absence from beauty magazines in particular is a double-edged sword, providing the message that they are outside the dominant beauty ideal, but also allowing some space for the creation of an alternate ideal. That is to say, there are competing beauty ideals that are community specific, that is, within a lesbian community, various racial-ethnic communities, and so forth.

Some scholars have argued that the increasing visibility of women of color in the entertainment industry (popular music, television, movies, modeling and fashion, etc.) has contributed to a diversification and expansion of previously very narrow beauty ideals. Celebrities like Beyonce Knowles, Kim Kardashian, Jennifer Lopez, Nikki Minaj, and others have highlighted their voluptuous figures and given rise to the term "bubble butt," referring to curvaceous rear ends, a contrast to the previous era's emphasis on slim physiques. Though it could be argued that this expansion of beauty standards to include physical attributes previously associated with women of color represents progress in the media, scholars like Naomi Wolf have pointed out that it is exactly the constant changing of beauty standards themselves that oppresses women—what she calls the "**beauty myth**" is the notion that beauty is objective and unchanging, when historical examination of beauty standards reveals continued changes in cultural standards about what constitutes beauty as well as variation from culture to culture about what physical beauty looks like. In this way, women are preoccupied with an ever-changing standard such that, as Wolf asserts, "[t]he beauty myth is always actually prescribing behaviour and not appearance."

Many women engage simultaneously in acts of accommodation and resistance, choosing to emulate the mainstream beauty ideal in some ways while rejecting other aspects of it. The work of scholars such as Connell, Hill Collins, Adair, and Duke, among many others, illustrates that questions about the symbolic dimensions of gender are intersected with race and class and not homogeneously connected to critiques of sexism or misogyny in ways that are generalizable to all men and women.

Bodies

One of the core issues that centered the second wave of feminism in the 1960s and 1970s was health care, particularly around women's access to bodily autonomy and choice within the medical industry. A notable contribution to feminist activism was the formation of the Boston Women's Health Book Collective, a group of twelve women in Boston whose activist concerns centered around women's access to accurate, women-centered knowledge about their bodies. These early advocacy efforts called attention to the ways that male-dominated medical practices were the products of patriarchal values; an even closer examination using an intersectional lens can pull apart how privilege and oppression as experienced in healthcare must be understood on multiple axes.

Within the medical industry, the four values of patriarchal culture identified by Allan Johnson (a society that is male-dominated, male-identified, male-centered, and obsessed with control) are evident and reveal women's oppression within the infrastructure, policy, and practices that reframe childbirth from a natural part of a woman's reproductive life cycle to a medical event of a pathological nature often requiring pharmaceutical and sometimes even surgical intervention. As the report "Evidence-Based Maternity Care" illustrates, many interventions to physiological childbirth are overused, while those that can offer equal benefit are underused, with women's ability to achieve physiological childbirth often undermined or questioned through medical practices. As the report explains,

> many practices that are disproved or appropriate for mothers and babies only in limited circumstances are in wide use. Conversely, numerous beneficial practices are underused because they offer limited scope for economic gain, are less compatible with predominant medical values and practices, or have only recently been favorably evaluated.
>
> (Sakala and Corry 9)

In a culture that privileges control, efficiency, and convenience over tolerance for the timing uncertainties of natural processes such as labor and delivery, the overuse of convenience methods such as induction of labor, episiotomies, and vacuum- and forceps-assisted deliveries predominate at levels well beyond the logical benefits to women and babies (see Table 4.3).

Table 4.3 Rate of Birth Interventions and Practices

Intervention or Practice	2000–2002	2005	2011–2012
Care provider used drugs or some other technique to try to cause labor to begin	44%	41%	41%
Had epidural or spinal analgesia for pain relief	63%	76%	67%
Midwife attended baby's birth	10%	8%	10%

(Continued)

Table 4.3 (Continued)

Intervention or Practice	2000–2002	2005	2011–2012
Had narcotics intravenously for pain relief	30%	22%	16%
Used no pain medication	20%	14%	17%
Doula provided supportive care during birth	5%	3%	6%
Obstetrician/gynecologist attended birth	80%	79%	70%
Family physician attended birth	4%	7%	6%
Had a spontaneous vaginal birth	64%	61%	59%
Had forceps or vacuum extraction	11%	7%	11%
Had cesarean section	24%	32%	31%
Used immersion in tub or pool for comfort	na	6%	8%
Used shower for comfort	na	4%	10%
Drank anything during labor	35%	43%	41%
Ate anything during labor	14%	15%	20%
Gave birth lying on back	na	57%	68%
Episiotomy	35%	25%	17%
Women who indicated a desire to exclusively breastfeed who received formula or water to supplement breast milk	47%	38%	29%

Source: Data provided by the *Listening to Mothers Surveys*[1] conducted by Childbirth Connection

A good example of this kind of intervention beyond levels of sound medical practice is the increase in deliveries by cesarean section. The rate of cesarean section—or surgical intervention in childbirth, both emergency and planned—has skyrocketed in the last several decades. As Sakala and Corry document, the C-section rate in the United States rose from 9.5 percent as recently as 1990 to 22.3 percent in 2005, and in 2010, the rate had risen to 32.8 percent, nearly a third of all births (Centers for Disease Control). The World Health Organization (WHO) estimated in 2010 that, in 2008, some 6.2 million C-sections were performed unnecessarily (and another 3.18 million should have been performed but weren't, primarily in developing countries with little access to advanced medical technology and facilities). In 1985, WHO declared, "[t]here is no justification for any region to have C-section rates higher than 10–15%" (Gibbons 4). In terms of privilege and oppression, these data reveal how the patriarchal medical profession imposes assumptions and values that serve to control women's choices, to normalize the medicalization of childbirth, and to present differential (and often medically inferior) care to a specific group served by this institution (women).

A closer look at the data, however, reveals that not all women have C-sections at the same rate. In their analysis of all recorded births from the year 2006 in the U.S., for example, Louise Roth and Megan Henley found that non-Hispanic Black, Hispanic/Latina, and Native American women had higher rates of delivery via C-section than non-Hispanic white and Asian women. Through an intersectional lens of privilege and oppression, the data show that women with race and class privilege use that privilege to, in the researchers' words, "avoid medically unnecessary cesarean deliveries rather than to request them" (207). On the flip side, Roth notes "pervasive racial-ethnic and socioeconomic disparities in maternity care (and) health care more generally, yet there has been little scrutiny of how overuse of cesarean deliveries might be linked to these disparities."

Similar disparities can be seen in the rates of pre term births and infant mortality rates. While 11.4 percent of all infants were born pre-term in 2013, that rate rose to 16.3 percent for non-Hispanic black infants; meanwhile, 25 percent of all preterm births (because of the greater number rather than percentage) are to Hispanic women. Pre-term birth is concerning because of its role as a leading cause of infant mortality (March of Dimes), and as the March of Dimes reports,

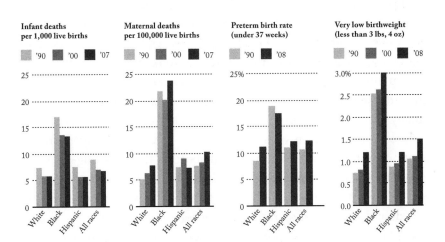

Figure 4.4 Infant Mortality Rates by Race

Source: www.npr.org/2011/07/08/137652226/-the-race-gap

"[b]lack women are about 60 percent more likely than white women to deliver babies early, and black infants are about 230 percent more likely than white infants to die before their first birthdays."

While researchers know that some risk factors are greater for black mothers including inadequate prenatal care, substance abuse, or health factors like obesity or diabetes, research also shows that

> [t]he gap does not narrow with age and educational attainment. In other words, white women's health outcomes improve as they climb the socioeconomic ladder and give birth in their 20s and early 30s, rather than in their teen years. Not so for black women, whose health problems seem to compound with age.
>
> (Norris)

Public health scholars have identified a phenomenon called "weathering" that is at work—the stressors of racism and social disadvantage are difficult to compensate for even with greater levels of educational attainment and socioeconomic resources.

The topic of women's reproductive control, particularly the female-controlled hormonal, oral contraceptive, illustrates how an intersectional lens can deepen our understanding of women's sexuality and the multiple identities that inflect it. As the PBS documentary, *The Pill*, explains, one of the early goals of the women's movement, after suffrage, was female-controlled birth control ("Timeline"). However, limiting conversations around women's access to birth control overlooks a number of the intra-group differences that shape women's needs: for example, lesbians may have different reproductive needs than heterosexual women; historically, many African American women's concerns had different emphases than white women; women with class privilege had a much larger array of options in terms of birth control and abortion than working-class and working-poor women; and marital status and age were, and continue to be, important in reflecting and determining a woman's reproductive needs and her level of reproductive control.

A look at the historical conditions out of which the female-controlled oral contraceptive emerged provides insight into the way institutions intersect and individual women's identities frame their experiences. Birth control activist Margaret Sanger opened a birth control clinic in the United States in 1916. With the financial backing of wealthy philanthropist Katharine Dexter McCormick, Sanger spearheaded the efforts on contraceptive research, ultimately collaborating with McCormick and scientist Gregory Pincus to explore hormonal birth control methods. An intersectional lens shows that social class played an important role in allowing Sanger and McCormick to advocate for access to female-controlled birth control, as did their respective educational achievements. McCormick had access to higher education; she earned a degree in biology from Massachusetts Institute of Technology—only the second woman to do so. Sanger pursued nursing training as a young woman.

In the development of the pill, two particular features deserve attention in order to illustrate how intersectional approaches can complicate and unpack discussions around reproductive control. Sanger and McCormick led the development of the new technology, but the scientific work was done by Gregory Pincus, and the human trials—required for any such drug—were led by Dr. John Rock. However, given that distributing contraceptives or information about contraceptives was illegal in most places in the United States, Rock sought out another region and population that could participate in the human clinical trials: Puerto Rico. Region and race play roles here in understanding the significance of the pill's development, as the Puerto Rican women who participated in the study were typically illiterate or semiliterate and were part of a developing industrial culture that was producing more opportunities for women's employment outside the home. Charges of racial discrimination—or put differently, racial and class exploitation—have been retrospectively alleged regarding this work because of the lack of what we now know as **informed consent**. Participants in modern-day studies such as these would have been required to receive a more substantial education about the potential side effects of the drug and would not have been participants for the length of time that they were. Because of the heavy dosages used in the early versions of the pill, close to 17 percent of study participants had significant side effects, and 25 withdrew because of the seriousness of those effects. One participant died of congestive heart failure. In this instance, participants' identities as working-class puertoriqueñas intersected with their gender in the lack of access to social power, information, and protection afforded them during the study process.

Objections from African American Communities

Emerging from past coercive sterilization practices imposed on African American women, controversy about black women's use of the pill complicated the discussion of reproductive control and the development of the oral contraceptive. A story in the *Nation* in 1974 documented multiple cases of coerced sterilization, such as two adolescent sisters who were sterilized after their mother, who was illiterate, was presented with misleading information about the nature of the procedure. Another case reported on the coerced sterilization of Nial Cox, 26, who was told her family would not be eligible for welfare benefits if she did not undergo the procedure. Against this backdrop and in the simultaneous cultural context of the Black Power movement, an outgrowth of the civil rights movement of the 1960s, African American men and women were justifiably suspicious of what they viewed as efforts on the part of whites to limit black fertility. Whereas for many white women the pill heralded a new level of self-determination and autonomy around controlling the timing and spacing of pregnancies, African Americans were concerned that oral contraception was "just another tool in the white man's efforts to curtail the Black population" (Roberts). Simultaneous public debates about the eugenics movement and research agendas focused on documenting the inferiority of immigrants and people of color provided reason for African Americans to believe that racial genocide was part of the explanation for the widespread availability of oral contraceptives. Within the black community, opinions were split, with many African American women welcoming access to a tool for reproductive control; however, other African American feminist activists, such as Toni Cade in her 1969 essay "The Pill: Genocide or Liberation?," drew attention to the lack of resources for women raising children: abysmal family leave policies; gendered divisions of labor around childrearing; abortion fatalities; and employment discrimination as framing the conversation for African American women around the use of the pill. What this history and ongoing practice reveals is not just the vexed relationship between African American women and birth control, but the critical importance of recognizing multiple identity factors and intragroup differences that will enrich and provide a finer-grained understanding of complex issues like those studied by feminist scholars—in this case, reproductive justice.

Case Study: 2016 Presidential Election

The 2016 U.S. presidential election was characterized by a contentious campaign, an outcome not predicted by most news pundits, and a resultant scramble by media commentators and scholars to make sense of what was for many an unexpected result. The two major political party candidates were positioned as polar opposites: the Republican candidate Donald Trump, a real estate mogul, reality TV star, and self-professed "political outsider" with no prior experience in government work and the Democratic candidate Hillary Clinton, with an extensive record of government service, a legal background, and leadership at the national and international level.

With polls showing Clinton in the lead up to the day of the election, her supporters eagerly anticipated her victory, using the hashtag #Imwith-her and creating a Facebook group, "Pantsuit Nation," which garnered over 1 million members who shared stories of advocating individually and publicly for inclusive values and empowerment of marginalized groups. Similar zeal was attributed to supporters of Donald Trump, whose campaign slogan, "Make America Great Again," positioned him as a "change" candidate who would break from the social, political, and policy work of the sitting president, Barack Obama. Further, some media headlines and punditry framed Trump supporters in terms of their race, class, and gender demographics, with the *New York Times* characterizing Trump's election as "a decisive demonstration of power by a largely over-looked coalition of mostly blue-collar white and working-class voters who felt that the promise of the United States had slipped their grasp amid decades of globalization and multiculturalism" (Flegenheimer and Barbaro). *The Guardian* wrote "the working-class white people who make up the bulk of Trump's fan base show up in amazing numbers for the candidate, filling stadiums and airport hangars, but their views, by and large, do not appear in our prestige newspapers" (Frank) while *The Atlantic* asserted "[t]he billionaire developer is building a blue-collar foundation" (Brownstein). These demographic analyses, especially those focused on gender lines, ultimately failed to have predictive or explanatory power when the votes were tallied on November 8, 2016. Analysis of the election results focused on a single axis (such as gender, class, or race) proves inadequate to a full explanation of the factors that shaped the results of the election. As Amanda Martinez observes in *Women's Studies in Communication*, "[w]e can assume little about women as a voting constituency, but we can enrich our understanding of women by centering intersectionalities that meaningfully and critically interrogate important differences" (Martinez 147). Single-axis lenses may lend themselves to easy generalizations about the election, but do not create an accurate account of who voted how and why, and who didn't vote at all.

Early accounts of the election focused heavily on analyzing the election results in ways suggesting that women as a collective group supported the first female presidential candidate for a major political party, while rhetoric surrounding hostility to globalism, economic decline, and multiculturalism drove men to support Trump. On first glance, this might seem true:

Table 4.4 All 2016 Presidential Election Exit Polls, CNN

Gender	Clinton	Trump	Other/No Answer
Male: 47%	41%	52%	7%
Female: 53%	54%	41%	5%

Data from www.cnn.com/election/results/exit-polls

A more fine-grained analysis, however, reveals the ways that race, educational attainment, social class, and gender intersect to shape voting patterns.

Table 4.5 Presidential Election Exit Polls, by Race and Gender

Voter demographic and percentage support:	Black men	Black women	Latinx men	Latinx women	White men	White women
Trump	13%	4%	32%	25%	62%	52%
Clinton	82%	94%	63%	69%	31%	37%

Data from www.cnn.com/election/results/exit-polls

What becomes apparent here is the fact that a majority of white women voters supported Trump, challenging the narrative of widespread support by women for Clinton as a candidate; women of color had far greater levels of support for Clinton.

A further analysis bears out the role of education, race, and gender as they intersect, with some data confirming the prevailing narrative and others challenging it; for example, the numbers do become more striking when education is factored in, with non-college-educated men supporting Trump at a rate of 71 percent—here, too, the gap widens for women, with a clear majority of white women without a college degree supporting Trump at 61 percent.

In addition, voter income—assumed to be a factor in terms of voter support for the two candidates' economic, domestic policy, and foreign policy platforms—proves to be negligible in terms of dictating whether a clear majority of voters support one candidate or the other. High-income voters supported each candidate at literally the same rate—47 percent, while lower-income and middle-class voters differed by just 4 percent in their support for the two candidates.

Last, it is as important to pay equal attention to those who chose not to vote or were excluded from voting as to those who did cast votes. In the 2016 election, a single-axis analysis of non-voters that attributes voter dissatisfaction with candidates or overall apathy to their decision not to vote is inadequate, as it fails to account for dramatic differences when looking at the relationship between race and voting status.

Comparing data between the 2012 and 2016 elections also yields more nuanced results. In the 2012 election, 13 percent of people who reported not voting cited dissatisfaction with candidates as their primary reason (Lopez and Flores). When this data is further broken out by race, however, we see a big gap, with white non-voters at 15 percent and black non-voters at 3 percent in the 2012 election. This shows that black non-voters were

Table 4.6 2016 Presidential Election Exit Polls, Whites and Educational Attainment

	White women college graduates	White women non college	White men college grad	White men non college grad
Clinton	51%	34%	39%	23%
Trump	44%	61%	53%	71%

Data from www.cnn.com/election/results/exit-polls

Table 4.7 2016 Presidential Election Nonvoter Dissatisfaction with Candidates or Campaign Issues Widespread across Demographic Groups

Among registered voters who did not vote, % who said not liking the candidates or campaign issues was main reason they did not vote

	2012	*2016*	*Diff*
All	13	25	+12
Men	14	25	+11
Women	12	24	+13
White	15	26	+11
Black	3	19	+16
Hispanic	9	25	+16
Asian	8	21	+14
Millennial	11	24	+13
Generation X	12	27	+15
Boomer	17	27	+10
Silent/Greatest	11	19	+9
U.S. born	13	25	+12
Foreign born	8	22	+14
Less than high school grad	12	23	+12
High school graduate	13	24	+11
Some college	14	26	+13
College+	11	25	+14
Northeast	12	24	+12
Midwest	16	28	+12
South	12	24	+12
West	11	24	+14

Note: Whites, blacks and Asians include only non-Hispanics. Hispanics are of any race. "Some college" includes those with two-year degrees.

Source: Pew Research Center analysis of the Current Population Survey, November Supplements for 2012 and 2016

www.pewresearch.org/fact-tank/2017/06/01/dislike-of-candidates-or-campaign-issues-was-most-common-reason-for-not-voting-in-2016/ft_17-06-01_nonvoters_demographics/

far less likely than white non-voters to stay home from the polls because of the perceived quality of the candidates.

By contrast, the 3 percent of registered black voters who did not vote in 2012 because of dissatisfaction with the candidates rose to 19 percent in 2016. However, this percentage did not reach the overall non-voting because of candidate dissatisfaction total of 26 percent. What this suggests is that white registered voter dissatisfaction seems to have had a stronger role in their decision not to participate in the election than it did for non-voting registered voters of color. Other analyses have looked at overall changes in voter turnout, broken down by race, with the finding that whites overall turned out in larger numbers in the 2016 election, as did Latinos, but black turnout fell by 4.7 percent compared to the 2012 election (Fraga et al.).

In short, it is important to be wary of election analyses that offer reductive pronouncements based on single-axis perspectives. This is especially true for the 2016 presidential election. As Allison Hurst writes, "who really put Trump into the White House? The short answer is, many of us did."

End of Chapter Elements

Evaluating Prior Knowledge

1. What previous uses have you heard of the term "intersections" or "intersect"? What other commonplace uses are there of these terms? What connotations or associations do you have with the term? Do these associations help you think more about this discipline-specific use of the term? In other words, how do those "commonsense" understandings of intersections help to amplify, elaborate, or illuminate your understanding of the material in this chapter?

2. Consider previous learning you've done in an educational context which may or may not explicitly have focused on gender, women, or power and privilege; for example, courses on history, in literature, politics and government, or psychology may address relevant topics. Can you identify any course materials, readings, lectures, or topics

that used an intersectional approach? If not, explain how your learning about that topic would have been enriched by using an intersectional lens.

Application Exercises

1. Watch the following clip from MTV's *Braless*, in which Franchesca Ramsey and Laci Green discuss intersectional feminism: www.youtube.com/watch?v=z-nmxnmt_XU. A few minutes into the clip, they name three feminist issues (equal pay, birth control and abortion access, and street harassment) and then succinctly explain how an intersectional approach to the issue differs from a non-intersectional approach. Choose another issue from the list below and describe what a non-intersectional or single-axis approach to the issue looks like, as opposed to an intersectional approach.
   a. "Staying at home" versus working outside the home for pay
   b. Gender violence
   c. Breastfeeding
   d. Beauty and body standards
   e. Mass incarceration
   f. Eating disorders
   g. Homelessness

2. Consider an area of your own interest or expertise (this could be a hobby, an academic major, or an important co-curricular activity you engage in), and identify an important issue, question, or controversy within that area of interest. How might an intersectional approach that accounts for multiple overlapping identities help you approach that issue? Share your findings with a classmate.

3. Choose a favorite film genre and screen at least three films in that genre. Take note of the number of women characters, the type of women characters, and relevant identity factors—marital status, educational attainment, race, class, sexual orientation. What conclusions can you draw about "women in X genre" of film based on your analysis? How does an intersectional approach help you with that analysis?

Skills Assessments

1. In 2014, two different women (one American and one Australian) made headlines when photos circulated online of them breast-feeding their babies while wearing cap and gown at their college graduations. Though the two images shared many similarities, the online response to them differed in significant ways. After reading about the two photos (www.buzzfeed.com/simoncrerar/breastfeed ing-student-goes-viral?utm_term=.ftJLwaAkw#.yc2qLk5YL and www.today.com/parents/breast-feeding-moms-college-gradu ation-photo-stirs-controversy-2D79780389) write a short essay in which you employ an intersectional lens to consider why the two photos received different responses.

2. Locate the following two articles through a Google search and develop an analysis in which you identity a) how successful the research study was at using an intersectional approach and b) how you would revise the study protocol or findings to be more intersectional.
   - Yong, Ed, "XY Bias: How Male Biology Students See Their Female Peers," *The Atlantic*, February 16, 2016.
   - Rivera, Lauren and Andras Tilcsik, "Research: How Subtle Class Cues Can Backfire on Your Resume," *Harvard Business Review*, December 21 2016.

3. Read Lisa Wade's brief discussion of the results of a 2015 survey of women working in STEM fields (https://thesocietypages. org/socimages/2015/07/02/nearly-half-of-black-and-latina-stem-workers-mistaken-for-janitors-and-assistants/) and analyze the findings. What have you have learned in this chapter (and in previous chapters) that would help you make sense of these findings? Be sure to refer to specific concepts and terms in your response.

Discussion Questions

1. In her classic essay "There Is No Hierarchy of Oppressions," Audre Lorde points to a local effort to censor LGBTQ content in works in school libraries. As an African American, she asserts,

I know that I cannot afford the luxury of fighting one form of oppression only. I cannot afford to believe that freedom from intolerance is the right of only one particular group. And I cannot afford to choose between the fronts on which I must battle these forms of discrimination. And when they appear to destroy me, it will not be long before they appear to destroy you.

Having read Chapter 4, how do you interpret Lorde's assertions? Reflect on how Lorde's comments elaborate on one or two of the chapter concepts.

2. Revisit the chapter case study on the 2016 presidential election, this time looking at the *candidates* rather than voter demographics through an intersectional lens. You might look not just at the major party candidates—Hillary Clinton and Donald Trump—but other contenders in the primary such as Bernie Sanders, Marco Rubio, Bill Richardson, Ben Carson, Chris Christie, or Jeb Bush. In what ways do you see race, social class, gender, or sexuality factoring into the campaign strategies, platforms embraced by candidates, or media representation?

3. In Chapter 4's opening illustration on breastfeeding through an intersectional lens, we often use gendered language when discussing breastfeeding, referring to mothers and of course breasts. But there is a growing recognition that not all parents who give birth identify as women, and some of those people may not have breasts. A recent article in *The Atlantic*, "What It's Like to Chestfeed," discusses this issue. Find the article here: www.theatlantic.com/health/archive/2016/08/chestfeeding/497015/. After reading it, please consider the following questions: how and where could the experience of these transmasculine parents be incorporated into the textbook discussion? And what are the implications of moving away from using gendered language when discussing infant feeding practices?

Writing Prompts

1. In 2012, then-15-year-old tennis player Taylor Townsend (an African American female) won the Australian Open junior title and was the top-ranked junior player in the world. Later that same year, however, the U.S. Tennis Association strongly discouraged her from

competing in the U.S. Open Junior Tennis Tournament, citing their concerns about her lack of physical conditioning. Thinking about the discussions in this chapter, consider the following questions: what does her experience reveal about the racial, gender, and class politics of the sport of women's tennis? In what ways can you "read" Townsend's experience through an intersectional lens that considers identity as well as institutional structures?

Figure 4.5 Tennis Player Taylor Townsend
Source: AP Photo/Darko Vojinovic

2. In June 2013, the World Health Organization released a report on the prevalence of physical and sexual violence against women globally. Review the key findings of the report "Global and Regional Estimates of Violence Against Women: Prevalence and Health Effects of Intimate Partner Violence and Non-partner Sexual Violence"[2] (www.who.int/reproductivehealth/publications/violence/9789241564625/en/) and conduct an intersectional analysis. What identity factors gesture toward or account for women's experiences? What policy interventions seem most promising?

3. A number of studies have documented the fact that race plays a big role in online dating, with some groups receiving more attention, in the form of messages, swipes, etc., than others. Do some Internet research on the subject to familiarize yourself with some of these studies (several are included in the suggested readings below), and then write an essay in which you summarize and analyze what (if anything) these studies say about how race intersects with gender and sexual identity to affect online dating. A few questions to consider: are queer online dating apps marked by racial hierarchies? If so, are the patterns the same as for heterosexual dating apps? If they differ, how?

4. Social media provides unprecedented opportunities for users to make identities important to them visible. For example, what has been referred to as Black Twitter is a cluster of trending hashtags that emerge in particular by black Twitter users, a population which is nearly double (proportionally) the African American population (13% of the U.S. population vs. an estimated 25% of Twitter users). Similarly, #rainbowrollcall offers a strategy for queer Twitter users to categorize their tweets, while #Icantbreathe and #blacklivesmatter are two hashtags intended to show solidarity with victims of state violence against African Americans. Explore some of the trends in hashtags that tweeters opt to use to "mark" their social media contributions in specific ways and write an essay about your findings.

Notes

1   http://transform.childbirthconnection.org/wp-content/uploads/2013/06/LTMIII_Pregnancy-and-Birth.pdf

2   www.who.int/mediacentre/news/releases/2013/violence_against_women_201306 20/en/

Works Cited

Abutaleb, Yasmeen. "Nudged by Hospitals, More U.S. Moms Are Breastfeeding: CDC." *Reuters*. 31 July 2013. www.reuters.com/article/us-usa-health-breastfeed ing-idUSBRE96U18E20130731. Accessed 6 July 2017.

Adair, Vivyan. "Branded with Infamy: Inscriptions of Poverty and Class in the United States." *Signs*, vol. 27, no. 2, 2002, pp. 451–471.

Bianchi, Suzanne M., Liana C. Sayer, Melissa A. Milkie, and John P. Robinson. "Housework: Who Did, Does, or Will Do It, and How Much Does It Matter?" *Social Forces*, vol. 91, no. 1, 2012, pp. 55–63.

Brownstein, Ronald. "The Billionaire Candidate and His Blue-Collar Following." *The Atlantic*. 11 September 2015. www.theatlantic.com/politics/archive/2015/09/the-bil lionaire-candidate-and-his-blue-collar-following/432783/. Accessed 5 July 2017.

Cade, Toni. "The Pill: Genocide or Liberation?" In *The Black Woman: An Anthology*. Ed. Toni Cade. Signet, 1970.

Centers for Disease Control and Prevention. "Births: Method of Delivery." 13 January 2013. www.cdc.gov/nchs/fastats/delivery.htm. Accessed 7 July 2017.

Childcare Aware. *Parents and the High Cost of Childcare*. 2016 Report. 21 June 2017. http://usa.childcareaware.org/advocacy-public-policy/resources/research/costof care/. Accessed 7 July 2017.

CNN Politics. "Exit Polls." 23 November 2016. www.cnn.com/election/results/exit-polls. Accessed 5 July 2017.

Collins, Patricia Hill. *Black Feminist Thought: Knowledge, Consciousness, and the Politics of Empowerment*. Psychology Press, 2000.

——. "Toward a New Vision: Race, Class, and Gender as Categories of Analysis and Connection." In *Oppression, Privilege, and Resistance: Theoretical Perspectives on Racism, Sexism, and Heterosexism*. Eds. Lisa Heldke and Peg O'Connor. McGraw Hill, 2004, pp. 529–543.

Combahee River Collective. "A Black Feminist Statement." In *Feminist Theory Reader: Local and Global Perspectives*. Eds. Carole R. McCann and Seung-kyung Kim. 3rd edition. Routledge, 2013, pp. 116–122.

Connell, Raewyn. "The Social Organization of Masculinity." *Feminist Theory Reader: Local and Global Perspectives*. Eds. Carole R. McCann and Seung-kyung Kim. 3rd edition. Routledge, 2013, pp. 252–263.

Crenshaw, Kimberlé W. "Mapping the Margins: Intersectionality, Identity Politics, and Violence Against Women of Color." *Stanford Law Review*, vol. 43, no. 6, 1991, pp. 1241–1299.

——. "Why Intersectionality Can't Wait." *The Washington Post*. 24 September 2015.

David, Deborah, and Robert Brannon, eds. *The Forty-Nine Percent Majority: The Male Sex Role*. Addison-Wesley, 1976.

Delgado, Richard, and Jean Stefancic. *Critical Race Theory: An Introduction*. New York University Press, 2012.

Dill, Bonnie Thornton, and Ruth Enid Zambrana. "Critical Thinking about Inequality: An Emerging Lens." *Feminist Theory Reader: Local and Global Perspectives*. Eds. Carole R. McCann and Seung-kyung Kim. 3rd edition. Routledge, 2013, pp. 176–186.

Duke, Lisa. "Black in a Blonde World: Race and Girls' Interpretations of the Feminine Ideal in Teen Magazines." *Journalism and Mass Communication Quarterly*, vol. 77, no. 2, 2000, pp. 367–392.

Flegenheimer, Matt, and Michael Barbaro. "Donald Trump Is Elected President in Stunning Repudiation of the Establishment." *New York Times*. 9 November 2016.

Fraga, Bernard L., Sean McElwee, Jesse Rhodes, and Brian Schaffner. "Why Did Trump Win? More Whites—and Fewer Blacks—Actually Voted." *The Washington Post*. 8 May 2017.

Frank, Thomas. "Millions of Ordinary Americans Support Donald Trump. Here's Why." *The Guardian*. 7 March 2016. www.theguardian.com/commentisfree/2016/mar/07/donald-trump-why-americans-support. Accessed 7 July 2017.

Freedman, Estelle. *No Turning Back: The History of Feminism and the Future of Women*. Ballantine Books, 2002.

Frisby, Cynthia M., and Erika Engstrom. "Always a Bridesmaid, Never a Bride: Portrayals of Women of Color in Bridal Magazines." *Media Report to Women*, vol. 34, no. 4, 2006, pp. 10–14.

Geraghty, Sheela R., Kiran Saluja, and Meredith Merchant. "Breastfeeding Disparities: Challenges and Solutions." *ICAN: Infant, Child, and Adolescent Nutrition*, vol. 4, no. 4, 2012, pp. 207–214.

Gibbons, Luz, et al. "The Global Numbers and Costs of Additionally Needed and Unnecessary Caesarean Sections Performed per Year: Overuse as a Barrier to Universal Coverage." *World Health Report 2010. Background Paper (30)*. 2010.

Givhan, Robin. "Can Obama Elevate the Look of Presidential Downtime? We Can Only Hope." *Washington Post*. 26 July 2009.

Goldberg, Abbie E. "'Doing' and 'Undoing' Gender: The Meaning and Division of Housework in Same-Sex Couples." *Journal of Family Theory and Review*, vol. 5, no. 2, 2013, pp. 85–104.

Grose, Jessica. "Why Does the Internet Hate Marissa Mayer's Baby?" *Slate*. 30 November 2012. www.slate.com/blogs/xx_factor/2012/11/30/yahoo_ceo_marissa_mayer_calls_her_baby_easy_cue_the_internet_rage.html. Accessed 6 July 2017.

Grzanka, Patrick R., ed. *Intersectionality: A Foundations and Frontiers Reader*. Westview Press, 2014.

Guy-Sheftall, Beverly, ed. *Words of Fire: An Anthology of African-American Feminist Thought*. New Press, 1995.

Hewlett, Sylvia Ann. *Off-Ramps and On-Ramps: Keeping Talented Women on the Road to Success*. Harvard Business School Press, 2007.

hooks, bell. *Feminist Theory from Margin to Center*. South End Press, 1984.

Howard, Greg. "Richard Sherman and the Plight of the Conquering Negro." *Deadspin*. 20 January 2014. http://deadspin.com/richard-sherman-and-the-plight-of-the-conquering-negro-1505060117. Accessed 7 July 2017.

Hull, Gloria T., Patricia Bell Scott, and Barbara Smith. *All the Women Are White, All the Blacks Are Men, But Some of Us Are Brave: Black Women's Studies*. The Feminist Press, 1982.

Hurst, Allison. "Have We Been Had? Why Talking about the Working-Class Vote for Trump Hurts Us." *Working-Class Perspectives*. 12 June 2017.

Katharine Dexter McCormick Library. "The Birth Control Pill: A History." *Planned Parenthood*. 15 August 2014.

Kivel, Paul. "The 'Act-Like-A-Man' Box." *Men's Lives*. Eds. Michael S. Kimmel and Michael A. Messner. 7th edition. Pearson, 2007, pp. 148–150.

Lopez, Gustavo, and Antonio Flores. "Dislike of Candidates or Campaign Issues Was Most Common Reason for Not Voting in 2016." *Fact Tank*. Pew Research Center. 1 June 2017.

Lorde, Audre. "There Is No Hierarchy of Oppressions." *LGBT Resource Center*. UC San Diego. https://lgbt.ucsd.edu/education/oppressions.html. Accessed 5 July 2017.

March of Dimes. "Racial and Ethnic Disparities in Birth Outcomes." 27 February 2015. www.marchofdimes.org/March-of-Dimes-Racial-and-Ethnic-Disparities_feb-27-2015.pdf.

Martinez, Amanda. "Monstrosities in the 2016 Presidential Election and Beyond: Centering Nepantla and Intersectional Feminist Activism." *Women's Studies in Communication*, vol. 40, no. 2, pp. 145–149.

Martinez, Elizabeth. "La Chicana." In *Feminist Theory Reader: Local and Global Perspectives.* Eds. Carole R. McCann and Seung-kyung Kim. 3rd edition. Routledge, 2013, pp. 113–115.

Miller, Claire Cain. "More Men Are Taking 'Women's' Jobs, Usually Disadvantaged Men." *New York Times.* 9 March 2017.

Moraga, Cherrie, and Gloria Anzaldua. *The is Bridge Called My Back, Writings by Radical Women of Color.* 4th edition. SUNY Press, 2015.

Mukherjee, Sy. "For Low-Income and Minority Women, Breastfeeding Is Often Easier Said Than Done." *ThinkProgress.* 1 August 2013. https://thinkprogress.org/for-low-income-and-minority-women-breastfeeding-is-often-easier-said-than-done-63381fb7f95e. Accessed 6 July 2017.

Norris, Michele. "Why Black Women, Infants, Lag in Birth Outcomes." National Public Radio. 8 July 2011. www.npr.org/2011/07/08/137652226/-the-race-gap. Accessed 7 July 2017.

Peck, Emily. "Under Fire, Netflix Defends Lopsided Parental Leave Policy." *Huffington Post.* 2 September 2015. www.huffingtonpost.com/entry/netflix-parental-leave-policy_us_55e7239ce4b0aec9f3556d1d. Accessed 7 July 2017.

"People and Events: Margaret Sanger." PBS.org. *The Pill.* 2001.

Petchesky, Barry. "Richard Sherman Explains What People Mean When They Call Him a Thug." *Deadspin.* 22 January 2014. http://deadspin.com/richard-sherman-explains-what-people-mean-when-they-cal-1506821800. Accessed 7 July 2017.

Pew Research Center. "Nonvoter Dissatisfaction with Candidates or Campaign Issues Widespread across Demographic Groups." 1 June 2017.

Reich, Robert. "Why 'Family Leave' Policies like Netflix's Are a Sham." *Christian Science Monitor.* 17 August 2015.

Roberts, Dorothy. "Forum: Black Women and the Pill." *Family Planning Perspectives,* vol. 32, no. 2, 2000.

Roth, Louise Marie, and Megan M. Henley. "Unequal Motherhood: Racial-Ethnic and Socioeconomic Disparities in Cesarean Sections in the United States." *Social Problems,* vol. 59, no. 2, 2012.

Sakala, Carol, and Maureen Corry. "Evidence-Based Maternity Care: What It Is and What It Can Achieve." Milbank Memorial Fund. 2008. www.nationalpartnership.org/research-library/maternal-health/evidence-based-maternity-care.pdf. Accessed 7 July 2017.

Smith, Barbara. "Racism and Women's Studies." *Frontiers: A Journal of Women's Studies,* vol. 5, no. 1, pp. 48–49.

Spelman, Elizabeth. *Inessential Women: Problems of Exclusion in Feminist Thought.* Beacon Press, 1988.

Swisher, Kara. "Physically Together: Here's the Internal Yahoo No-Work-From-Home Memo for Remote Workers and Maybe More." *All Things.* 22 February 2013.

http://allthingsd.com/20130222/physically-together-heres-the-internal-yahoo-no-work-from-home-memo-which-extends-beyond-remote-workers/. Accessed 7 July 2017.

Thompson, Becky. "Multiracial Feminism: Recasting the Chronology of Second Wave Feminism." In *Feminist Theory Reader: Local and Global Perspectives*. Eds. Carole R. McCann and Seung-kyung Kim. 3rd edition. Routledge, 2013, pp. 56–67.

"Timeline: The Pill, 1951–1990." PBS.org. *The Pill*. 2002.

Truth, Sojourner. "Ain't I a Woman." Modern History Sourcebook. Fordham University. https://sourcebooks.fordham.edu/mod/sojtruth-woman.asp. Accessed 6 July 2017.

Tuchman, Gaye. "Introduction: The Symbolic Annihilation of Women by the Mass Media." In *Hearth and Home: Images of Women in the Mass Media*. Eds. Gaye Tuchman, Arlene Kaplan Daniels, and James Benet. Oxford University Press, 1978, pp. 3–38.

United States Department of Labor. "Fact Sheet #28: The Family and Medical Leave Act." *Wage and Hour Division*. 25 July 2013. Web.

U.S. Census Bureau. "State and County Quick Facts." 11 June 2014. www.census.gov/quickfacts/. Accessed 7 July 2017.

Vallas, Rebecca, and Shawn Fremstad. "Disability Is a Cause and Consequence of Poverty." *Talk Poverty*. 19 September 2014. https://talkpoverty.org/2014/09/19/disability-cause-consequence-poverty/. Accessed 7 July 2017.

Wade, Lisa. "Nearly Half of Black and Latina Scientists Mistaken for Janitors or Assistants." *Sociological Images*. 2 July 2015. https://thesocietypages.org/socimages/2015/07/02/nearly-half-of-black-and-latina-stem-workers-mistaken-for-janitors-and-assistants/. Accessed 6 July 6 2017.

Wagner, Kyle. "The Word Thug Was Uttered 625 Times on TV Monday." *Deadspin*. 21 January 2014. http://deadspin.com/the-word-thug-was-uttered-625-times-on-tv-yesterday-1506098319. Accessed 7 July 2017.

Wendell, Susan. *The Rejected Body*. Routledge, 1996.

Wolf, Naomi. *The Beauty Myth: How Images of Beauty Are Used Against Women*. Harper Collins, 1991.

Working Mother Magazine. "Working Mother Best Companies for Hourly Workers: Executive Summary 2010." Working Mother Magazine. 2010.

Suggested Readings

A Matter of Life and Death: Fatal Violence Against Transgender People in America 2016. Human Rights Campaign and Trans People of Color Coalition. 2016.

Babcock, Richard. "Sterilization: Coercing Consent." *Nation*. 12 January 1974.

"Breastfeeding." *Women's Health USA*. U.S. Department of Health and Human Services. 2010. Web.

Carlson, Nicholas. "Marissa Mayer Had a Baby Boy!" *Business Insider*. 1 October 2012. Web.

Chow, Kat and Elise Hu. "Odds Favor White Men, Asian Women on Dating App." *National Public Radio: Code Switch*. 30 November 2013.

Curington, Celeste, Ken-Hou Lin, and Jennifer Lundquist. "Dating Partners Don't Always Prefer 'Their Own Kind': Some Multiracial Daters Get Bonus Points in the Dating Game." *The Society Pages*. 9 July 2015.

De la Cretaz, Britini. "5 Reasons You Should Care About Breastfeeding Even If You're Not a Nursing Parent." Everyday Feminism. 9 August 2015. http://everydayfem inism.com/2015/08/why-care-about-breastfeeding/. Accessed 6 July 2017.

Epstein, Rebecca, Jamilia J. Blake, and Thalia Gonzalez. "Girlhood Interrupted: The Erasure of Black Girls' Childhood." Georgetown Law Center on Poverty and Inequality. 2017.

Fein, Sara, Lawrence Grummer-Strawn, and Raju Tonse. "Chapter 3: Infant Feeding." *Infant Feeding Practices Study II*. Centers for Disease Control and Prevention. www.cdc.gov/breastfeeding/data/ifps/results/ch3/table3–4.htm. Accessed 6 July 2017.

Freedman, Estelle. *No Turning Back: The History of Feminism and the Future of Women*. Ballantine Books, 2002.

Ginty, Molly. "Detroit Team Shrinks Breastfeeding Disparities." Women's E-News. 22 June 2015. http://womensenews.org/2015/06/detroit-team-shrinks-breast feeding-disparities/. Accessed 5 July 2017.

Grzanka, Patrick R., ed. *Intersectionality: A Foundations and Frontiers Reader*. Westview Press, 2014.

Guy-Sheftall, Beverly, ed. *Words of Fire: An Anthology of African-American Feminist Thought*. New Press, 1995.

Hang, Maykao Yangblongsua, and Tru Hang Thao. "Hmong Women's Peace." In *Transforming a Rape Culture*. Eds. Emilie Buchwald, Pamela R. Fletcher, and Martha Roth. 2nd edition. Milkweed Editions, 2005, pp. 201–210.

Harrison, Jeff. "C-Sections a Measure of Ethnic, Economic Disparities." 13 April 2012. https://sbs.arizona.edu/news/c-sections-measure-ethnic-economic-disparities. Accessed 7 July 2017.

Heymann, Jody, Alison Earle, and Jeffrey Hayes. "The Work, Family, and Equity Index: How Does the United States Measure Up?" McGill University Institute for Health and Social Policy. Project on Global Working Families. 2008.

Hill Collins, Patricia. *Black Feminist Thought: Knowledge, Consciousness, and the Politics of Empowerment*. Routledge, 1991.

hooks, bell. *Feminist Theory: From Margin to Center*. South End Press, 1984.

Hull, Gloria T., Patricia Bell Scott, and Barbara Smith. *All the Women Are White, All the Blacks Are Men, But Some of Us Are Brave: Black Women's Studies*. The Feminist Press, 1982.

International Labour Organization. "More Than 120 Nations Provide Paid Maternity Leave." 16 February 1998. Web.

Jacknowitz, Alison. "Increasing Breastfeeding Rates: Do Changing Demographics Explain Them?" *Women's Health Issues*, vol. 17, 2006, pp. 84–92. Web.

Law, Victoria. "A Look at How Media Writes Women of Color." *Bitch Magazine*. 17 November 2014. www.bitchmedia.org/post/how-media-writes-woc-or-doesnt-twitter-conversation. Accessed 5 July 2017.

Marks, Lara. *Sexual Chemistry: A History of the Contraceptive Pill*. Yale University Press, 2001.

Moraga, Cherrie, and Gloria Anzaldua. *This Bridge Called My Back, Writings by Radical Women of Color*. 4th edition. SUNY Press, 2015.

Mukherjee, Sy. "For Low-Income and Minority Women, Breastfeeding Is Often Easier Said Than Done." *ThinkProgress*. 1 August 2013.

Mula, Rick. "Wonky Wednesday: Racism in Gay Online Dating." *National LGBTQ Task Force*. No date.

Planned Parenthood. "Issue Brief: The Birth Control Pill: A History." *Planned Parenthood*. March 2013.

Quinlan, Casey. "New Data Shows the School-to-Prison Pipeline Starts as Early as Preschool." *Think Progress*. 7 June 2016.

Schulte, Brigid. "What Gay Couples Get About Relationships That Straight Couples Often Don't." *The Washington Post*. 4 June 2015.

Simms, Margaret, Karina Fortuny, and Everett Henderson. "Racial and Ethnic Disparities among Low-Income Families." LIWF Fact Sheet. *Urban Institute*. August 2009.

Sokoloff, Natalie J. "Domestic Violence at the Crossroads: Violence Against Poor Women and Women of Color." *Women's Studies Quarterly*, vol. 32, no. 3/4, 2004, pp. 139–147.

Solis, Marie. "Meet Moya Bailey, the Black Woman Who Created the Term 'Misogynoir.'" *Mic*. 30 August 2016.

Solod, Lisa. "Marissa Mayer and the Great Class Divide." *Huffington Post*. 27 February 2013. Web.

"The School-to-Prison Pipeline." *Teaching Tolerance*, vol. 43, 2013.

Time Magazine. "A Brief History of Birth Control." *Time*. 3 May 2010. Web.

5

FEMINIST PRAXIS

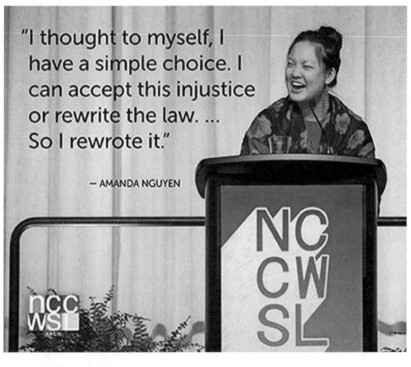

Figure 5.1 Amanda Nguyen

Source: https://pbs.twimg.com/media/DBvICshXsAAi30K.jpg

Opening Illustration

Amanda Nguyen is a sexual assault survivor. She is also the founder of a national nonprofit called Rise, which, according to its website, is "spearheading the effort to enshrine the rights of survivors of sexual assault in law." As a survivor of sexual assault, Nguyen quickly realized that "the system meant to protect and deliver justice is broken" (Arter). After experiencing sexual assault in 2013 while a college student in Massachusetts, Nguyen went to the hospital, where medical staff completed a rape kit, collecting evidence that could potentially be used to prosecute the perpetrator. At the time, however, Massachusetts law stipulated that her rape kit could be destroyed after six months unless she filed an extension (which she would have to do again every subsequent six months), in spite of the fact that the statute of limitations for pressing charges is fifteen years. Nguyen astutely understood that the "six-month rule makes me live my life by date of rape" (Bess), and upon investigation, she found that other states didn't have that requirement. She came to the realization that "[j]ustice shouldn't be dependent on geography. It's completely unconscionable that a survivor in one state would have a completely different set of rights than a survivor in another state." More broadly, as Neesha Arter puts it, Nguyen came to believe that "current legal protections were insufficient and in complete disarray." From that first-hand experience of victimization (and subsequent revictimization by the state), Nguyen began an intense process of research and self-education about the issue. From there came the idea for Rise and for a bill of rights for survivors of sexual assault.

With the help of Senator Jeanne Shaheen of New Hampshire and many other legislators (the bill had 51 co-sponsors, both Democrat and Republican), the Sexual Assault Survivors' Rights Act was introduced in Congress in February of 2016, passed in September of 2016, and signed into law by President Barack Obama the next month. The bill was carefully crafted to receive bipartisan support, and indeed passed unanimously, an extremely rare occurrence; as Nguyen writes in an open letter on the Rise website, "[b]efore Rise came along, only 20 bills, or 0.016% in modern United States history, had passed through Congress with unanimous support. Ours became the 21st." The bill affirms survivors' right to not be charged a fee to have forensic evidence collected after a rape; their right to not have their rape kit destroyed for 20 years or until the statute of limitations runs out, whichever comes first; and the right to be informed of the results of their rape kit, as well as a copy of any filed police reports relating to the assault (Cauterucci).

While passage of the bill represents a huge victory, it is ultimately only the first step in a larger struggle. As of 2017, Nguyen and members of Rise are engaged in the process of introducing similar legislation in all 50 states of the U.S., because most sexual assault and rape cases are prosecuted at the state level, rather than at the federal level. Nguyen asserts,

> [t]his movement is grounded in the belief that the voices of ordinary citizens matter—no matter the background, no matter the age. That's why it is named Rise—to remind us that a small group of thoughtful, committed citizens can rise up and change the world.

Amanda Nguyen's experience of navigating the criminal justice system in the wake of her experience of rape provides a powerful reminder of the persistence of rape culture, but the actions she has taken and the support she has received from many people and institutions shows that many are invested in upsetting and dismantling it. These actions illustrate the threshold concept in Chapter 5, feminist praxis. In this chapter, we explore the strategies that feminist activists and educators use to effect change that supports gender justice.

A Feminist Stance

- Stresses the importance of locating oneself within structures of privilege and oppression;
- analyzes how systems of privilege and oppression operate in a number of contexts (for example, in one's personal life and relationships, in experiences of one's body, in societal institutions, etc.);
- prioritizes generating visions for social change and identifying strategies for bringing about that change.

Why a Threshold Concept?

The field of Women's and Gender Studies in the United States arose out of and as a result of second-wave feminism. In fact, many early practitioners in the field referred to it as the scholarly or academic arm of the women's movement, suggesting not just that it arose from the movement, but that it was literally a part of that social movement for change. Although it is now granted that the academic field and feminist social movements operate independently, the concept of praxis is still considered central to the field. As the earlier chapters of this book have made clear, the threshold concepts of the social construction of gender, privilege and oppression, and intersectionality provide ways of seeing, thinking, and knowing that help us describe and diagnose social problems that are rooted in inequality. In this chapter, we will build on the knowledge and skills gained from the previous chapters and learn about how feminists *apply* their knowledge and skills in the service of tackling those problems. We will also consider whether and how we might join them.

Framing Definitions and Related Concepts

In *Transforming Scholarship: Why Women's and Gender Studies Students Are Changing Themselves and the World*, Michele Tracy Berger and Cheryl Radeloff define feminist praxis as the "integration of learning with social justice" (44). As they go on to explain, for students of Women's and Gender Studies, "[p]raxis is about applying one's knowledge to challenge oppressive systems and unequal traditions" (44). The same pertains to scholars in the field, as Sharlene Hesse-Biber notes in her introduction to *Feminist Research Practice:*

> [o]ne of the main goals of feminist research projects is to support social justice and social transformation; these projects seek to study and to redress the many inequities and social injustices that continue to undermine and even destroy the lives of women and their families.
>
> (3)

Many instructors in the field even think about their teaching as a form of praxis in which they seek to raise students' awareness and consciousness of their location in systems of privilege and oppression.

Activism and praxis are related concepts but not synonymous. Praxis, the intersection of theory and practice, involves a visible and deliberate set of actions informed by theory, by research, and by evidence. As Charlotte Bunch explains in "Not By Degrees: Feminist Theory and Education," theory is useful because it helps guide, and therefore strengthen, activism; without it, she argues, we run the risk of falling into the "'any action/no action' bind. When caught in this bind, one may go ahead with action—any action—for its own sake, or be paralyzed, taking no action for lack of a sense of what is 'right.'" Bunch envisions a two-way street between theory and activism, in which theory guides activism, and then the knowledge gained from engaging in activism is used to revise and refine one's theory. As she puts it, "[t]heory thus both grows out of and guides activism in a continuous, spiraling process." As we saw in the Opening Illustration, the legislation that Amanda Nguyen helped write and shepherd through Congress was shaped by theory-informed research and evidence.

Many practitioners of Women's and Gender Studies have sought to help students cultivate knowledge and skills that support their ability to link their classroom learning with their experiences outside of the classroom. This focus can be seen in many of the hallmarks of Women's and Gender Studies courses; these key features of WGS courses serve as the foundation on which the threshold concept of feminist praxis is built.

- *Critical thinking:* although critical thinking is often identified as an important goal of a postsecondary education generally, Women's and Gender Studies places an especially high premium on critical approaches to everyday assumptions or "commonsense" understandings of the world. For example, Berger and Radeloff note that one of the most important concepts students in such programs grasp is the social construction of gender, which often involves stripping away "naturalized" ideas about men, women, gender, and sexuality, and reexamining assumptions about how gender operates both as a system and on an interpersonal level. Another example is that of privilege, oppression, and inequality. As one student wrote,

> I learned that some issues I saw as personal shortcomings were actually the result of structural inequality directed at women. It also helped me to interpret the situations of other women in my family in this light. This was liberating, to say the least.
>
> (Berger and Radeloff 151)

Students in Women's and Gender Studies develop the ability to strip away and "re-see" the world, calling into question previous assumptions, a foundation of critical thinking.

- *Empowerment and leadership:* two interconnected features of a Women's and Gender Studies education that support feminist praxis are students' development of empowerment and leadership. Linking empowerment with self-confidence, Berger and Radeloff note that being empowered means being able to stand up for oneself, to challenge prevailing assumptions, and to act on one's convictions. Shrewsbury defines the women's studies classroom as built on a foundation of empowerment, or what she describes as a "concept of power as energy, capacity, and potential rather than as domination" (10). By developing self-confidence and becoming empowered to have a vision and act on that vision, students educated in Women's and Gender Studies can exercise leadership, but a particular kind of leadership that involves collaboration, responsibility, and respect. Berger and Radeloff identify the development of negotiation skills, responsibility, presentation abilities, and collaborative learning as outgrowths of a feminist education.
- *Community and community engagement:* Carolyn Shrewsbury identified a sense of community in her 1993 essay "What Is Feminist Pedagogy?" as key to the feminist classroom, but it's also an important dimension of feminist praxis—developing a sense of communal identity, shared purpose, and collective values and then translating that into action in the service of those shared goals are central to the notion of community engagement. Many instructors in Women's and Gender Studies seek to help students develop a sense of

community identity and "build connections and relationships inside and outside of [the] workplace, family, and neighborhoods" (Berger and Radeloff 161).

• *Connecting knowledge and experiences and applying knowledge for social transformation:* Amy Levin, in her 2007 report to the National Women's Studies Association summarizing assessment practices in national programs, identified the application of academic knowledge to the world outside the classroom as an important learning goal in WGS courses. Many Women's and Gender Studies classrooms incorporate an "action research" or consciousness-raising project in which students are asked to do original research, engage in an advocacy or activism project, or in some other way connect the academic learning they do with the world outside the classroom. As Levin notes, successful students in Women's and Gender Studies courses are able to take what they learned—whether it's how to use an intersectional lens to approach a complex problem, how to apply standpoint theory, or a shifting understanding of gender as socially constructed—and integrate that knowledge with their own lived experiences and that of others. A current example of this kind of focus is the Know Your IX project, which is a campaign designed to both educate college students about their rights under Title IX, and empower them to advocate for change on their campuses based on what they learn about their school's compliance with Title IX (or lack thereof).

But moving from the broad and general to the concrete and specific, we can ask the question, how to get started with this kind of thinking and action? In Chapter 1 of *Fight Like a Girl: How to Be a Fearless Feminist*, Megan Seely lays out twelve action steps in a kind of how-to guide for those new to activism. The first three are: 1) Define the issue that you want to raise awareness on; 2) Work with other activists, and dialogue the issue to clarify the feminist analysis of the problem and the solution; and 3) Decide what action to take (20). As a result of learning about the first three threshold concepts, you have been introduced to a large number of issues, and have likely read a variety of feminist perspectives on those issues. What this chapter shines a light on are the actions and strategies that can be used to tackle the issue(s). In what follows, we outline some of the different approaches to activism that make up feminist praxis.

Feminist action: an event or phenomenon that raises awareness and/ or creates change on issues of patriarchy, gender systems, the intersectionality of identities and oppressions, and/or the overall structural inequalities experienced by women. Some examples include participating in an organized event, like a march, rally, candlelight vigil, protest, or sit-in; raising awareness about a feminist issue through traditional and/ or social media; organizing a speak-out about a pressing feminist issue; hosting an ongoing book club or discussion circle to discuss books by feminist authors; calling for a boycott; hosting a benefit to raise money for a local feminist nonprofit agency; and creating a petition and gathering signatures.

Membership and participation in formal and organized activist organizations: an array of organizations, agencies, commissions, and foundations exist that illustrate the principle of feminist praxis and whose advocacy emerged from a small group of dedicated activists. Organizations are varied and emerge from a wide range of local contexts and catalysts; however, organizations galvanize around a particular issue or focus. This can be the product of a small or large group of like-minded individuals, or the brainchild of one particularly ambitious leader. For example, the National Organization for Women (NOW) emerged from the Third National Conference of Commissions on the Status of Women in 1966, where a group of similarly interested professionals, activists, and other participants discussed priorities for social justice for women. Out of that conference and the leadership of writer and activist Betty Friedan, the formal, nonprofit organization NOW was formed. Similarly, the group 9to5 originated from a small group of office workers whose gatherings to discuss sexism in the workplace led to the establishment of a formal, nonprofit group with a national policy agenda around workplace equity. Planned Parenthood, currently a network of public health clinics as well as an advocacy organization, has been around for nearly 100 years and was the product of both action and activism on the part of Margaret Sanger. More recently, INCITE!, an organization focused on combating violence against women of color, came about after a group organized a conference in 2000. The conference organizers were frustrated with feminist organizations that marginalized women of color, and so sought to fill that gap of analysis and activism. Since then, their work has expanded to include gender nonconforming and trans people of color. Their structure has multiple parts: their website lists city-based grassroots chapters of INCITE!, working groups, and affiliate groups, as well as a national collective. They also continue to host conferences around the country that bring together scholars, students, and activists who are engaged in analyzing, organizing, and mobilizing around issues of gendered violence against people of color. Many of these organizations predate the rise of Internet activism, although they almost all now have strong online presences. For those looking to get involved in their local communities, a good place to start would be to research where you'll find the nearest chapter of NOW, 9to5, INCITE!, or Planned Parenthood.

Activism with limited capital: although large-scale, organized, and formal organizations can effect change in ways that exert influence over institutions and policies, smaller-scale and locally based activism can also bring about change in local communities. A good example of this is Shelby Knox, whose local activism on the topic of comprehensive sex education versus abstinence-only education became the subject of a PBS documentary, *The Education of Shelby Knox*. As a 15-year-old high school sophomore in a Texas high school, Knox identified as a supporter of abstinence-only education and a politically conservative Southern Baptist. Over the course of the documentary period, Knox struggles to reconcile her school's abstinence-only education with the high rates of teenage pregnancy and sexually transmitted disease among her peers. Ultimately, Knox's participation in a teen group consulting with local government and an unsuccessful year-long campaign to convince the local school board to discontinue its abstinence-only sex education policy leads to her self-redefinition as a liberal Democrat. She could not accept the basic principles upon which her school's health education curriculum was founded, and eventually continued her education in college and beyond as a political science major and now as the Director of Women's Rights Organizing for Change.org, as well as an organizer, public speaker, and commentator.

Other types of activities blend these types of activism, operating with limited capital to create a formal or informal organization. At Colby College, for example, starting in 2012, student Jonathan Kalin created "Party with Consent," a movement that includes events and products that emerged counter to a series of fraternity-initiated apparel items labeled "Party with Sluts." Kalin responded by organizing social gatherings centered on critical, reflective practice:

> "I don't know how different those parties feel to students than a party that is not labeled Party With Consent, but I think that putting this language out there in the community invites people to reflect and consider, 'Am I doing the things I want to be doing? Is this consistent with the experience I want to have?' I think a big part of the movement is just posing that question," said Director of Campus Life Jed Wartman.
>
> (Ohm)

Feminism as text: in "From a Mindset to a Movement: Feminism Since 1990," Astrid Henry observes that "the feminism that emerged in the mid-1990s developed primarily through the publication of individually authored texts. Texts named the generation, texts energized it, and reading texts became a way of participating in the contemporary movement" (173). While written texts have always been an important part of feminism, they are uniquely central to feminists of the past 20 years, both because third-wave feminism focused less on the formation of face-to-face activist groups, and also because the rise of third-wave feminism roughly coincided with the explosion of Internet technologies. Today, feminist ideas continue to flourish both in books and online on blogs and various social media sites, including Tumblr, Instagram, Twitter, and Facebook. This has been a boon for feminism; as Henry points out, "a fourteen-year-old girl today is much more likely to discover feminism online than at her local library or bookstore. That means she is much more likely to discover feminism in the first place" (176). The immediacy of the Internet has allowed feminists, especially young feminists, to respond to, analyze, and theorize about the world around them as events unfold in real-time, and to reach and engage one another in the discussion of feminist ideas instantaneously. From there, it is easy to see how the Internet has increasingly become the space in which feminist action is organized and undertaken, as will be discussed in the next section.

Online activism: feminist activism has increasingly moved online and has demonstrated that it can produce tangible results. Julie Zeilinger boldly claims that "[t]he Internet is one of the greatest things ever to happen to the modern feminist movement" (140), citing its capacity for community building, organizing, and consciousness raising in particular. In terms of activism, online petitions are one prominent tactic of digital feminism. For example, a number of petitions at Change.org have resulted in "victories" for women's rights, such as a petition to Sprint to change its fees for victims of domestic violence,[1] and another Change.org petition launched to request that the South African government tackle the national problem of "corrective rape,"[2] or the rape of lesbians in order to convert them to heterosexuality. As a result of the petition, the South African Parliament agreed to convene a National Task Team to end the practice of "corrective" rape.

Online feminism is not without its critics, however. **Slacktivism** is a derisive term that has been coined to reflect what some have critiqued as "easy" actions that can be taken through, for example, social media, and that sometimes become a substitute for what many perceive as more demanding forms of activism such as letter-writing campaigns, lobbying legislators, protests and rallies, or other types of advocacy. With the ease of signing online petitions, posting Facebook status updates, sharing links and blogs, or **tweeting** one's views, slacktivist approaches have garnered skepticism about their effectiveness in terms of bringing about social change. Zeilinger humorously admits that it makes sense when older generations of feminists "watch us tapping away on our computers," they may think, "'Um, no, I think you're confused. That's not activism, that's actually the ancient art of sitting on your ass'" (140).

Those involved with online feminist organizing see petitions as a starting point, however, rather than an end in themselves. In "Girls Tweeting (Not Twerking) Their Way to Power," Courtney Martin refers to what is called the **ladder of engagement**, whereby "someone signs a petition, before long they're creating their own, then running a full-fledged campaign." Martin makes clear that online feminist organizing should and does distinguish between short-term and long-term "wins." **Online activism** is still in its early years, and those who are invested in it are currently doing the hard work of figuring out what both its potentials and its limitations are.

Another form of online feminist activism involves the creation and circulation of hashtags on Twitter. For example, #solidarityisforwhitewomen was created by Mikki Kendall as a way to critique the tendency of some white feminists to exclude or marginalize the issues of women of color. Writing on the blog Racialicious, blogger Lindsey Yoo argues that the hashtag "led to robust and much-needed discussions that unmasked the tendency of all progressive circles to work in silos instead of calling for *true* solidarity across multiple race and gender identities." In this instance, the hashtag was used primarily to facilitate an internal conversation among feminists to air grievances and call for change.

As mentioned in Chapter 3, the #yesallwomen hashtag sprang up in the immediate aftermath of the Isla Vista, California shootings in late May 2014, in which a young man set out on a killing spree motivated by his hatred of women, as demonstrated in videos he posted online and in a 140-page "manifesto." Within three days, 1.5 million tweets using the hashtag had been made. The #yesallwomen hashtag served the purpose of raising consciousness and awareness about the ubiquity of sexism in our culture, and gendered violence in particular, as people wrote posts expressing their experiences of living in a patriarchal culture. According to Sasha Weiss, "[t]here is something about the fact that Twitter is primarily designed for speech—for short, strong, declarative utterance—that makes it an especially powerful vehicle for activism, a place of liberation." In this way, Twitter is a forum with instant, global reach that is suited, to reference the title of a famous essay by Audre Lorde, to the transformation of silence into language and action. In her essay, Lorde writes, ". . . [a]nd where the words of women are crying to be heard, we must each of us recognize our responsibility to seek those words out, to read them and share them and examine them in their pertinence to our lives" (43). Discussion in the aftermath of the Isla Vista shootings focused on how the misogynist views of the shooter, as well as the views expressed in the anti-feminist men's rights online forums he frequented, are a part of the fabric of our culture. In addition, the #yesallwomen hashtag references and is intended as a retort to a sentiment expressed by those attempting to derail or dismiss feminist critiques of sexism, #notallmen.

Popular hashtags in recent years include Janet Mock's #girlslikeus (focused on trans women); the African American Policy Forum's #sayhername (created to raise awareness of police brutality against African American women and girls); #whyistayed and #whyileft, which inspired speak-outs about the misconceptions surrounding intimate partner violence; Laura Bates's #everydaysexism, which is connected to the Everyday Sexism project (everydaysexism.com); and #effyourbeautystandards, created by plus-sized model Tess Holliday, and #metoo, which exploded in late 2017 around issues of sexual harassment and assault.

Everyday activism: while the quote from Megan Seely at the beginning of this section suggests that feminist praxis is by definition undertaken by and with a group, this is not necessarily the case. There is increasing recognition that another component of feminist praxis is individual, everyday actions that reject or challenge oppressive practices. Jessica Valenti's *Full Frontal Feminism: A Young Woman's Guide to Why Feminism Matters* dedicates a chapter to identifying "acts of everyday feminism," ways that individual life choices can challenge oppressive practices. Regarding sex, Valenti argues that women should educate themselves, refuse to participate in "slut-bashing," take control of their sexuality, and think critically about exhibitionist behaviors. She encourages young women to critically scrutinize popular culture and mass media, and to reject misogynist male-targeted publications like *Maxim* and *Playboy*. Regarding dating and marriage, Valenti advocates that (heterosexual) women pay their own way rather than expecting men to do so, and also strongly advocates that women not take their husband's name when they get married. Valenti also identifies reproductive rights as an area for **everyday activism**, exhorting women to take birth control, volunteer at a local clinic, find out local pharmacies' policies on providing women with birth control and emergency contraception, and call out public attitudes that are anti-choice. She also encourages women to talk to the men in their lives about feminism, and to reject dieting and beauty standards. In her book *A Little F'd Up: Why Feminism Is Not a Dirty Word*, Julie Zeilinger argues that the individualization of feminism is a hallmark of the third wave, and points to an emphasis on the rejection of sexist social norms and self-acceptance in the face of societal pressure to conform to those norms, as in the body positivity movement.

Everyday feminist acts can also be undertaken by men, as the *XO Jane* article "35 Practical Steps Men Can Take To Support Feminism" makes clear. The post identifies and explicates specific everyday actions that cisgender and straight men can take to support feminist movement, including admonitions to do

> 50% (or more) of emotional support work in your intimate rela-tionships and friendships, consume cultural products produced by women, and educate yourself about sexual consent and make sure there is clear, unambiguous communication of consent in all your sexual relationships.
>
> (Clark)

But in addition to living one's politics through individual choices in your personal life about what to do and wear (or not), what to buy (or not), and who to date and/or be intimate with (or not), everyday activ-ism can extend into other places and roles, including the workplace. A growing body of research, for example, has focused on document-ing the existence and negative effects of implicit or unconscious bias in many arenas. Implicit biases are biases that we have that are below the conscious level, and are based on internalized stereotypes about margin-alized groups that help reinforce and perpetuate systems of oppression. An important kind of individual, everyday activism that everyone can engage in is to bring those implicit biases to a conscious level and work against them. Given the large body of research that backs up the exis-tence and negative effects of implicit bias, this is a powerful example of feminist praxis.

One way to become aware of implicit biases is by taking the Implicit Association Test. Jessica Bennett, author of *Feminist Fight Club: An Office Survival Manual (For a Sexist Workplace)*, offers concrete strategies (aimed at both women and men) for working against implicit gender bias in the workplace; one tip has to do with instituting a "no inter-ruption" rule to help ensure that women's voices are heard in meetings.

Implicit racial bias in the workplace (most notably, in the criminal justice system) has also been amply documented, and can be worked against; in her article, "Implicit Bias Means We're All Probably at Least a Little Bit Racist," Jenee Desmond-Harris lists six approaches to combating implicit bias: counter-stereotypic training; exposure to individuals who defy stereotypes; intergroup contact; education efforts aimed at raising awareness of implicit bias; taking the perspective of others; and mindfulness-meditation techniques. Tackling our own implicit biases is a micro-level activist strategy, but it can have lasting, wide-reaching effects as we consider how countering those biases will impact how we act and how we treat members of marginalized groups in our friend circles, in encounters with strangers in public, and in our roles as workers and parents.

Bystander intervention: another related type of everyday activism is **bystander intervention**. Bystander intervention is a technique for preventing rape and sexual assault by teaching people (bystanders) to intervene when they spot a situation (on the street, at a party, in their residence hall, etc.) that seems headed in that direction. According to E.J. Graff, bystander intervention programs teach "young men and women that they can look out for others in trouble, and show them how to intervene without confrontation or danger." These programs are offered by organized activist organizations such as Green Dot, Men Can Stop Rape, Coaching Boys into Men, and Mentors in Violence Prevention, but the technique itself, once taught, can be modeled and practiced by individuals as they go about their everyday lives. Bystander intervention programs are a good example of praxis; social science researchers have begun to study whether they are effective, as measured by, for example, a drop in reported cases of sexual assault and rape on a campus that has instituted a program. As the results of these studies emerge, they will be used to modify existing bystander intervention programs.

Misconception Alert

"I'm not a member of group x, so I can't be a part of their movement." Some people mistakenly think that they have to be a member of a marginalized group in order to be an advocate or activist for that cause. By this mistaken logic, men can't be feminists, and straight people can't be a part of the LGBTQ movement. Nothing could be further from the truth, however. The operative term here is "ally," which Andrea Ayvazian defines as "a member of a dominant group in our society who works to dismantle any form of oppression from which she or he receives the benefit" (724). Allies have many important roles to play in creating social change, but one of the most important, perhaps, is their role in working with other members of their dominant group. PFLAG's "Guide to Being a Straight Ally," for example, invites straight allies to "[b]e part of the solution even if you're not part of the GLBT community" by challenging heterosexist and homophobic comments, jokes, and stereotypes:

> [w]hether it is around the water cooler, at a restaurant, or with your kids on the way to soccer practice, speaking up changes minds. And the more you do it, you'll find that the less your help is actually needed as people on the whole begin to change.

Resistance to Feminist Praxis

It is important to remember that feminist praxis, and Women's and Gender Studies education, are not embraced by all. As discussed in Chapter 1, there are those who believe that the aims of feminist movement have been achieved over the course of the last 150 years, and therefore that there is no longer a need for further feminist activism. The perpetuation of this idea that feminism is no longer needed is a form of resistance to challenging sexism and is one aspect of a phenomenon known as **backlash**. In the context of feminism, the term was popularized by journalist Susan Faludi's book of the same name, *Backlash: The Undeclared War against American Women*. Published in 1991, Faludi's book documented media and public discourse that she identified as a form of cultural backlash against the advances of the second wave of the women's movement in the 1960s and 1970s, which had been a tidal wave of social and cultural change in key areas such as workplace equality and pay equity, reproductive rights, and changing social norms around gender expectations for women. Calling into question the conclusions of media pundits and writers who claimed that feminism was to blame for women's purported ennui and dissatisfaction with their "liberation," Faludi indicts such claims as part of a larger cultural resistance to true liberation and equality for women.

Backlash against feminism and other progressive social movements continues in the 21st century, but its forms have shifted over time. In addition to overt rejection and demonization of feminism, we are now seeing what Susan J. Douglas terms "enlightened sexism," which she describes as "more nuanced and much more insidious" (11). Enlightened sexism

> takes the gains of the women's movement as a given, and then uses them as permission to resurrect retrograde images of girls and women as sex objects, bimbos, and hootchie mamas still defined by their appearance and their biological destiny.
>
> (10)

The nuance or subtlety that Douglas refers to comes from the fact that these retrograde images are often presented ironically, with a level of self-awareness that they're sexist, which positions the viewer or consumer of the images as in on the joke. In a post on her blog, Feminist Frequency, entitled "Retro Sexism and Uber Ironic Advertising," Anita Sarkeesian uses the term "retro sexism" to analyze advertisements that use this type of irony, and she argues that advertisers do this in order to simultaneously present sexist images while distancing themselves from them.

According to Douglas, media stories about women **opting out** of the workforce are another aspect of enlightened sexism. A 2003 *New York Times* story, the "Opt-Out Revolution," suggested that feminism had failed in its aims to liberate women through access to education and economic self-sufficiency and that, instead, professional and educated women were returning in droves to the home, "opting out" of the hectic demands of the workplace for the halcyon sanctuary of domesticity.

A range of cultural and media responses have questioned these assumptions from multiple angles. For example, an August 2013 *New York Times* story claimed "The Opt-Out Generation Wants Back In," asserting that those women who had "opted" for domestic responsibilities over paid labor were realizing that "opting out" of careers and opting in to unpaid work subsidized by a working partner's labor was unsustainable. Article author Judith Warner uses the case study of Sheila O'Donnel to illustrate the consequences of "opting out":

> [e]ven with the reduced schedule, the stresses of life in a two-career household put an overwhelming strain on her marriage. There were ugly fights with her husband about laundry and over who would step in when the nanny was out sick. "All this would be easier if you didn't work," O'Donnel recalled her husband saying. "I was so stressed," she told me. "I said, This is ridiculous. We'd made plenty of money. We'd saved plenty of money."

Subsequently, in describing the case of O'Donnel, as well as the seismic economic changes since the initial "opt-out" story was published in 2003, Warner claims that individual women have reconsidered their decisions in light of the personal sacrifices and uncertainty and dependence that such a "choice" engenders.

A number of feminist theorists and critics have argued that the current cultural obsession with girls' and women's physical appearance in terms of the shape, size, and sexiness of their bodies is a form of backlash against feminism. Gender norms for girls and women have inarguably changed in significant ways over the past 50 years as a result of feminism, but even as women have greater freedoms in many areas of life, there is a corresponding greater scrutiny of their bodies. Sandra Bartky, for example, points out that "[w]omen are no longer required to be chaste or modest, to restrict their sphere of activity to the home, or even to realize their properly feminine destiny in maternity." Instead, she argues, "normative femininity is coming more and more to be centered on woman's body—not its duties and obligations or even its capacity to bear children, but its sexuality, more precisely, its presumed heterosexuality and its appearance" (41–42). Further, Bartky argues that the latter type of control only started to assume greater importance as the former waned as a result of feminist struggles to redefine women's roles. Jessica Valenti calls it a distraction: "[t]he more we're worked up about how fat we are or how hot we want to be, the less we're worried about the things that really matter, the things that will affect our lives" (199–200). In other words, reorienting women's attention to their physical appearances is as much about directing women's behavior and time as it is surveilling their appearances and conformity to a narrowly defined ideal of feminine beauty.

A related term is **postfeminism**, which rests on the premise that the aims of feminist movement(s) have been achieved and that we live in a society where women experience a full range of choices equal to those of men, or as Angela McRobbie explains, "post-feminism positively draws on and invokes feminism as that which can be taken into account, to suggest that equality is achieved, in order to install a whole repertoire of new meanings which emphasise that it is no longer needed" (255). Another definition uses postfeminism interchangeably or as an alternate to the term "backlash."

A different but related form of backlash can be seen in recent transphobic efforts to force transgender people to use public restrooms that correspond with the sex assigned on their birth certificate, as opposed to using the bathroom that corresponds with their gender identity. These anti-trans policies, bills, and referenda can be seen as a reactionary response to the growing visibility of trans people in our society, and the recent legal and political gains made by and for them. An especially insidious aspect of some of these anti-trans efforts is that they have attempted to garner support by claiming that they are championing (cisgender) girls' and women's safety. These appeals claim that allowing trans women to use women's restrooms will lead to violence against women and girls in those spaces, as trans women are, in this transphobic view, really men who dress in women's clothing in order to prey on women and girls. But as Alex Berg succinctly articulated in a recent article,

> invoking women's safety while ignoring real violence faced by women and girls on college campuses, on the street and in their own homes is nothing more than a veil for hate. This so-called

protection is a justification for transphobia—and as cisgender women, we're done being your excuse.

Another form of backlash can occur at the micro level, and takes the form of potential negative personal consequences to individuals in the workplace who engage in what one research study refers to as "diversity-valuing behaviors." The study, reported in the *Harvard Business Review*, demonstrated that employees who engaged in these behaviors, "whether they respected cultural, religious, gender, and racial differences, valued working with a diverse group of people, and felt comfortable managing people from different racial or cultural backgrounds" did not benefit from them in terms of how their bosses rated their competence or performance and in fact,

> women and nonwhite executives who were reported as frequently engaging in these behaviors were rated much *worse* by their bosses, in terms of competence and performance ratings, than their female and nonwhite counterparts who did not actively promote balance. For all the talk about how important diversity is within organizations, white and male executives aren't rewarded, career-wise, for engaging in diversity-valuing behavior, and nonwhite and female executives actually get punished for it.

What we want to highlight here is that actively valuing diversity within a range of environments has differential consequences, and these should be recognized; it also showcases the importance of the roles of allies from a range of demographic sectors toward achieving diversity goals. Johnson and Hekman's research suggests that those within the mythical norm may not be rewarded for the work, but if they engage in it they are not punished, and their actions have the long-term potential to shift the workplace culture so that members of marginalized groups can engage in diversity-valuing behavior without fear of repercussion.

Finally, backlash includes cultural, media, and interpersonal reactions to movements like Black Lives Matter, which was discussed in Chapter 3. Black Lives Matter began as a reaction against "extrajudicial killings of Black people by police and vigilantes" and has extended into a larger movement for racial justice. Reactionary hashtags and products like "All Lives Matter" and "Blue Lives Matter" bumper stickers and posters aim to shift the public narrative about and undercut the attention to the very real risks and effects faced by people of color when interacting with institutions broadly and law enforcement specifically; reframing the narrative is an example of how social movements are not necessarily lockstep narratives of progress.

Understanding the causes and manifestations of backlash is a necessary skill for those engaged in feminist praxis.

Misconception Alert

White men are frequently victims of "reverse discrimination." One misconception about feminism and feminist movement is that not only have the goals of feminist movement been achieved, but that in fact women (or other groups such as men of color) have distinct advantages over men, or that men are significantly disadvantaged by women's achievements or by affirmative action and equity efforts. As a brief review of key issues shows, in fact reverse discrimination is uncommon, partly because, by using a macro lens as outlined in Chapter 3, we can see how systems of privilege and oppression interact to grant some groups privileges and withhold them from others. In this system, white men are usually an advantaged group. In this sense, feminism in the popular imagination is at odds on some key issues with the demographic and statistical realities of women's lives in the United States and globally.

Although there have been important achievements in improving the quality of life for many women in the United States and internationally, demographic and statistical realities reveal that, in fact, there is a good deal of work to be done to bring about gender equity, particularly because such claims about feminism having reached its goals typically operate under the assumption that the goals of middle-class, white women are the goals of feminist movement. However, feminist movement takes many forms and serves a broad spectrum of women's needs. For example:

- Women and girls globally experience high rates of violence and cultural sexism ranging from son preference to dowry deaths to sex-selective abortion.

- Female circumcision, the nonmedical removal of all or part of a women's genitalia, persists across many parts of Africa, Asia, North America, and Europe.
- Males outnumber females three to one in family films. In contrast, females make up just over 50 percent of the population in the United States. Even more staggering is the fact that this ratio, as seen in family films, is the same as it was in 1946 (Geena Davis Institute on Gender in the Media).
- As UNICEF reports, women are dramatically underrepresented in national representative and legislative bodies, making up just 17 percent of elected representatives, and 6 percent of heads of state (UNICEF).
- Although women have made substantial gains in efforts for economic justice, wage inequalities continue to persist. According to 9to5.org, an advocacy organization for women workers,

> a significant pay gap exists for women and people of color. Women earn 77 cents for every dollar earned by men in 2011 annual earnings. For women of color the gap is even wider— African-American women earn only 69 cents and Latinas just 60 cents for every dollar earned by males, the highest earners.
>
> (9to5)

- Legislative efforts such as the Paycheck Fairness Act aim to reduce this gap, but women still make less than their male coworkers.
- As the National Center for Education Statistics explains, "Title IX of the Education Amendments of 1972 protects people from discrimination based on sex in education programs and activities that receive federal financial assistance." As a result of this legislative act, there is some cultural perception that equity for women in athletics has led to inequities or disadvantages for men. However, the Women's Sports Foundation explains that, in fact, men's participation in athletics is increasing; they observe:

> [t]his misinformation campaign takes the focus away from the facts that (1) women continue to be significantly underrepresented among high school and college athletes, (2) the gap between men's and women's sports participation and support

is not closing and (3) it is the wealthiest athletic programs in NCAA Division I-A that are dropping men's minor sports, typically because they are shifting these monies to compete in the football and men's basketball arms race.

(Women's Sports Foundation)

On the whole, female athletes receive fewer scholarship dollars ($965 million female vs. $1.15 billion male) and fewer athletic participation opportunities (3.2 million female vs. 4.5 million male) than male athletes. A news story in the *Christian Science Monitor* reveals the more common explanation for the elimination of men's sports:

[t]he NCAA also points out that non-revenue men's sports are often cut to provide more funds for the two big revenue sports, football and basketball. In 2006, for instance, Rutgers University dropped men's tennis, a team with a budget of approximately $175,000. The National Women's Law Center points out that Rutgers spent about $175,000 in the same year on hotel rooms for the football team—for home games.

(Goodale)

Anchoring Topics through the Lens of Feminist Praxis

Work and Family

There is a wide range of feminist praxis that focuses on issues related to work and family. Some takes the form of formal organizations focused on achieving economic justice for women as workers and mothers. Other examples include programs focused on addressing racial disparities in breastfeeding rates, as well as the high-profile initiative to bail mothers out of jail for Mother's Day, thereby raising awareness in the general public about the bail system in the U.S. and the impact of mass incarceration on women.

MomsRising: serves as a kind of clearinghouse that takes multiple approaches to activism on behalf of women. They are focused on a range of issues including maternity and paternity leave, flexible work options, health care access, early childhood education, and paid sick leave. Since 2006, the group has been engaged in organizing grassroots activists, for example, providing online resources for lobbying legislators to support fair wages or family leave. MomsRising also hosts a blog where women can share their stories on the topics supported by the organization; it also aims to "amplify women's voices and issues in the national dialogue and in the media" in order to advocate for positive social and legislative change that will support work–life balance.

Pride at Work: Pride at Work is a nonprofit organization that focuses on identifying issues of mutual importance to the labor movement and the LGBTQ community. According to their website, they focus both on improving the climate for LGBTQ people in labor unions and on forging connections between the labor movement and LGBTQ communities. Members of the organization recognize that labor unions can be an important source of protection from discrimination in the workplace for LGBTQ people; for example, they point out that in 33 states, union contracts are the "only legal form of protection against employment discrimination for transgender working people." They also note that OSHA (Occupational Safety and Health Administration) offers guidelines for restroom access for transgender employees, noting that access to a restroom is a workplace safety and health issue for all employees, and uniquely so for transgender employees. Among other things, Pride at Work offers support and trainings to labor unions seeking to be more inclusive of their membership.

Mother Nurture: the Opening Illustration in Chapter 4 focused on intersectional approaches to breastfeeding. In Detroit, MI, a program called Mother Nurture has been created, building on the work of a diverse group of health activists and health care professionals. The program focuses on addressing the racial disparities in breastfeeding rates and has done so by drawing on the wealth of research findings that have documented the disparities, pinpointed their sources, and studied the most effective means of shrinking them, making the program an excellent example of feminist praxis. For example, according to Molly Ginty, studies have shown that "people of different ethnicities were significantly more receptive to receiving health information when it was delivered by someone with whom they identified— someone who looked like them, talked like them, and was in their same peer group." As a result, Mother Nurture has focused on providing training to African American women to become breastfeeding peer counselors and lactation consultants.

Mama's Bail Out Day: in the lead up to Mother's Day in 2017, a coalition of more than 20 organizations across the United States worked together to provide bail money for over 100 women. Actions like this are a part of the larger Movement for Black Lives, the platform for which lays out the case for abolishing money bail because the bail system is racially discriminatory and disproportionately negatively impacts low-income people. As noted on the National Bail Out website,

> [p]re-trial incarceration has catastrophic effects on our communities in particular. Black people are over two times more likely to be arrested and once arrested are twice as likely to be caged before trial. Our LGBTQ and gender nonconforming family are targeted and caged at even more alarming rates, and once in jail are significantly more likely to be sexually and physically abused.

People who cannot afford to post bail, even in amounts of only a few hundred dollars, are consigned to sit in jail while awaiting trial, perhaps losing their jobs, their housing, and sometimes even losing custody of their children. Many plead guilty to charges against them, even if they are innocent, in an effort to be released from jail more quickly. Actions like Mama's Bail Out Day serve dual purposes; a small percentage of incarcerated people are literally freed through community bail funds, and the publicity surrounding the action raises the level of awareness in the broader community about this aspect of inequality in the criminal justice system. Allies can also donate money to one of the many community bail funds. As law professor Jocelyn Simonson puts it, "this unprecedented coordination of efforts to bail out poor people of color exemplifies the kind of mass acts of resistance that can disrupt the status quo in the criminal-justice system."

Language, Images, and Symbols
Although critical to the development of social norms and assumptions around gender, language, images, and symbols can be particularly

challenging to reshape. Unlike work and family or reproductive rights—which are often subject at least in part to public policy (whether laws, regulations, funding priorities, initiatives, etc.), symbolic representations of gender in the form of art, music, popular culture, literature, film, are much less subject to such forms of social and political legislation, and so activism around language, images, and symbols takes different approaches to critiquing, reframing, and influencing symbolic representations of women, gender, and race.

One group, active since the 1980s, is the Guerrilla Girls. Following an exhibit at the Museum of Modern Art on "An International Survey of Painting and Sculpture," protests about the white, male, Eurocentric, and U.S.-centric content of the "international survey" emerged. Feminists in the art world critiqued the exclusion of women and people of color from important temporary exhibits such as these, and that critique broadened out to include an analysis of whose work was included in museums' permanent collections and exhibited in commercial galleries. They created colorful, sarcastic, and humorous posters and posted them as a way to draw attention to the art world's gender and racial disparity. As the group themselves explains, the Guerrilla Girls are

> a bunch of anonymous females who take the names of dead women artists as pseudonyms and appear in public wearing gorilla masks. We have produced posters, stickers, books, printed projects, and actions that expose sexism and racism in politics, the art world, film and the culture at large.

Highlighting the exclusion of women artists and artists of color from mainstream galleries, the loosely organized group engages in a range of activities from demonstrations to "flash mob" type protests, to billboards and posters as well as authoring books and public letters.

A similar effort to reshape media representation of girls and women across many types of media is the Institute on Gender and Media, founded by actress Geena Davis in 2004. The institute takes a three-pronged approach to changing the "media landscape" around gender representations, including research, education, and advocacy. First, as the sponsor of research studies, the organization is able to support investigations into media representations, providing a sound and robust empirical foundation for its education and advocacy. For example, the institute has sponsored studies of industry leaders' perceptions of gender in family films, investigations into gender disparities both on-screen and behind the camera, and assessments of the portrayal of occupations in G-rated, family films. Such research investigations have allowed the institute to draw important conclusions, for example, about the representation of women in particular fields, such as the finding that in one study, not a single female character was depicted in medical science, executive business, or politics (Smith 2). The institute uses this research in two equally important ways. First, the institute and its organizational partners seek to educate stakeholders and leaders about the impact of gender representations in media. In other words, the institute reaches out to the *makers* of media in an attempt to shape the content that they produce. They also reach out to *consumers* of media; the institute offers an array of web-based resources including lessons and curricula that can be used by teachers in a variety of settings to teach critical thinking and media literacy skills to young people. Finally, the institute engages in advocacy by providing public presentations, consulting with professional and industry groups, using social media, and interfacing and partnering with other organizations such as UN Women and the Girl Scouts.

Feminist praxis can take other forms around symbolic representation— such as the #notbuyingit Twitter campaign initiated by *Missrepresentation.org*, a nonprofit social action campaign and media organization emerging from the documentary of the same name, written and directed by Jennifer Siebel Newsom. *Miss Representation* focused on making visible the underrepresentation and degrading representations of women in the media. The #notbuyingit campaign is one way that organizations can use social media to highlight, critique, and mobilize action about symbolic representation, in this case, products that offer stereotyped, degrading, or harmful messages. For example, an August 2013 tweet highlighted an Etsy product, a glass with the message "You've Just Been Roofied" that reveals itself at the bottom after the drinker has finished the beverage. One of the goals of the campaign is to call attention to such products and hold manufacturers accountable

for misogynist products as well as to discourage consumers from pur-
chasing them.

Another powerful example of hashtag activism focused on representations is #oscarssowhite, created by April Reign in 2015, which was
briefly mentioned in the Case Study at the end of Chapter 1. Reign
coined the hashtag in response to the nomination list of the four
categories for acting which included no people of color among its
20 nominees. In 2016, #oscarsstillsowhite emerged when a similar
slate of white nominees was announced for the four categories in 2015
films, even though two commercially and critically successful films—
Creed and *Straight Outta Compton*—featured performances by highly
praised actors like Samuel Jackson, Will Smith, and Idris Elba. It's hard
to know the specific impact of Reign's hashtag activism precisely on
subsequent years, but the 2017 nomination list had a record number of
African American nominees and saw the most black Academy Award
winners in the history of the awards.

Bodies

A key focus of feminist activism has been the idea that women have
a right to control their own bodies. There is a long history of feminist
organizing around the issues of rape, sexual assault, and street harassment. In its earliest forms, this activism focused on marital violence and
was sometimes linked to the temperance movement, as many saw alco-
hol as the chief cause of men's violence against their wives and children.
It was not until the second wave of feminism, however, that the impact
of feminist efforts began to be felt. A brief discussion of this activism
over the past 40 years reveals both continuity and change in terms of its
targets, tone, tactics and strategies.

A well-established form of activism around violence against women
is the international movement Take Back the Night. Starting in 1976 in
Brussels, Belgium, this activist effort uses marches, protests, and demonstrations as well as candlelight vigils and accompanying speakers to
call for the elimination of violence against women. Take Back the Night
marches are a symbolic reclamation of public space after dark, which
girls and women are taught to fear through the messages they receive

about their responsibility in protecting themselves against attack. The Take Back the Night Foundation, established in 1999, describes its goals as follows: "[t]he Take Back The Night Foundation seeks to end sexual assault, domestic violence, dating violence, sexual abuse and all other forms of sexual violence. We serve to create safe communities and respectful relationships through awareness events and initiatives" ("About"). Take Back the Night marches are especially prevalent on college campuses, where they continue to play a crucial role in raising young people's awareness of these issues and also provide a powerful forum for survivors to speak and heal. Critiques of the movement have centered on the potential implication that "stranger rape" and nighttime attacks in the bushes are the primary form of sexual violence against women, when in fact a small minority of sexual assaults are committed by someone unknown to the victim.

Similar in its goals but different in its tone and tactics is the **Slut-Walk** movement. SlutWalks began after a police officer at a safety forum at York University in January 2011 claimed that women "should avoid dressing like sluts in order not to be victimized." Outraged, a grassroots and social media campaign led by Heather Jarvis and Sonya Barnett emerged in major cities across the United States and Canada in which thousands took to the streets with chants and signs to protest the victim-blaming attitude reflected in Constable Michael Sanguinetti's comments. Even though the officer later apologized, his comments set off hundreds of organized SlutWalks, starting with the April 3 march in Toronto. The foundation of SlutWalk is the rejection of the idea that women's sexuality, sexual behavior, or sexual expression is the cause of sexual violence against women or of rape culture. Marchers come together in their rejection and condemnation of victim-blaming. SlutWalks proved to be controversial, even among feminists, however, in part because some feminists reject the idea that "slut" can be co-opted or repurposed because of its sexist and patriarchal origins. Rebecca Traister, for example, wrote that

> [s]cantily clad marching seems weirdly blind to the race, class, and body-image issues that usually (rightly) obsess young femi-nists and seems inhospitable to scads of women who, for various reasons, might not feel it logical or comfortable to express their

revulsion at victim-blaming by donning bustiers. So whereas the mission of SlutWalks is crucial, the package is confusing and leaves young feminists open to the very kinds of attacks they are battling.

Many women of color also pointed out that because of racialized stereotypes that construct them as hypersexualized, they have an even more ambivalent relationship to the term "slut."

A controversial activist strategy related to combating rape and sexual assault is the practice of posting (physically and/or virtually) the names of alleged perpetrators. In the past, names might have been posted on a photocopied flyer and posted in women's restrooms or in residence halls on campus, whereas now the names might circulate online. In spring of 2014 an unknown person or persons posted a list of four names under the heading "Rapists on Campus" around the campus of Columbia University. The act received national attention, in large part because Columbia was already in the news as a result of 23 students filing a federal complaint against the university alleging the mishandling of sexual assault cases. According to CNN, the complaint alleges "the Ivy League university discouraged students from reporting sexual assaults, allowed perpetrators to remain on campus, sanctioned inadequate disciplinary actions for perpetrators and discriminated against students based on their sexual orientation" (Crook). Whereas some defended this approach as a way of empowering students to protect themselves when the university administration had failed to do so, others rightly pointed out this tactic's potential for abuse.

Another way that feminist activism around violence has changed in the last 40 years is that it increasingly includes (and is sometimes led by) men. The White Ribbon Campaign, based in Canada, describes itself as the "world's largest movement of men and boys working to end violence against women and girls, promote gender equity, healthy relationships and a new vision of masculinity." Primarily educational in its focus, the White Ribbon Campaign offers workshops, conferences, and trainings. An organization whose focus is more parallel to Take Back the Night and SlutWalks is Walk a Mile in Her Shoes, which is an international men's march that features men walking in high heels. While lauded for raising men's awareness of gendered violence and facilitating their active involvement in the movement against it, this event has been criticized for not always being thoughtful about the way it is organized and advertised. More specifically, some local marches have played up the idea that men walking in "women's" shoes is funny, thereby reinforcing rather than challenging traditional constructions of masculinity. One response to this is for march organizers to challenge attendees' assumptions by reminding them that not all women wear heels, and not all who wear heels are women. Another example is the activist group Men Can Stop Rape, a nonprofit organization engaging in education programs, awareness building campaigns, and training projects with the goal of combating men's violence against women. The organization "mobilizes men to use their strength for creating cultures free from violence, especially men's violence against women," and operates from the assumption that men are "vital allies with the will and character to make healthy choices and foster safe, equitable relationships" ("What We Do"). Their 2014 "Take a Stand" campaign provides strategies for bystander intervention—ways men (and women) can support women who are in uncomfortable or dangerous situations (see Figure 5.2 for an example of a public awareness campaign of this nature).

Activism around street harassment has further gained new visibility in recent years as a result of the creation of **Hollaback**. Hollaback, which is described as a "non-profit and movement to end street harassment," is a good example of activism that has been enhanced by technological innovation. According to the website, "[a]t Hollaback!, we leverage technology to bring voice to an issue that historically has been silenced, and to build leadership within this movement to break the silence." It was inspired by one woman who was so fed up by her experience of street harassment that she decided to take out her phone and snap a picture of the man who was masturbating on the subway while staring at her. She initially took her complaint to the police, but they did nothing, so she posted the photo online, and the story eventually got considerable media attention. In response, a group of young people decided to start a blog where people could share their experiences of street harassment. From there, the project has grown to include the creation and dissemination of a mobile app that people can use to document the nature and location of street harassment. On an individual level, it can

Figure 5.2 Bystander Intervention

Source: Men Can Stop Rape (www.mencanstoprape.org)

be empowering for someone who has experienced harassment to fight back by documenting their experience and connecting with others who have had similar experiences. On a broader level, to do so also contributes to the collection of data that can be used when approaching police and policy makers about addressing the issue. Importantly, Hollaback employs an intersectional approach to street harassment, rightly pointing out that street harassment can be "sexist, racist, transphobic, homophobic, ableist, sizeist and/or classist. It is an expression of the interlocking and overlapping oppressions we face and it functions as a means to silence our voices and 'keep us in our place.'"

Case Study: The Spark Movement

In 2010, the American Psychological Association published the "Report of the APA Task Force on the Sexualization of Young Girls," the results of work conducted by a subcommittee of the national organization of the field of psychology. The group was charged to

> examine and summarize the best psychological theory, research, and clinical experience addressing the sexualization of girls via media and other cultural messages, including the prevalence of these messages and their impact on girls, and include attention to the role and impact of race/ethnicity and socioeconomic status.

Defining early sexualization as the objectification of girls and women, exclusive value attached to the sexual attributes of individuals, and inappropriate imposition of sexuality on a person, the group's report documented the ample evidence of sexualization of young girls, as well as the cognitive, emotional, psychological, and physical harms caused by early sexualization. The group made recommendations for future directions for research, public policy, practice, education, and training, and as a result of that report, the Spark Movement emerged.

The Spark Movement describes itself as "a girl-fueled, intergenerational activist organization working to ignite and foster an antiracist gender justice movement to end violence against women and girls and promote girls' healthy sexuality, self-empowerment and well-being." They do so "by providing feminist, girl-focused training, consulting services, curricula and resources." Their website has pages that are addressed to and for girls, while other pages are for adult educators and activists who work with girls. The movement illustrates feminist praxis because of its blending of research, education, training, and "everyday activism," such as publicly critiquing those products that objectify, stereotype, and demean girls and women through protest, social media, or other methods. Some of the organization's victories include launching a Change.org petition asking *Seventeen* Magazine to include at least one photo spread each issue that included "unaltered images" (Bluhm). Other recent efforts include providing resources for tagging gender stereotyped toys in store aisles with the note "You've Been Sparked" to invite shoppers to recognize such stereotypes or sexualized products, and Spark Activist Theater, with online toolkits available to launch activist performances within one's community. Another ongoing project involves a collaboration with Google's Field Trip app called "Women on the Map." Those involved in the project identified and wrote profiles of over 100 women around the world who have made history, and then linked them to particular geographical spots. According to the Spark Movement website, "[w]hen you download Field Trip and turn on Spark's Women on the Map, your phone will buzz when you approach a place where a woman made history."

The Spark Movement directs activist efforts through its blog (which features posts by both girls and adults), recommendations for taking action (such as a recent fundraising campaigns directed at supporting girl activists), and documenting efforts to intervene in harmful practices or correcting gaps in education and training (such as a national effort to educate athletic coaches about sexual assault prevention). The work of the Spark Movement illustrates how activism can emerge from research and inform policy and practice. It also shows that awareness of injustice and the agency to address injustice is not the sole province of adults.

Misconception Alert

I'm only one person and can't make a difference, being an activist is a full-time job, activism is all about marching in the streets. When taking a Women's and Gender Studies course, students sometimes feel overwhelmed and unsure how to take action. As this chapter demonstrates, however, there are large- and small-scale activist efforts that any one individual can take—and that *allies* are critical to the achievement of social justice.

End of Chapter Elements

Evaluating Prior Knowledge

1. Think about past educational experiences you've had in school. To what degree have you seen intersections between your classroom learning, or academic knowledge, and your lived experience? Which classes most commonly "translated" into your non-school life? Which seemed disconnected?

2. Think about the key terms presented in this chapter, including feminist praxis, ally, backlash, rape culture, postfeminism, and activism. Which of these have you used previously in your everyday vocabulary? Which take on new meanings in the context of this chapter material?

Application Exercises

1. Spend a day paying careful attention to gender dynamics in your own life—to interactions with friends, family, and coworkers; to your workplace culture, practices, or discourse; to your own use of language and ways of communicating. Framing your discussion in terms of feminist praxis, reflect on how you see threshold concepts from the texts manifested in your everyday experiences and how you might engage in "everyday activism."

2. What are the activist organizations on your campus and in your community? What issues are these organizations working on, and how? Do you know anyone who is connected to one or more of them? What opportunities do they provide for getting involved? In your opinion, are there pressing issues on your campus and/or in your community that are *not* currently being addressed by an activist organization? If so, what are they?

3. Visit the website of one of the following organizations. In what ways do you see the organization engaged in feminist praxis?
   a. http://9to5.org/
   b. www.incite-national.org/home

    c.   www.feministfrequency.com/
    d.   www.transequality.org/
    e.   www.ihollaback.org/
    f.   http://upsettingrapeculture.com/
    g.   www.womensmediacenter.com
    h.   www.onebillionrising.org/
    I.   www.knowyourix.org/

Skills Assessments

1. Read Abigail Jones' article, "The Fight to End Period Shaming Is Going Mainstream," published in *Newsweek* in April of 2016, and write an analytical response that uses concepts and framework from Chapter 5 as a lens. What forms is menstrual activism taking, and in what institutions, both in the U.S. and in other parts of the world? How, where, and why is backlash experienced by menstrual activists? In what ways is menstrual activism informed by research and data?

2. Select an anti-feminist or pro-feminist website and thoroughly explore the site, paying attention to both the content of the site and how the site functions. Answer the following short-answer prompts with several paragraphs each, drawing on specific examples from the website.

   a. Summarize the overall point of view of the website.

   b. How does the website connect to a broader feminist movement?

   c. What opportunities for activism/action beyond reading does the website offer?

   d. How does the website situate feminism within a broader framework of interlocking oppressions/intersectionality?

   e. Describe how the website acknowledges the social construction of gender, privilege, and oppression (or resists such a construction).

   f. Describe the role that community and/or collaboration plays in the website. Is it supported or acknowledged? Is it suggested as a value?

   g. Analyze the persona of the website—that is, analyze the tone, mood, and "personality" of the website. Here, you should draw from both visual and textual cues that contribute to the overall persona of the website.

h. Finally, drawing on your previous answers, evaluate the website's effectiveness as an anti-feminist or pro-feminist site. This answer should be longer than your previous answers, and should synthesize the elements from questions a through g.

Discussion Questions

1. Think about some of the recommendations made throughout this chapter for small- and large-scale activism. Are there ways that you have engaged in activism? Describe your previous experiences.
2. What are the major barriers or challenges to social change? What are the major barriers or challenges to your personal involvement in activism for social justice?
3. One of the goals of a feminist perspective is "the importance of locating oneself within structures of privilege and oppression" and to "analyze" how systems of privilege and oppression operate in a number of contexts (for example, in one's personal life and relationships, in experiences of one's body, in societal institutions, etc.). How does your personal social location connect to a larger social structure? What forms of feminist praxis would be most appropriate and comfortable for you to engage in, based on that location? Which would be uncomfortable and why?

Writing Prompts

1. Feminist praxis is the ability to apply and/or enact feminist theoretical principles to your own life and experience. Create a self-reflection or narrative that demonstrates your participation in and analysis of a feminist event or act of social change of which you were a part. This will include supporting documentation (e.g., photos, documents, Internet coverage) of the event/action. Write a personal narrative reflection describing and analyzing a particular experience/event/action in which you have participated that meets the criteria of feminism action offered in this chapter. Collect and

assemble a series of artifacts that document your participation in this event. Write an essay in which you:

a. Explain the event
b. Explain/describe your documentation and how they represent the event
c. Describe your role in the event
d. Address your perception of the outcome of the event
e. Connect your experience in this event to the definition of feminist action

2. Building on Megan Seely's "action plan" in *Fight Like a Girl*, review the first three of her twelve-step approach to engaging in feminist praxis.

1) Define the issue that you want to raise awareness on;
2) Work with other activists, and dialogue the issue to clarify the feminist analysis of the problem and the solution; and
3) Decide what action to take.

(20)

Write an essay in which you get started on a praxis plan that uses these first three steps, documenting your interest in the issue (and demonstrating familiarity with research and evidence on that issue); researching the current work (and organizations or groups involved in it) on the topic; and laying out action steps you could take to effect change.

Notes

1   www.change.org/petitions/sprint-improve-policies-to-keep-domestic-violence
     victims-safe
2   www.change.org/petitions/south-africa-take-action-to-stop-corrective-rape

Works Cited

9to5.org. "We Need the Paycheck Fairness Act." 9to5.org. http://9to5.org/we-need-the-paycheck-fairness-act/. Accessed 7 July 2017.

"About Take Back the Night." *Take Back the Night.org.* 2013. https://takebackthenight.org/. Accessed 7 July 2017.

"About: What Is Hollaback?" *Hollaback! You Have the Power to End Street Harassment.* 2014. www.ihollaback.org/about/. Accessed 7 July 2017.

APA Task Force on the Sexualization of Young Girls. "Report of the Task Force on the Sexualization of Young Girls." *American Psychological Association*. 2010. www.apa.org/pi/women/programs/girls/report.aspx. Accessed 7 July 2017.

Arter, Neesha. "Navigating the Broken System Was Worse than the Rape Itself." *New York Times: Women in the World*. 4 February 2016. http://nytlive.nytimes.com/womenintheworld/2016/02/04/amanda-nguyen-is-taking-the-fight-for-sexual-violence-survivors-civil-rights-all-the-way-to-the-white-house/. Accessed 7 July 2017.

Ayvazian, Andrea. "Interrupting the Cycle of Oppression: The Role of Allies as Agents of Change." *Race, Class, and Gender in the United States: An Integrated Study*. Ed. Paula Rothenberg. 7th edition. Worth, 2007, pp. 724–730.

Bartky, Sandra. "Foucault, Feminism, and the Modernization of Patriarchal Power." *The Politics of Women's Bodies*. Ed. Rose Weitz. Oxford University Press, 1998, pp. 25–45.

Belkin, Lisa. "The Opt-Out Revolution," *New York Times*, 26 October 2003, www.nytimes.com/2003/10/26/magazine/the-opt-out-revolution.html. Accessed 19 December 2017.

Bennett, Jessica. "How Not to Be Manterrupted in Meetings." *Time*. 20 January 2015.

Berg, Alex. "Stop Using Women and Girls to Justify Transphobia." *Huffington Post*. 23 February 2017. www.huffingtonpost.com/entry/stop-using-women-and-girls-to-justify-transphobia_us_58ae0c33e4b01406012f7e80. Accessed 7 July 2017.

Berger, Michele, and Cheryl Radeloff. *Transforming Scholarship: Why Women's and Gender Studies Students Are Changing Themselves and the World*. Routledge, 2011.

Bess, Gabby. "The Sexual Assault Survivor Saving Untested Rape Kits from the Trash." *Broadly*. 2 February 2016. https://broadly.vice.com/en_us/article/4xkzwj/the-sexual-assault-survivor-saving-untested-rape-kits-from-the-trash. Accessed July 7 2017.

Bluhm, Julia. "*Seventeen Magazine:* Give Girls Images of Real Girls!" *Change.org*. July 2012. www.change.org/p/seventeen-magazine-give-girls-images-of-real-girls. Accessed 7 July 2017.

Bunch, Charlotte. "Not by Degrees: Feminist Theory and Education." *Feminist Theory: A Reader*. Eds. Wendy Kolmar and Frances Bartkowski. 4th edition. McGraw Hill, 2013, pp. 12–15.

Cauterucci, Christina. "The U.S. Is One Step Closer to a Federal Sexual Assault Survivors' Bill of Rights." *Slate*. 7 September 2016. www.slate.com/blogs/xx_factor/2016/09/07/congress_unanimously_passes_a_sexual_assault_survivors_bill_of_rights.html. Accessed 7 July 2017.

Clark, Pamela. "35 Practical Steps Men Can Take to Support Feminism." *XO Jane*. 13 June 2014, www.xojane.com/issues/feminism-men-practical-steps. Accessed 7 July 2017.

Cobble, Dorothy Sue, Linda Gordon, and Astrid Henry. *Feminism Unfinished*. W.W. Norton, 2014.

Crook, Lawrence. "Alleged 'Rapist List' Appears around Columbia University." CNN.com. 15 May 2014. www.cnn.com/2014/05/14/us/columbia-university-flier-rapes/index.html. Accessed 7 July 2017.

Desmond-Harris, Jenee. "Implicit Bias Means We're All Probably at Least a Little Bit Racist." *Vox*. 15 August 2016. www.vox.com/2014/12/26/7443979/racism-implicit-racial-bias. Accessed 7 July 2017.

Douglas, Susan J. *Enlightened Sexism: The Seductive Message that Feminism's Work Is Done*. Henry Holt, 2010.

The Education of Shelby Knox. Directed by Marion Lipschitz and Rose Rosenblatt, Women Make Movies, 2005.

Faludi, Susan. *Backlash: The Undeclared War against American Women*. Crown, 1991.

Geena Davis Institute on Gender in the Media. "Research Informs and Empowers." *SeeJane.org*. 27 May 2014. https://seejane.org/research-informs-empowers/. Accessed 7 July 2017.

Ginty, Molly. "Detroit Team Shrinks Breastfeeding Disparities." *Women's eNews*. 22 June 2015. http://womensenews.org/2015/06/detroit-team-shrinks-breastfeeding-disparities/. Accessed 7 July 2017.

Goodale, Gloria. "40 Years Later, Title IX Is Still Fighting Perception It Hurts Men's Sports." *Christian Science Monitor*. 23 June 2012. www.csmonitor.com/USA/Education/2012/0623/40-years-later-Title-IX-is-still-fighting-perception-it-hurt-men-s-sports. Accessed 7 July 2017.

Graff, E.J. "Building a Respect Culture." *American Prospect*. 9 January 2013. http://prospect.org/article/building-respect-culture. Accessed 7 July 2017.

Guerrilla Girls. "Guerrilla Girls: Reinventing the 'F' Word: Feminism." 2011. www.guerrillagirls.com/#open. Accessed 7 July 2017.

Hesse-Biber, Sharlene. *Feminist Research Practice: A Primer*. SAGE, 2014.

INCITE!: Women of Color against Violence, eds. *Color of Violence: The INCITE! Anthology*. South End Press, 2006.

Johnson, Stefanie K., and David R. Hekman. "Women and Minorities Are Penalized for Promoting Diversity." *Harvard Business Review*. 23 March 2016. https://hbr.org/2016/03/women-and-minorities-are-penalized-for-promoting-diversity. Accessed 7 July 2017.

Levin, Amy. *Questions for a New Century: Women's Studies and Integrative Learning, a Report to the National Women's Studies Association*. 2007. www.nwsa.org/Files/Resources/WS_Integrative_Learning_Levine.pdf. Accessed 7 July 2017.

Lorde, Audre. *Sister Outsider*. Crossing Press, 1984.

Martin, Courtney E. "Girls Tweeting (Not Twerking) Their Way to Power." *New York Times*. 4 September 2013.

McRobbie, Angela. "Post-Feminism and Popular Culture." *Feminist Media Studies*, vol. 4, no. 3, 2004, pp. 255–264.

National Center for Education Statistics. "Fast Facts: Title IX." *Institute of Education Sciences*. 2011. https://nces.ed.gov/fastfacts/display.asp?id=93. Accessed 7 July 2017.

National Organization for Women. "Founding: Setting the Stage." 3 June 2013. Web.

Ohm, Rachel. "Colby Student's 'Party with Consent' Gets the Nod at 30 Campuses." *Portland Press Herald*. 25 May 2014.

Parents and Friends of Lesbians and Gays. "Guide to Being a Straight Ally." 1st edition.

Sarkeesian, Anita. "Retro Sexism and Uber Ironic Advertising." *Feminist Frequency*. 21 September 2012. https://feministfrequency.com/video/retro-sexism-uber-ironic-advertising/. Accessed 7 July 2017.

Seely, Megan. *Fight Like a Girl: How to Be a Fearless Feminist*. New York University Press, 2007.

Shrewsbury, Carolyn. "What Is Feminist Pedagogy?" *Women's Studies Quarterly*, vol. 3, no. 4, 1993, pp. 8–16.

Simonson, Jocelyn. "Bail Keeps These Moms in Jail on Mother's Day. So Strangers Are Posting It for Them." *Washington Post.* 12 May 2017.

Smith, Stacy L., Marc Choueiti, and Jessica Stern. "Occupational Aspirations: What Are G-Rated Films Teaching Children about the World of Work?" *Geena Davis Institute on Gender in Media.* 2012. https://seejane.org/wp-content/uploads/key-findings-occupational-aspirations-2013.pdf. Accessed 7 July 2017.

Spark Movement. "About Us." *Spark Movement.* April 2017. www.sparkmovement.org/about/. Accessed 7 July 2017.

Traister, Rebecca. "Ladies, We Have a Problem." *New York Times.* 20 July 2011.

UNICEF. "The State of the World's Children: Women and Children, The Double Dividend of Gender Equality." 2007. www.unicef.org/publications/files/The_State_of_the_Worlds__Children__2007_e.pdf. Accessed 26 August 2013.

Valenti, Jessica. *Full Frontal Feminism: A Young Woman's Guide to Why Feminism Matters.* Seal Press, 2007.

——. "SlutWalks and the Future of Feminism." *Capital Times.* 8 June 2011. Web.

Warner, Judith. "The Opt-Out Generation Wants Back In." *New York Times.* 7 August 2013.

Weiss, Sasha. "The Power of #yesallwomen." *New Yorker.* 26 May 2014.

"What We Do: Our Mission and Vision." *Men Can Stop Rape.* www.mencanstoprape.org/Our-Mission-History/. Accessed 5 June 2014.

White Ribbon Australia. "White Ribbon Australia: Fact Sheet 1—Origin of the Campaign." 2017. www.whiteribbon.org.au/understand-domestic-violence/facts-violence-women/. Accessed 7 July 2017.

Women's Sports Foundation. "Title IX Myths and Facts." 2011. www.womenssportsfoundation.org/advocate/title-ix-issues/what-is-title-ix/title-ix-myths-facts/. Accessed 7 July 2017.

Yoo, Lindsey. "Solidarity Is for White Women and Asian People Are Funny." *Filthy Freedom: Race, Sexuality, Culture.* 22 August 2013. www.filthyfreedom.com/blog/solidarity-is-for-white-women-and-asian-people-are-funny. Accessed 7 July 2017.

Zeilinger, Julie. *A Little F'd Up: Why Feminism Is Not a Dirty Word.* Seal Press, 2012.

Suggested Readings

Ayvazian, Andrea. "Interrupting the Cycle of Oppression: The Role of Allies as Agents of Change." In *Race, Class, and Gender in the United States: An Integrated Study.* Ed. Paula Rothenberg. 7th edition. Worth, 2007, pp. 724–730.

Baumgardner, Jennifer, and Amy Richards. *Grassroots: A Field Guide for Feminist Activism.* Farrar, Strauss, and Giroux, 2004.

Baxandall, Rosalyn, and Linda Gordon, eds. *Dear Sisters: Dispatches from the Women's Liberation Movement.* Basic Books, 2001.

Bennett, Jessica. *Feminist Fight Club.* Harper Wave, 2016.

——. "How Not to Be Manterrupted in Meetings." *Time.* 20 January 2015.

Collins, Patricia Hill. *On Intellectual Activism.* Temple University Press, 2012.

Desmond-Harris, Jenee. "Implicit Bias Means We're All Probably At Least a Little Bit Racist." *Vox*. 15 August 2016. www.vox.com/2014/12/26/7443979/racism-implicit-racial-bias. Accessed 7 July 2017.

Feinberg, JonaRose Jaffe. "Postfeminism." In *The Women's Movement Today: An Encyclopedia of Third-Wave Feminism*. Ed. Leslie Heywood. Greenwood Press, 2006.

Finley, Laura, and Emily Reynolds Stringer. *Beyond Burning Bras: Feminist Activism for Everyone*. Praeger, 2010.

Frank, Gillian. "Anti-Trans Bathroom Nightmare Has Its Roots in Racial Segregation." *Slate*. 10 November 2015. www.slate.com/blogs/outward/2015/11/10/anti_trans_bathroom_propaganda_has_roots_in_racial_segregation.html. Accessed 7 July 2017.

Hernandez, Daisy, and Bushra Rehman, eds. *Colonize This! Young Women of Color on Today's Feminism*. Seal Press, 2002.

Kingcade, Tyler. "This Is Why Every College is Talking About Bystander Intervention." *HuffPost*. 8 February 2016. www.huffingtonpost.com/entry/colleges-bystander-intervention_us_56abc134e4b0010e80ea021d. Accessed 7 July 2017.

Marcotte, Amanda. *Get Opinionated: A Progressive's Guide to Finding Your Voice (and Taking a Little Action)*. Seal Press, 2010.

Parents and Friends of Lesbians and Gays. "Guide to Being a Straight Ally." www.pflag.org/sites/default/files/guide%20to%20being%20a%20straight%20ally.pdf. Accessed 7 July 2017.

Rush, Curtis. "Cop Apologizes for 'Sluts' Remark at Law School." *Toronto Star*. 18 February 2011.

Stampler, Laura. "SlutWalks Sweep the Nation." *Huffington Post*. 20 April 2011. www.huffingtonpost.com/2011/04/20/slutwalk-united-states-city_n_851725.html. Accessed 7 July 2017.

Stewart, Nikki Ayanna. "Transform the World: What You Can Do with a Degree in Women's Studies." *Ms.*, Spring 2007, pp. 65–66.

Sullivan, J. Courtney, and Courtney E. Martin. *Click: When We Knew We Were Feminists*. Perseus Books, 2010.

Turner, Cory. "Bias Isn't Just a Police Problem, It's a Preschool Problem." *NPR*. 28 September 2016. www.npr.org/sections/ed/2016/09/28/495488716/bias-isnt-just-a-police-problem-its-a-preschool-problem. Accessed 7 July 2017.

Valenti, Jessica. *Full Frontal Feminism: A Young Woman's Guide to Why Feminism Matters*. Seal Press, 2007.

Zeilinger, Julie. *A Little F'd Up: Why Feminism Is Not a Dirty Word*. Seal Press, 2012.

Glossary

#notallmen: A Twitter hashtag created by men's rights activists to contradict the effort to make visible and to critique sexism and violence

#yesallwomen: A Twitter hashtag created in response to #notallmen to call out misogynist violence and sexism

ableism: Institutionalized practices and individual actions and beliefs that posit the able-bodied as the norm. It works to promote negative images of disabled women, such as the myth that it is not possible for someone with a disability to have a positive and equal relationship

act-like-a-man box: Paul Kivel's articulation of masculine gender norms and expectations that men are socialized to adhere to

activism: Conscious efforts to raise awareness about a social problem and and/or to bring about social change

allies: Defined by Andrea Ayvazian as "a member of a dominant group in our society who works to dismantle any form of oppression from which she or he receives the benefit"

backlash: Popularized by journalist Susan Faludi in her book of the same name, and refers to media sources who claimed that feminism was to blame for women's dissatisfaction with the results of feminist activism. Characterizes these claims as part of a larger cultural resistance to true liberation and equality for women

beauty myth: In Naomi Wolf's 1991 book of the same name, she argued that orienting women's attention to their physical appearances is as much about directing women's behavior and time as it is surveilling their appearances and conformity to a narrowly defined ideal of female beauty

bootstraps myth: The idea that upward class mobility is not only possible but probable, and that individual will and hard work are the only requisites for moving out of poverty and into the middle class

bystander intervention: A technique for preventing rape and sexual assault, which teaches people (bystanders) to intervene when they spot a situation (on the street, at a party, in their residence hall, etc.) which seems headed in that direction

cisgender: A person who experiences congruence between their gender assignment and gender identity

cissexual: A person who experiences congruence between their assigned sex and their gender identity

classism: Oppression based on social class or socioeconomic status

compulsory heterosexuality: Social messaging, policies, and practices that privilege heterosexual behavior and identity

consumer capitalism: An economic and social theory building on the definition of capitalism as an economic system based on private goods, private property, the accumulation of wealth, and free market economics and laws of supply and demand. Consumer capitalism adapts this economic theory to cultural value attached to aspirational consumption and consumerism

contraception: Reproductive technologies that prevent pregnancy

crowdsourcing: Social media platforms that allow multiple users to contribute to the building of a text, database, or website

double bind: When an individual faces two equally problematic choices (e.g., for a woman, being sexually active, or choosing not to be sexually active)

egalitarian: A belief in human equality, especially with respect to social, political, and economic rights and privileges

electoral politics: Processes associated with the democratic principles of representative government

Equal Rights Amendment (ERA): Proposed constitutional amendment introduced in 1923 as an effort to cast in policy equal rights for women. It reads: "[e]quality of rights under the law shall not be denied or abridged by the United States or by any state on account of sex." The amendment was never ratified

everyday activism: The notion that activism happens on a daily basis, with everyday actions that may reject or challenge oppressive practices

Family and Medical Leave Act (FMLA): An act passed in 1993 that guarantees U.S. employees twelve weeks of unpaid leave to attend to family responsibilities or personal illness

female genital cutting/female circumcision: Procedures involving partial or total removal or modification of the external female genitalia or other injury to the female genital organs for cultural or other nonmedical reasons

feminine mystique: Concept introduced by Betty Friedan in her 1963 book of the same name, arguing that domestic responsibilities alone were unfulfilling to middle-class, educated women

femininity: Socially defined principles associated with the feminine gender

feminism/feminist: The social and political movement advocating for women's equality

feminist action: Associated with achieving the goals and aims of feminism

Freudian: Refers to the work of Sigmund Freud, the "father of psychoanalysis," who developed influential theories about human psychology

gender: A social concept referring to a complex set of characteristics and behaviors prescribed for a particular sex by society and learned through the socialization process. The socially treated expectations for the looks, behavior, and functions of that sex are, however, often perceived as innate and not learned. Identifies people as feminine or masculine; *see also* social constructionism

gender assignment and gender status: The gender assigned to a baby when born, translated into gender-specific treatment and socialization throughout childhood

gender comportment/expression: The expression of the gendered sense of self, which Susan Stryker defines as "bodily actions such as how we use our voices, cross our legs, hold our heads, wear our clothes, dance around the room, throw a ball, walk in high heels"

gender display: The presentation of self as a kind of gendered person through dress, cosmetics, adornments, and both permanent and reversible body markers

gender identity: A person's gendered sense of self

gender ranking: Social value attached to masculine and feminine attributes (with higher value attached to masculinity)

gender socialization: The processes (social feedback, institutional organization, policies) that communicate socially appropriate roles for boys and men and girls and women; *see also* social constructionism

gender wage gap: The common gap between men's and women's earnings, with women generally receiving lower pay

gendered double standard: A double standard of behavior for men and women (e.g., in the workplace and in personal relationships), where the same behavior is judged very differently depending on whether the person engaging in the behavior is a man or woman

hegemonic feminism: According to Chela Sandoval, a feminism that was "white led, marginalize[d] the activism and world views of women of color, focuse[d] mainly on the United States, and treat[ed] sexism as the ultimate oppression"

heteronormativity: Cultural, material, and institutional messages and policies that validate and encourage heterosexuality

heterosexism: Attitudes, actions, and institutional practices that privilege heterosexuality and subordinate people on the basis of their gay, lesbian, bisexual, or transgender orientation

Hollaback: A nonprofit online-based activist movement to end street harassment

homophobia: The irrational fear, distrust, hatred of, and discrimination against homosexuals

honor killings: A tradition whereby a man is obliged to kill a close female blood relative if she does something that is believed to tarnish the family honor

horizontal hostility: Whereby members of marginalized groups police each other's behavior and/or appearance. Horizontal hostility happens when a member of a marginalized group identifies with the values of the dominant group

horizontal segregation of labor: Describes the segregation of men and women into different occupational/professional fields

ideology: Ideas, attitudes, and values that represent the interests of a group of people. Cultures generally support a dominant ideology, as well as several other minor or less powerful ideological systems. People who accept the dominant beliefs of a culture are more successful within the culture and thus part of the dominant ideology. The dominant ideology includes the ideas, attitudes, and values that represent the interests of the dominant group(s); for example, the ideological role of the idealized nuclear family is to devalue other family forms

infanticide: The murder of infants; historically a strategy for reproductive control in the absence of other forms of contraceptive technology

informed consent: The practice by which participants in modern-day medical research studies receive a substantial education about the potential side effects and outcomes of participation in such a study

institutions: Social arrangements that have survived over time and become standard or "normalized" so that we forget they are only one possible response or way of organizing a situation. For example, the nuclear family, the military, and a capitalist economy all provide formulas for routine action (like scripts for the actors), backed up by ideology that stresses their rightness as well as their being the only possibility

internalized oppression: Attitudes and behavior of some oppressed people that reflect the negative, harmful, stereotypical beliefs of the dominant group directed at oppressed people; when a victim of oppression accepts her situation as natural, normal, or deserved and enables her oppression to take place at least partly through her own efforts; the behaviors include holding negative beliefs about people in their own group. An example of internalized sexism is the view of some women that they and other women are inferior to men, which causes them to adopt oppressive attitudes and behaviors toward women

intersectionality: The ways multiple forms of oppression and identity interact to create someone's experience of and access to social influence and individual and institutional power

intersex: Defined by the Intersex Society of North America as "a general term used for a variety of conditions in which a person is born with a reproductive or sexual anatomy that doesn't seem to fit the typical definitions of female or male"

intimate partner violence: Physical, emotional, sexual, or other forms of violence and abuse that take place between intimate partners

ladder of engagement: Within the context of activism, Courtney Martin refers to this process whereby "someone signs a petition, before long they're creating their own, then running a full-fledged campaign"

LGBTQ: Acronym for lesbian, gay, bisexual, transgender, and queer or questioning; reflects a range of sexual and gender identities and orientations distinct from traditional heterosexuality

macro/micro: Macro refers to viewing social issues from a structural, institutional, and global perspective; micro refers to the individual or local perspective on such issues

mansplaining: Popularized by Rebecca Solnit and defined by urbandictionary.com as "[t]o explain in a patronizing manner, assuming total ignorance on the part of those listening"

marked and unmarked: One of the markers of privilege is invisibility, and one of the ways this invisibility manifests is through identity terms and labels. In other words, dominant groups that are a part of the mythical norm have the privilege of being unmarked and unremarkable because of their presumed neutrality and normality

masculine god language: Linguistic and imagery conventions referring to and conceptualizing God as male, despite theologians' claims that God is not to be considered in sexual terms at all, despite such terminology

masculinity: The set of characteristics or attributes traditionally ascribed to maleness

mythical norm: A dominant group and a marginalized group; one group is considered the norm, with their counterpart being the "other." According to Audre Lorde, the mythical norm is "usually defined as white, thin, male, young, heterosexual, christian, and financially secure"

objectification: Attitudes and behaviors by which people treat others as if they were "things"; the objectification of women through advertising images

occupational segregation of labor: Explains the pay gap by noting that even when men and women have the same occupation, women tend to be represented in lower ranks than men within the same occupation. Explains the pay gap in terms of the tendency for occupations mainly held by men to have substantially higher pay rates and status as compared to those mainly held by women. Cf. vertical segregation of labor

online activism: A form of feminist activism taking place online, including social media activities, online petitions, and community building

oppression: Prejudice and discrimination directed toward a group and promoted by the ideologies and practices of multiple social institutions. The critical elements differentiating oppression from simple prejudice and discrimination are that it is a group phenomenon and that institutional power and authority are used to support prejudices and enforce discriminatory behaviors in systematic ways. Everyone is socialized to participate in oppressive practices, either as direct and indirect perpetrators or passive beneficiaries, or—as with some oppressed peoples—by directing discriminatory behaviors at members of one's own group

opting out: Emerged in the 1990s; suggests that feminism had failed in its aims to liberate women through access to education and economic self-sufficiency and that, instead, professional and educated women were returning to stay-at-home motherhood

patriarchy: Literally, rule of the fathers; a family, social group, or society in which men hold power and are dominant figures; a social order in which men, for the most part, have primary access to resources and hence to power and authority that they use to maintain themselves in power and resources

the personal is political: A feminist and women's studies idea that came about in the second wave; it is a starting point for explaining how things taken as personal or idiosyncratic have broader social, political, and economic causes and consequences. In other words, situations that we are encouraged to view as personal are actually part of broader cultural patterns and arrangements

postfeminism: The premise that the aims of feminist movement(s) have been achieved and that we live in a society where women experience a full range of choices equal to those of men

praxis: The intersection of theory and practice, involving a visible and deliberate set of actions informed by theory, by research, and by evidence

privilege: Benefits and power from institutional inequalities; individuals and groups may be privileged without realizing, recognizing, or even wanting it

racism: Racial prejudice and discrimination supported by institutional power and authority. In the United States, racism is based on the ideology of white (European) supremacy and is used to the advantage of white people and the disadvantage of peoples of color. Also, a system of advantage based on race. In this sense, racism is not a personal ideology based on racial prejudice, but a system involving cultural messages and institutional practices and policies as well as the beliefs and actions of individuals. Also defined by antiracist educators as "prejudice plus power"

rape culture: As defined by Lynn Phillips, a lecturer in communication at the University of Massachusetts–Amherst, "a culture in which dominant cultural ideologies, media images, social practices, and societal institutions support and condone sexual abuse by normalizing, trivializing and eroticizing male violence against women and blaming victims for their own abuse"

Rape Shield Laws: A set of policies that emerged in the 1970s and 1980s on the state level preventing a rape victim's past sexual history from being used as evidence in a rape trial

Roe v. Wade: Landmark 1973 Supreme Court case that made abortion legal

sex: The specific biological categories of female and male; identification by sex is based on a variety of factors including chromosomal patterns, hormonal makeup, and genital structures

sex/gender system: A set of interrelated biological, institutional, psychological, and ideological elements that classifies people by biological sex; organizes a division of labor that patterns productive and reproductive activities; instills within individuals an internalized self-definition as woman or man; and promotes itself as true, proper, and appropriate

sexism: Material and ideological prejudice and discrimination based on sex and gender enacted and supported by institutional authority

sexual orientation: A term suggesting a person's preferred sexuality

slacktivism: A derisive term that has been coined to reflect what some have critiqued as "easy" actions that can be taken through, for example, social media, and that sometimes become a substitute for what many perceive as more demanding forms of activism such as letter-writing campaigns, lobbying legislators, protests and rallies, or other types of advocacy

slut shaming: Social messaging that judges women's sexual conduct

SlutWalk: A grassroots and social media campaign led by Heather Jarvis and Sonya Barnett that emerged in major cities across the United States and Canada, in which organized thousands took to the streets with chants and signs to protest victim-blaming attitudes for sexual assault

social constructionism: The view that gender, race, and sexual orientation are defined by human beings operating out of particular cultural contexts and ideologies. The definitions are systematically transmitted, and attitudes and behaviors purported to be appropriate are learned through childhood socialization and life experience. In this view, for example, heterosexuality, manhood, and womanhood are learned—socially constructed—not innate

socioeconomic status (SES): Economic and social indicators of groups generally defined by a combination of income, occupation, educational attainment, and accumulated wealth; sometimes referred to as social class, SES is also communicated by various language, cultural, and taste markers/associations

sociological imagination: Foundational concept of the discipline of sociology posited by C. Wright Mills, who argues that "the individual can understand his own experience and gauge his own fate only by locating himself within his period, that he can know his own chances in life only by becoming aware of those of all individuals in his circumstances"

suffrage: The right to vote and have representation in participatory democracy

symbolic annihilation: Described by Tuchman and colleagues in 1978 as the relative absence of marginalized groups in the mass media, which has the effect of signaling to the public that these groups are less important and beneath notice

Take Back the Night: An activist effort that began in 1976 in Brussels, Belgium. It uses marches, protests, and demonstrations as well as candlelight vigils and accompanying speakers to call for the elimination of violence against women

threshold concept: Defined by Meyer and Land as a core disciplinary concept that is both troublesome and transformative and that allows students to enter into new ways of disciplinary thinking

Title IX: This part of the Educational Amendments of 1972 guarantees equal participation in any educational program or activity that receives federal financial resources. Though primarily associated with advancing women's equal participation in athletic activities, Title IX also affected women's achievement of postsecondary degrees, pay equity within schools, and any other discrimination taking place within an educational setting

trans*: A shortened term to encompass the various gender- and sexuality-based identities that depart from the mythical heterosexual and binary gender norms

transgender: An individual for whom there is a lack of congruence between their gender assignment and gender identity

transphobia: Julia Serano defines this as "an irrational fear of, aversion to, or discrimination against people whose gendered identities, appearances, or behaviors deviate from societal norms"

Twitter/tweeting: Social media platform that allows users to post links and messages of fewer than 140 characters

vertical segregation of labor: Explains the pay gap by noting the fact that even in fields where there is a more even mix of men and women working, women tend to be clustered in positions with lower pay and prestige

Violence Against Women Act (VAWA): A U.S. law passed in 1994 that offered coordinated efforts to develop awareness and prevent violence

waves: Most commonly used to describe chronological groupings of feminist activism in the United States

Women's and Gender Studies (WGS): An interdisciplinary academic field of study emerging from feminist movement in the 19th and 20th centuries; examines the experiences, status, and disciplinary contributions of women in academic and extra-academic sites of inquiry

women's liberation: Second-wave feminist activism in the United States in the 1960s

work–life balance: The relationship between the policies and lived experiences of working families, particularly those who are managing the demands of paid labor with the demands of personal and work responsibilities, including childcare and eldercare

INDEX

Note: **bold** page numbers indicate tables; *italic* page numbers indicate figures; numbers preceded by n are chapter endnote numbers.

legal/criminal justice systems 192–193; and social construction of gender 37, 49–51, *see also* prisons, women in
lesbianism/lesbians 7, 147, 167, 201
Leslie, Sarah-Jane 39
Levin, Amy 197
Lewis, John *114*, 115
LGBTQ 16, 19, 25, 181–182, 206, 214, 215, 236
Lincoln, Anne E. 78
literature, women's 17
Little Miss Sunshine 44
Lockwood, Penelope 70
Lorber, Judith 33, 71
Lord of the Rings 43, **44**
Lorde, Audre 92, 95, 181–182, 202, 237

McClintock, Mary Ann: "White Privilege" 11
McCormick, Katharine Dexter 173
Mcintosh, Peggy 95–97, 99–100
McRobbie, Angela 209
Mama's Bail Out Day 215
man-hating 6–7
mansplaining 113–114, 236
marriage 9, 10, *10*, 12, 152–153; and name-changing 69–70, 203; and privilege/oppression 102, 104–105, 106–107; promotion programs 111–112; same-sex xv, 105, 120–121, *see also* domestic violence
Martin, Courtney: "Girls Tweeting (Not Twerking) Their Way to Power" 201–202
Martin, Trayvon 97
Martinez, Amanda: *Women's Studies in Communication* 176
Martinez, Elizabeth: "La Chicana" 146–147
masculinity 7, 19, 38, 51, **51**, 52–53, 54, 81, 104, 163–165, 221, 237; and academic fields 80; and bodies/clothing 71, 73, 163; and class/race 153–154, 163, 164–165; four dictates of 153–154; and labor market

158–159; negatives outcomes of 56; and privilege/oppression 92; ranking of 164; reimagining 55–57; violent 123, 164; writing prompts on 82, *see also* gender ranking
maternity care *see* childbirth
maternity leave 156–157, 213
Matsuda, Mari 91, 103
Maxim 5, 6, 7, 203
Mayer, Marissa 156, 158
media x, 60, 73, 203, 207–208, 216–218; advertisements 76, 82, 207; feminine beauty ideal in 165–168; and gender socialization 37; objectification of women in 16; and rape culture 123; stereotypes/misconceptions of feminism in 5; and symbolic annihilation 165, 239
medical industry 168–169
medical professions 63, 77–78
Men Can Stop Rape 221, *222*
menstrual activism 16, 226
metacognition 103
Meyer, Jan ix–x, 239
middle class 125, 126, 153, 157, 161, 177; women/feminism 7–8, 13, 54, 147–148, 167, 211
military 13, 16
Milkman, Katherine 68–69
Miller, Claire Cain 159
Million Dollar Baby 44, **44**
Mills, C. Wright 31–32; *Sociological Imagination* 32, 238–239
Miss Representation 217–218
Mock, Janet 203
MomsRising 213–214
Montoya, Bobby 36
Moraga, Cherie 147
moral development 58
Mormon church 42
Mother Nurture program 214–215
mother/motherhood 18, 58, 65, *see also* breastfeeding
Mott, Lucretia 11
Movement for Black Lives xv, 215
Ms. Magazine 8, 29, 118